# ETHICAL ISSUES IN THE COURTS

A Companion to Philosophical Ethics

Second Edition

Julie C. Van Camp
California State University, Long Beach

WADSWORTH
CENGAGE Learning

Australia • Brazil • Japan • Korea • Mexico • Singapore • Spain •
United Kingdom • United States

# WADSWORTH
## CENGAGE Learning

**Ethical Issues in the Courts: A Companion to Philosophical Ethics, Second Edition**
Julie C. Van Camp

For product information and technology assistance, contact us at **Cengage Learning Customer & Sales Support, 1-800-354-9706**

For permission to use material from this text or product, submit all requests online at **www.cengage.com/permissions**
Further permissions questions can be emailed to **permissionrequest@cengage.com**

Library of Congress Control Number: 2005922428

ISBN-13: 978-0-495-00574-2
ISBN-10: 0-495-00574-6

**Wadsworth**
10 Davis Drive
Belmont, CA 94002-3098
USA

Cengage Learning is a leading provider of customized learning solutions with office locations around the globe, including Singapore, the United Kingdom, Australia, Mexico, Brazil, and Japan. Locate your local office at: **www.cengage.com/international**

Cengage Learning products are represented in Canada by Nelson Education, Ltd.

To learn more about Wadsworth, visit **www.cengage.com/wadsworth**

Purchase any of our products at your local college store or at our preferred online store **www.ichapters.com**

Printed in Canada
2 3 4 5 6 7 11 10 09 08

# CONTENTS

# PREFACE

This collection provides excerpts from 73 important court decisions considering ethical issues studied in courses in philosophy, political science, and other disciplines in the humanities and social sciences. This new edition includes 14 new cases, including the latest decisions on euthanasia, gay marriage, the pledge of allegiance, affirmative action, business ethics, computer ethics, and other topics of urgent contemporary concern.

The study of legal cases is increasingly common in undergraduate courses. Pre-law students, regardless of major, are eager to learn about important court decisions in the nation's history. Given the pervasiveness of the law in contemporary life, all students, regardless of future career plans, should be introduced to major cases that will affect their own lives, whether on assisted suicide or affirmative action or free speech on the Internet.

Court decisions also are interesting and important to students as applications of theoretical principles encountered in their course work. The centrality of good reasoning, consideration of alternative viewpoints, and close scrutiny of key terminology in these decisions use analytical skills paramount in undergraduate education.

Although these decisions are available in print law libraries and many on-line legal databases, the complete texts can be intimidating for undergraduates. They typically are very long, with extensive legal citations, as well as technical and procedural material not significant for the ethical issues being studied. Casebooks used in the law schools consist of edited decisions, but they too include distracting technical material, and none focuses exclusively on the issues in typical undergraduate courses.

The cases here have been edited primarily for use in undergraduate classrooms. To conserve space, ellipses have not been used where text has been omitted. Words not in the original decision are indicated in square brackets [ ]. The glossary at the end of this volume provides definitions appropriate for undergraduate students of legal terminology.

Although most court decisions include extensive citations to prior legal authority, these have been omitted to focus directly on the reasoning about the ethical issues at hand. One major difference between legal reasoning and reasoning in philosophy is the role of appeals to authority. In the law, such appeals to precedent (*"stare decisis"*) are an essential element of the reasoning. In contrast, in philosophy and critical thinking in general, appeals to authority are shunned. Students who want to learn more about precedents will encounter them in law school or can look up the full text of decisions.

On the Wadsworth Web site, philosophy.wadsworth.com, students can obtain additional information about these cases and instructors can obtain suggested exam questions and other instructional aids.

I am enormously grateful to Peter Adams at Wadsworth Publishing for his encouragement of this project and to Steve Wainwright and Lee McCracken for their support for this second edition. I also appreciate the suggestions of several reviewers: Bob McArthur, Colby College; Barbara Carlson, Clark University; Win-Chiat Lee, Wake Forest University; Phillip Spivey, University of Central Arkansas. My greatest thanks go to my students at California State University, Long Beach, for sharing with me the excitement of learning about law and philosophy.

*Julie C. Van Camp*

# CHAPTER 1. HUMAN LIFE: BEGINNINGS AND ENDINGS

## Abortion

## ROE v. WADE
### 410 U.S. 113 (U.S. Supreme Court, 1973)

This appeal present[s] constitutional challenges to state criminal abortion legislation. The Texas statutes under attack here are typical of those that have been in effect in many States for approximately a century.

We forthwith acknowledge our awareness of the sensitive and emotional nature of the abortion controversy, of the vigorous opposing views, even among physicians, and of the deep and seemingly absolute convictions that the subject inspires. One's philosophy, one's experiences, one's exposure to the raw edges of human existence, one's religious training, one's attitudes toward life and family and their values, and the moral standards one establishes and seeks to observe, are all likely to influence and to color one's thinking and conclusions about abortion. In addition, population growth, pollution, poverty, and racial overtones tend to complicate and not to simplify the problem. Our task, of course, is to resolve the issue by constitutional measurement, free of emotion and of predilection.

The Texas statutes that concern us here make it a crime to "procure an abortion," except with respect to "an abortion procured or attempted by medical advice for the purpose of saving the life of the mother."

Jane Roe, a single woman, instituted this federal action in March 1970. She sought a declaratory judgment that the Texas criminal abortion statutes were unconstitutional on their face, and an injunction restraining the defendant from enforcing the statutes.

It perhaps is not generally appreciated that the restrictive criminal abortion laws in effect in a majority of States today are of relatively recent vintage. Those laws, generally proscribing abortion or its attempt at any time during pregnancy except when necessary to preserve the pregnant woman's life, are not of ancient or even of common law origin. Instead, they derive from statutory changes effected, for the most part, in the latter half of the 19th century.

Three reasons have been advanced to explain historically the enactment of criminal abortion laws in the 19th century and to justify their continued existence. It has been argued that these laws were the product of a Victorian social concern to discourage illicit sexual conduct. A second reason is concerned with abortion as a medical procedure. Thus, it has been argued that a State's real concern in enacting a criminal abortion law was to protect the pregnant woman, that is, to restrain her from submitting to a procedure that placed her life in serious jeopardy. The third reason is the State's interest -- some phrase it in terms of duty -- in protecting prenatal life. Some of the argument for this justification rests on the theory that a new human life is present from the moment of conception.

The Constitution does not explicitly mention any right of privacy. In a line of decisions, however, going back perhaps as far as 1891, the Court has recognized that a right of personal privacy, or a guarantee of certain zones

1

of privacy, does exist under the Constitution. In varying contexts, the Court or individual Justices have, indeed, found at least the roots of that right in the First Amendment; in the Fourth and Fifth Amendments; in the penumbras of the Bill of Rights; in the Ninth Amendment; or in the concept of liberty guaranteed by the Fourteenth Amendment. These decisions make it clear that only personal rights that can be deemed "fundamental" or "implicit in the concept of ordered liberty" are included in this guarantee of personal privacy. They also make it clear that the right has some extension to activities relating to marriage; contraception; family relationships; and childrearing and education.

This right of privacy is broad enough to encompass a woman's decision whether or not to terminate her pregnancy. The detriment that the State would impose upon the pregnant woman by denying this choice altogether is apparent. Specific and direct harm medically diagnosable even in early pregnancy may be involved. Maternity, or additional offspring, may force upon the woman a distressful life and future. Psychological harm may be imminent. Mental and physical health may be taxed by child care. There is also the distress, for all concerned, associated with the unwanted child, and there is the problem of bringing a child into a family already unable, psychologically and otherwise, to care for it. In other cases, the additional difficulties and continuing stigma of unwed motherhood may be involved.

On the basis of elements such as these, some argue that the woman's right is absolute and that she is entitled to terminate her pregnancy at whatever time, in whatever way, and for whatever reason she alone chooses. With this we do not agree. We conclude that the right of personal privacy includes the abortion decision, but that this right is not unqualified, and must be considered against important state interests in regulation.

The Constitution does not define "person" in so many words [and] the use of the word is such that it has application only post-natally. None indicates, with any assurance, that it has any possible pre-natal application.

[T]ogether with our observation that, throughout the major portion of the 19th century, prevailing legal abortion practices were far freer than they are today, persuades us that the word "person," as used in the Fourteenth Amendment, does not include the unborn.

We need not resolve the difficult question of when life begins. When those trained in the respective disciplines of medicine, philosophy, and theology are unable to arrive at any consensus, the judiciary is not in a position to speculate as to the answer.

We repeat, however, that the State does have an important and legitimate interest in preserving and protecting the health of the pregnant woman, and that it has still *another* important and legitimate interest in protecting the potentiality of human life. These interests are separate and distinct.

To summarize: A state criminal abortion statute of the current Texas type, that excepts from criminality only a lifesaving procedure on behalf of the mother, without regard to pregnancy stage and without recognition of the other interests involved, is violative of the Due Process Clause of the Fourteenth Amendment.

(a) For the stage prior to approximately the end of the first trimester, the abortion decision and its effectuation must be left to the medical judgment of the pregnant woman's attending physician.

(b) For the stage subsequent to approximately the end of the first tri-mester, the State, in promoting its interest in the health of the mother, may, if it chooses, regulate the abortion procedure in ways that are reasonably related to maternal health.

(c) For the stage subsequent to viability, the State in promoting its interest in the potentiality of human life may, if it chooses, regulate, and even proscribe, abortion except where it is necessary, in appropriate medical judgment, for the preservation of the life or health of the mother.

Our conclusion means, of course, that the Texas abortion statutes, as a unit, must fall.

DISSENT: I have difficulty in concluding, as the Court does, that the right of "privacy" is involved in this case. The fact that a majority of the States reflecting, after all, the majority sentiment in those States, have had restrictions on abortions for at least a century is a strong indication that the asserted right to an abortion is not "so rooted in the traditions and con-science of our people as to be ranked as fundamental." Even today, when society's views on abortion are changing, the very existence of the debate is evidence that the "right" to an abortion is not so universally accepted as the appellant would have us believe.

## DISCUSSION QUESTIONS

(1) Is the abortion controversy primarily a moral issue? A religious issue? A legal issue? Is public agreement or compromise possible?

(2) What should "privacy" mean in the context of the abortion debate?

(3) Should the fetus be considered a "person" morally? legally? What are the implications of this issue?

(4) Are consequences (either positive or negative) for the mother, the fetus, the doctor, or the society at large relevant in this debate?

## PLANNED PARENTHOOD OF SOUTHEASTERN PENNSYLVANIA v. CASEY
### 505 U.S. 833 (U.S. Supreme Court, 1992)

Liberty finds no refuge in a jurisprudence of doubt. Yet 19 years after our holding that the Constitution protects a woman's right to terminate her pregnancy in its early stages, *Roe v. Wade*, that definition of liberty is still questioned. At issue in these cases are five provisions of the Pennsylvania Abortion Control Act of 1982.

Before any of these provisions took effect, five abortion clinics and one physician representing himself as well as a class of physicians who provide abortion services, brought this suit seeking declaratory and injunctive relief. Each provision was challenged as unconstitutional on its face.

After considering the fundamental constitutional questions resolved by *Roe*, principles of institutional integrity, and the rule of *stare decisis*, we are led to conclude this: the essential holding of *Roe v. Wade* should be retained and once again reaffirmed.

Men and women of good conscience can disagree, and we suppose some always shall disagree, about the profound moral and spiritual implications of terminating a pregnancy, even in its earliest stage. Some of us as individuals find abortion offensive to our most basic principles of morality, but that cannot control our decision. Our obligation is to define the liberty of all, not to mandate our own moral code. The underlying constitutional issue is whether the State can resolve these philosophic questions in such a definitive way that a woman lacks all choice in the matter, except perhaps in those rare circumstances in which the pregnancy is itself a danger to her own life or health, or is the result of rape or incest.

[T]hough the abortion decision may originate within the zone of conscience and belief, it is more than a philosophic exercise. Abortion is an act fraught with consequences for others: for the woman who must live with the implications of her decision; for the persons who perform and assist in the procedure; for the spouse, family, and society which must confront the knowledge that these procedures exist, procedures some deem nothing short of an act of violence against innocent human life; and, depending on one's beliefs, for the life or potential life that is aborted. Though abortion is conduct, it does not follow that the State is entitled to proscribe it in all instances. That is because the liberty of the woman is at stake in a sense unique to the human condition and so unique to the law. The mother who carries a child to full term is subject to anxieties, to physical constraints, to pain that only she must bear. That these sacrifices have from the beginning of the human race been endured by woman with a pride that ennobles her in the eyes of others and gives to the infant a bond of love cannot alone be grounds for the State to insist she make the sacrifice. Her suffering is too intimate and personal for the State to insist, without more, upon its own vision of the woman's role, however dominant that vision has been in the course of our history and our culture. The destiny of the woman must be shaped to a large extent on her own conception of her spiritual imperatives and her place in society.

[W]e recognize that no judicial system could do society's work if it eyed each issue afresh in every case that raised it. Indeed, the very concept of the rule of law underlying our own Constitution requires such continuity over time that a respect for precedent is, by definition, indispensable.

[F]or two decades of economic and social developments, people have organized intimate relationships and made choices that define their views of themselves and their places in society, in reliance on the availability of abortion in the event that contraception should fail. The ability of women to participate equally in the economic and social life of the Nation has been facilitated by their ability to control their reproductive lives. The Constitution serves human values, and while the effect of reliance on *Roe* cannot be exactly measured, neither can the certain cost of overruling *Roe* for people who have ordered their thinking and living around that case be dismissed.

We have seen how time has overtaken some of *Roe*'s factual assumptions: advances in maternal health care allow for abortions safe to the mother later in pregnancy than was true in 1973, and advances in neonatal care have advanced viability to a point somewhat earlier. But these facts go only to the scheme of time limits on the competing interests, and the divergences from the factual premises of 1973 have no bearing on the validity of *Roe*'s central holding, that viability marks the earliest point at which the State's interest in fetal life is constitutionally adequate to justify a legislative ban on nontherapeutic abortions. Whenever it may occur, the attainment of viability may continue to serve as the critical fact; which is to say that no change in *Roe*'s factual underpinning has left its central holding obsolete, and none supports an argument for overruling it.

The Court's duty in the present cases is clear. Whether or not a new social consensus is developing on that issue, its divisiveness is no less today than in 1973, and pressure to overrule the decision, like pressure to retain it, has grown only more intense. A decision to overrule *Roe*'s essential holding under the existing circumstances would address error, if error there was, at the cost of both profound and unnecessary damage to the Court's legitimacy, and to the Nation's commitment to the rule of law. It is therefore imperative to adhere to the essence of *Roe*'s original decision, and we do so today.

We conclude the line should be drawn at viability, so that before that time the woman has a right to choose to terminate her pregnancy. [T]he concept of viability is the time at which there is a realistic possibility of maintaining and nourishing a life outside the womb, so that the independent existence of the second life can in reason and all fairness be the object of state protection that now overrides the rights of the woman.

The trimester framework no doubt was erected to ensure that the woman's right to choose not become so subordinate to the State's interest in promoting fetal life that her choice exists in theory but not in fact. We do not agree, however, that the trimester approach is necessary to accomplish this objective. We reject the trimester framework, which we do not consider to be part of the essential holding of *Roe*.

The very notion that the State has a substantial interest in potential life leads to the conclusion that not all regulations must be deemed unwarranted. Not all burdens on the right to decide whether to terminate a pregnancy will be undue. In our view, the undue burden standard is the appropriate means of reconciling the State's interest with the woman's constitutionally protected liberty.

[T]he statute requires that at least 24 hours before performing an abortion a physician inform the woman of the nature of the procedure, the health risks of the abortion and of childbirth, and the "probable gestational age of the unborn child." Because the informed consent requirement facilitates the wise exercise of that right, it cannot be classified as an interference with the right *Roe* protects.

Pennsylvania's abortion law provides that no physician shall perform an abortion on a married woman without receiving a signed statement from the woman that she has notified her spouse that she is about to undergo an abortion.

In well-functioning marriages, spouses discuss important intimate decisions such as whether to bear a child. But there are millions of women in this country who are the victims of regular physical and psychological abuse at the hands of their husbands. Should these women become pregnant, they may have very good reasons for not wishing to inform their husbands of their decision to obtain an abortion. We must not blind ourselves to the fact that the significant number of women who fear for their safety and the safety of their children are likely to be deterred from procuring an abortion. It is an undue burden, and therefore invalid.

We next consider the parental consent provision. [W]e reaffirm today that a State may require a minor seeking an abortion to obtain the consent of a parent or guardian, provided that there is an adequate judicial bypass procedure.

Our Constitution is a covenant running from the first generation of Americans to us and then to future generations. Each generation must learn anew that the Constitution's written terms embody ideas and aspirations that must survive more ages than one. We accept our responsibility not to retreat from interpreting the full meaning of the covenant in light of all of our precedents. We invoke it once again to define the freedom guaranteed by the Constitution's own promise, the promise of liberty.

DISSENT: [Q]uite simply, the issue in these cases [is] not whether the power of a woman to abort her unborn child is a "liberty" in the absolute sense; or even whether it is a liberty of great importance to many women. Of course it is both. The issue is whether it is a liberty protected by the Constitution of the United States. I am sure it is not. I reach that conclusion for the same reason I reach the conclusion that bigamy is not constitutionally protected -- because of two simple facts: (1) the Constitution says absolutely nothing about it, and (2) the longstanding traditions of American society have permitted it to be legally proscribed.

The whole argument of abortion opponents is that what the Court calls the fetus and what others call the unborn child is a human life. Thus, whatever answer *Roe* came up with after conducting its "balancing" is bound to be wrong, unless it is correct that the human fetus is in some critical sense merely potentially human. There is of course no way to determine that as a legal matter; it is in fact a value judgment. Some societies have considered newborn children not yet human, or the incompetent elderly no longer so.

## DISCUSSION QUESTIONS

(1) How important is *stare decisis* (precedent) in this controversy? Does reliability in the nation's laws provide needed stability to American life or does it force the country into continuing deference to previous decisions, regardless of their correctness?

(2) What would be examples of "undue burden" on a woman seeking an abortion? On what basis should these be determined by the Court?

### STENBERG v. CARHART
530 U.S. 914 (U.S. Supreme Court, 2000)

We again consider the right to an abortion. Millions of Americans believe that life begins at conception and consequently that an abortion is akin to causing the death of an innocent child; they recoil at the thought of a law that would permit it. Other millions fear that a law that forbids abortion would condemn many American women to lives that lack dignity, depriving them of equal liberty and leading those with least resources to undergo illegal abortions with the attendant risks of death and suffering. Taking account of these virtually irreconcilable points of view, aware that constitutional law must govern a society whose different members sincerely hold directly opposing views, and considering the matter in light of the Constitution's guarantees of fundamental individual liberty, this Court, in the course of a generation, has determined and then redetermined that the Constitution offers basic protection to the woman's right to choose.

Three established principles determine the issue before us. First, before "viability the woman has a right to choose to terminate her pregnancy." Second, "a law designed to further the State's interest in fetal life which imposes an undue burden on the woman's decision before fetal viability" is unconstitutional. An "undue burden is shorthand for the conclusion that a state regulation has the purpose or effect of placing a substantial obstacle in the path of a woman seeking an abortion of a nonviable fetus." Third, "subsequent to viability, the State in promoting its interest in the potentiality of human life may, if it chooses, regulate, and even proscribe, abortion except where it is necessary for the preservation of the life or health of the mother."

We apply these principles to a Nebraska law [which] reads: "No partial birth abortion shall be performed in this state, unless such procedure is necessary to save the life of the mother whose life is endangered by a physical disorder, physical illness, or physical injury, including a life-endangering physical condition caused by or arising from the pregnancy itself."

The statute defines "partial birth abortion" as: "an abortion procedure in which the person performing the abortion partially delivers vaginally a living unborn child before killing the unborn child and completing the delivery."

It defines "partially delivers vaginally a living unborn child before killing the unborn child" to mean: "deliberately and intentionally delivering into the vagina a living unborn child, or a substantial portion thereof, for the purpose of performing a procedure that the person performing such procedure knows will kill the unborn child and does kill the unborn child."

The law classifies violation of the statute as a "Class III felony" carrying a prison term of up to 20 years, and a fine of up to $ 25,000. It also provides for the automatic revocation of a doctor's license to practice medicine in Nebraska. We hold that this statute violates the Constitution.

Dr. Leroy Carhart is a Nebraska physician who performs abortions in a clinical setting. He brought this lawsuit in Federal District Court seeking a declaration that the Nebraska statute violates the Federal Constitution, and asking for an injunction forbidding its enforcement. [T]he District Court held the statute unconstitutional. On appeal, the Eighth Circuit affirmed.

Because Nebraska law seeks to ban one method of aborting a pregnancy, we must describe and then discuss several different abortion procedures.

1. About 90% of all abortions in the United States take place during the first trimester of pregnancy. [T]he predominant abortion method is "vacuum aspiration," which involves insertion of a vacuum tube into the uterus to evacuate the contents. Such an abortion is typically performed on an outpatient basis under local anesthesia. Vacuum aspiration is considered particu-

larly safe. The procedure's mortality rates for first trimester abortion are 5 to 10 times lower than those associated with carrying the fetus to term. Complication rates are also low. As the fetus grows in size, however, the vacuum aspiration method becomes increasingly difficult to use.

2. Approximately 10% of all abortions are performed during the second trimester of pregnancy. The most commonly used procedure is called "dilation and evacuation" (D&E). That procedure (together with a modified form of vacuum aspiration used in the early second trimester) accounts for about 95% of all abortions performed from 12 to 20 weeks of gestational age.

3. D&E "refers generically to transcervical procedures performed at 13 weeks gestation or later." D&E involves (1) dilation of the cervix; (2) removal of at least some fetal tissue using nonvacuum instruments; and (3) the potential need for instrumental disarticulation or dismemberment of the fetus or the collapse of fetal parts to facilitate evacuation from the uterus. The breech extraction version of the intact D&E is also known commonly as "dilation and extraction," or D&X. Despite the technical differences, intact D&E and D&X are sufficiently similar for us to use the terms interchangeably. There are no reliable data on the number of D&X abortions performed annually. Estimates have ranged between 640 and 5,000 per year.

The question is whether Nebraska's statute violates the Federal Constitution. We conclude that it does for at least two reasons. First, the law lacks any exception "for the preservation of the health of the mother." Second, it "imposes an undue burden on a woman's ability" to choose a D&E abortion, thereby unduly burdening the right to choose abortion itself.

The standard depends on the state regulations "promoting [the State's] interest in the potentiality of human life." The Nebraska law does not directly further an interest "in the potentiality of human life" by saving the fetus in question from destruction, as it regulates only a method of performing abortion. Nebraska describes its interests differently. It says the law "shows concern for the life of the unborn," "prevents cruelty to partially born children," and "preserves the integrity of the medical profession." But we cannot see how the interest-related differences could make any difference to the question at hand, namely, the application of the "health" requirement.

[T]he governing standard requires an exception "where it is necessary, in appropriate medical judgment for the preservation of the life or health of the mother," for this Court has made clear that a State may promote but not endanger a woman's health when it regulates the methods of abortion.

Nebraska fails to demonstrate that banning D&X without a health exception may not create significant health risks for women, because the record shows that significant medical authority supports the proposition that, in some circumstances, D&X would be the safest procedure.

Even if the statute's basic aim is to ban D&X, its language makes clear that it also covers a much broader category of procedures. The language does not track the medical differences between D&E and D&X -- though it would have been a simple matter, for example, to provide an exception for the performance of D&E and other abortion procedures.

In sum, using this law some present prosecutors and future Attorneys General may choose to pursue physicians who use D&E procedures, the most commonly used method for performing previability second trimester

8

abortions. All those who perform abortion procedures using that method must fear prosecution, conviction, and imprisonment. The result is an undue burden upon a woman's right to make an abortion decision. We must consequently find the statute unconstitutional.

DISSENT: I am optimistic enough to believe that, one day, *Stenberg v. Carhart* will be assigned its rightful place in the history of this Court's jurisprudence beside *Korematsu* and *Dred Scott*. The method of killing a human child proscribed by this statute is so horrible that it evokes a shudder of revulsion. [T]he Court must know that demanding a "health exception" is to give live-birth abortion free rein. The notion that the Constitution, designed "to secure the Blessings of Liberty to ourselves and our Posterity," prohibits the States from banning this visibly brutal means of eliminating our half--born posterity is absurd.

[W]hat I consider to be an "undue burden" is different from what the majority considers to be an "undue burden" -- a conclusion that can not be demonstrated true or false by factual inquiry or legal reasoning. It is a value judgment, dependent upon how much one respects the life of a partially delivered fetus, and how much one respects the freedom of the woman who gave it life to kill it.

## DISCUSSION QUESTIONS

(1) What requirements must a state legislature meet if it wants to ban late term abortions? Do these requirements strike the appropriate balance between the rights of the woman and the rights of the unborn fetus?

(2) Is "undue burden" on the woman a matter of factual inquiry? Legal reasoning? Value judgments? What factors are most important to you in determining what constitutes an "undue burden"?

### Euthanasia and Assisted Suicide

### IN THE MATTER OF KAREN QUINLAN
70 N.J. 10 (Supreme Court of New Jersey, 1976)

The central figure in this tragic case is Karen Ann Quinlan, a New Jersey resident. At the age of 22, she lies in a debilitated and allegedly moribund state at Saint Clare's Hospital in New Jersey. The litigation has to do, in final analysis, with her life -- its continuance or cessation -- and the responsibilities, rights and duties, with regard to any fateful decision concerning it, of her family, her guardian, her doctors, the hospital, the State through its law enforcement authorities, and finally the courts of justice.

The matter is of transcendent importance, involving questions related to the definition and existence of death; the prolongation of life through artificial means developed by medical technology undreamed of in past generations of the practice of the healing arts; the impact of such durationally indeterminate and artificial life prolongation on the rights of the incompetent, her family and society in general; the bearing of constitutional right and the scope of judicial responsibility.

On the night of April 15, 1975, for reasons still unclear, Karen Quinlan ceased breathing for at least two 15 minute periods. She was taken by ambulance to [a] Hospital. There she had a temperature of 100 degrees, her pupils were unreactive and she was unresponsive even to deep pain.

Three days later, [the doctor] found her comatose with evidence of decortication, a condition relating to derangement of the cortex of the brain causing a physical posture in which the upper extremities are flexed and the lower extremities are extended. She required a respirator to assist her breathing. An electroencephalogram (EEG) measuring electrical rhythm of the brain was performed and [the doctor] characterized the result as "abnormal but it showed some activity."

[E]xpert physicians characterized Karen as being in a "chronic persistent vegetative state," defined as a "subject who remains with the capacity to maintain the vegetative parts of neurological function but who. . . no longer has any cognitive function."

Because Karen's neurological condition affects her respiratory ability she requires a respirator to assist her breathing. Attempts to "wean" her from the respirator were unsuccessful and have been abandoned.

Although she does have some brain stem function and has other reactions one normally associates with being alive, such as moving, reacting to light, sound and noxious stimuli, blinking her eyes, and the like, the quality of her feeling impulses is unknown. She grimaces, makes stereotyped cries and sounds and has chewing motions.

No form of treatment which can cure or improve that condition is known or available. As nearly as may be determined, she can never be restored to cognitive or sapient life. Even with regard to the vegetative level the prognosis is extremely poor.

It is the issue of the constitutional right of privacy that has given us most concern. Here a loving parent seeks authorization to abandon specialized technological procedures which can only maintain for a time a body having no potential for resumption or continuance of other than a "vegetative" existence.

We have no doubt that if Karen were herself miraculously lucid for an interval (not altering the existing prognosis of the condition to which she would soon return) and perceptive of her irreversible condition, she could effectively decide upon discontinuance of the life-support apparatus, even if it meant the prospect of natural death.

We have no hesitancy in deciding that no external compelling interest of the State could compel Karen to endure the unendurable, only to vegetate a few measurable months with no realistic possibility of returning to any semblance of cognitive or sapient life.

Although the Constitution does not explicitly mention a right of privacy, Supreme Court decisions have recognized that a right of personal privacy exists and that certain areas of privacy are guaranteed under the Constitution. Presumably this right is broad enough to encompass a patient's decision to decline medical treatment under certain circumstances.

The claimed interests of the State in this case are essentially the preservation and sanctity of human life and defense of the right of the physician to administer medical treatment according to his best judgment. We think that the State's interest *contra* weakens and the individual's right to privacy grows as the degree of bodily invasion increases and the prognosis dims. Ultimately there comes a point at which the individual's rights overcome the State interest. It is for that reason that we believe Karen's choice, if she were competent to make it, would be vindicated by the law.

Our affirmation of Karen's independent right of choice, however, would ordinarily be based upon her competency to assert it. The sad truth, however, is that she is grossly incompetent and we cannot discern her supposed choice based on the testimony of her previous conversations with friends, where such testimony is without sufficient probative weight.

If a putative decision by Karen to permit this non-cognitive, vegetative existence to terminate by natural forces is regarded as a valuable incident of her right of privacy, as we believe it to be, then it should not be discarded solely on the basis that her condition prevents her conscious exercise of the choice. The only practical way to prevent destruction of the right is to permit the guardian and family of Karen to render their best judgment, as to whether she would exercise it in these circumstances.

[P]hysicians distinguish between curing the ill and comforting and easing the dying; that they refuse to treat the curable as if they were dying or ought to die, and that they have sometimes refused to treat the hopeless and dying as if they were curable. We think these attitudes represent a balanced implementation of a profoundly realistic perspective on the meaning of life and death and that they respect the whole Judeo-Christian tradition of regard for human life. Yet this balance is particularly difficult to apply in the context of the development by advanced technology of sophisticated and artificial life-sustaining devices.

[T]here must be a way to free physicians, in the pursuit of their healing vocation, from possible contamination by self-interest or self-protection - concerns which would inhibit their independent medical judgments for the well-being of their dying patients.

The most appealing factor seems to us to be the diffusion of professional responsibility for decision. Moreover, such a system would be protective to the hospital as well as the doctor in screening out a case which might be contaminated by less than worthy motivations of family or physician. Decision-making within health care should be controlled primarily within the patient-doctor-family relationship.

Having concluded that there is a right of privacy that might permit termination of treatment in the circumstances of this case, we consider the relationship of that right to the criminal law. We believe that the ensuing death would not be homicide but rather expiration from existing natural causes. [E]ven if it were to be regarded as homicide, it would not be unlawful.

We thus arrive at the formulation of the declaratory relief which we have concluded is appropriate to this case. Upon the concurrence of the guardian and family of Karen, should the responsible attending physicians conclude that there is no reasonable possibility of Karen's ever emerging from her present comatose condition to a cognitive, sapient state and that the life-support apparatus now being administered to Karen should be discontinued, they shall consult with the hospital "Ethics Committee" or like body of the institution in which Karen is then hospitalized. If that consultative body agrees that there is no reasonable possibility of Karen's ever emerging from her present comatose condition to a cognitive, sapient state, the present life-support system may be withdrawn and said action shall be without any civil or criminal liability therefor on the part of any participant, whether guardian, physician, hospital or others.

## DISCUSSION QUESTIONS

(1) Is Karen a "person" with moral and legal rights? Given that she is not competent, who should be allowed to make decisions about the continuation of her treatment, and on what basis should these decisions be made?

(2) Does this court recognize a distinction between "active" and "passive" euthanasia?

(3) The Court sets up an elaborate system of review for making the euthanasia decision. Does this process resolve "slippery slope" problems? Is there a possibility of abuse? Is the process too cumbersome?

## CRUZAN v. DIRECTOR, MISSOURI DEPARTMENT OF HEALTH
497 U.S. 261 (U.S. Supreme Court, 1990)

Petitioner Nancy Beth Cruzan was rendered incompetent as a result of severe injuries sustained during an automobile accident. Nancy's parents and coguardians sought a court order directing the withdrawal of their daughter's artificial feeding and hydration equipment after it became apparent that she had virtually no chance of recovering her cognitive faculties. The Supreme Court of Missouri held that, because there was no clear and convincing evidence of Nancy's desire to have life-sustaining treatment withdrawn under such circumstances, her parents lacked authority to effectuate such a request. We now affirm.

On the night of January 11, 1983, Nancy Cruzan lost control of her car in Missouri. The vehicle overturned, and Cruzan was discovered lying face down in a ditch without detectable respiratory or cardiac function. Paramedics were able to restore her breathing and heartbeat at the accident site, and she was transported to a hospital in an unconscious state. An attending neurosurgeon diagnosed her as having sustained probable cerebral contusions compounded by significant anoxia (lack of oxygen). The Missouri trial court found that permanent brain damage generally results after 6 minutes in an anoxic state; it was estimated that Cruzan was deprived of oxygen from 12 to 14 minutes. She remained in a coma for approximately three weeks, and then progressed to an unconscious state in which she was able to orally ingest some nutrition. In order to ease feeding and further the recovery, surgeons implanted a gastrostomy feeding and hydration tube in Cruzan with the consent of her then husband. Subsequent rehabilitative efforts proved unavailing. She now lies in a Missouri state hospital in what is commonly referred to as a persistent vegetative state: a condition in which a person exhibits motor reflexes but evinces no indications of significant cognitive function. The State of Missouri is bearing the cost of her care.

After it had become apparent that Nancy Cruzan had virtually no chance of regaining her mental faculties, her parents asked hospital employees to terminate the artificial nutrition and hydration procedures. All agree that such a removal would cause her death. The employees refused to honor the request without court approval. The parents then sought and received authorization from the state trial court for termination. The Supreme Court of Missouri reversed by a divided vote.

We granted *certiorari* to consider the question of whether Cruzan has a right under the United States Constitution which would require the hospital to withdraw life-sustaining treatment under these circumstances.

The Fourteenth Amendment provides that no State shall "deprive any person of life, liberty, or property, without due process of law." The principle that a competent person has a constitutionally protected liberty interest in refusing unwanted medical treatment may be inferred from our prior decisions.

But determining that a person has a "liberty interest" under the Due Process Clause does not end the inquiry; "whether respondent's constitutional rights have been violated must be determined by balancing his liberty interests against the relevant state interests."

An incompetent person is not able to make an informed and voluntary choice to exercise a hypothetical right to refuse treatment or any other right. Such a "right" must be exercised for her, if at all, by some sort of surrogate. Missouri requires that evidence of the incompetent's wishes as to the withdrawal of treatment be proved by clear and convincing evidence. The question is whether the United States Constitution forbids the establishment of this requirement by the State. We hold that it does not.

The choice between life and death is a deeply personal decision of obvious and overwhelming finality. We believe Missouri may legitimately seek to safeguard the personal element of this choice through the imposition of heightened evidentiary requirements. A State is entitled to guard against potential abuses in such situations. Finally, we think a State may properly decline to make judgments about the "quality" of life that a particular individual may enjoy, and simply assert an unqualified interest in the preservation of human life to be weighed against the constitutionally protected interests of the individual.

The Supreme Court of Missouri held that the testimony at trial did not amount to clear and convincing proof of the patient's desire to have hydration and nutrition withdrawn. The testimony at trial consisted primarily of Nancy Cruzan's statements, made to a housemate about a year before her accident, that she would not want to live should she face life as a "vegetable," and other observations to the same effect. The observations did not deal with withdrawal of medical treatment or of hydration and nutrition.

If the State were required by the United States Constitution to repose a right of "substituted judgment" with anyone, the Cruzans would surely qualify. But we do not think the Due Process Clause requires the State to repose judgment on these matters with anyone but the patient herself. Close family members may have a strong feeling -- a feeling not at all ignoble or unworthy, but not entirely disinterested, either -- that they do not wish to witness the continuation of the life of a loved one which they regard as hopeless, meaningless, and even degrading. But there is no automatic

13

assurance that the view of close family members will necessarily be the same as the patient's would have been had she been confronted with the prospect of her situation while competent.

DISSENT: Our Constitution is born of the proposition that all legitimate governments must secure the equal right of every person to "Life, Liberty, and the pursuit of Happiness." The Court would make an exception here. It permits the State's abstract, undifferentiated interest in the preservation of life to overwhelm the best interests of Nancy Cruzan, interests which would, according to an undisputed finding, be served by allowing her guardians to exercise her constitutional right to discontinue medical treatment.

## DISCUSSION QUESTIONS

(1) As most people do not execute "living wills" which authorize the discontinuance of medical treatment, what evidence of consent should be sufficient to meet the Court's requirement of "clear and convincing proof"?

(2) The U.S. Supreme Court never reviewed the *Quinlan* decision. Based on the reasoning here, how would it have ruled?

## BUSH v. SCHIAVO
### No. SC04-925 (Supreme Court of Florida, 2004)

The narrow issue in this case requires this Court to decide the constitutionality of a law passed by the Legislature that directly affected Theresa Schiavo, who has been in a persistent vegetative state since 1990. This Court concludes that the law violates the fundamental constitutional tenet of separation of powers and is therefore unconstitutional both on its face and as applied to Theresa Schiavo.

The resolution of the discrete separation of powers issue presented in this case does not turn on the facts of the underlying guardianship proceedings that resulted in the removal of Theresa's nutrition and hydration tube. The underlying litigation, which has pitted Theresa's husband, Michael Schiavo, against Theresa's parents, turned on whether the procedures sustaining Theresa's life should be discontinued. However, the procedural history is important because it provides the backdrop to the Legislature's enactment of the challenged law.

Theresa Marie Schindler was born on December 3, 1963, and married Michael Schiavo on November 10, 1984. Michael and Theresa moved to Florida in 1986. They were happily married and both were employed. They had no children.

On February 25, 1990, their lives changed. Theresa suffered a cardiac arrest as a result of a potassium imbalance. Michael called 911, and Theresa was rushed to the hospital. She never regained consciousness.

Since 1990, Theresa has lived in nursing homes with constant care. She is fed and hydrated by tubes. The staff changes her diapers regularly. She has had numerous health problems, but none have been life threatening.

For the first three years after this tragedy, Michael and Theresa's parents, Robert and Mary Schindler, enjoyed an amicable relationship.

However, that relationship ended in 1993 and the parties literally stopped speaking to each other. In May of 1998, eight years after Theresa lost consciousness, Michael petitioned the court to authorize the termination of life-prolonging procedures. By filing this petition, which the Schindlers opposed, Michael placed the difficult decision in the hands of the court.

After a trial, the guardianship court issued an extensive written order authorizing the discontinuance of artificial life support. The trial court found by clear and convincing evidence that Theresa Schiavo was in a persistent vegetative state and that Theresa would elect to cease life-prolonging procedures if she were competent to make her own decision. This order was affirmed on direct appeal, and we denied review.

The evidence is overwhelming that Theresa is in a permanent or persistent vegetative state. [A] persistent vegetative state is not simply a coma. She has cycles of apparent wakefulness and apparent sleep without any cognition or awareness. As she breathes, she often makes moaning sounds. Theresa has severe contractures of her hands, elbows, knees, and feet.

[T]he difficult question that faced the trial court was whether Theresa Schiavo, not after a few weeks in a coma, but after ten years in a persistent vegetative state that has robbed her of most of her cerebrum and all but the most instinctive of neurological functions, with no hope of a medical cure but with sufficient money and strength of body to live indefinitely, would choose to continue the constant nursing care and the supporting tubes in hopes that a miracle would somehow recreate her missing brain tissue, or whether she would wish to permit a natural death process to take its course and for her family members and loved ones to be free to continue their lives. After due consideration, we conclude that the trial judge had clear and convincing evidence to answer this question as he did.

Although the guardianship court's final order authorizing termination of life-prolonging procedures was affirmed on direct appeal, the litigation continued because the Schindlers began an attack on the final order. We denied review, and Theresa's nutrition and hydration tube was removed on October 15, 2003.

On October 21, 2003, the Legislature enacted [legislation], and the Governor issued [an] executive order to stay the continued withholding of nutrition and hydration from Theresa. The nutrition and hydration tube was reinserted pursuant to the Governor's executive order.

The cornerstone of American democracy known as separation of powers recognizes three separate branches of government--the executive, the legislative, and the judicial--each with its own powers and responsibilities. In Florida, the constitutional doctrine has been expressly codified in the Florida Constitution, which not only divides state government into three branches but also expressly prohibits one branch from exercising the powers of the other two branches.

Similarly, the framers of the United States Constitution recognized the need to establish a judiciary independent of the legislative branch. Indeed, the desire to prevent Congress from using its power to interfere with the judgments of the courts was one of the primary motivations for the separation of powers established at this nation's founding.

[T]he Act, as applied in this case, resulted in an executive order that

effectively reversed a properly rendered final judgment and thereby constituted an unconstitutional encroachment on the power that has been reserved
for the independent judiciary. [W]e further conclude that the Act is unconstitutional on its face because it delegates legislative power to the Governor.

[The] standardless, open-ended delegation of authority by the Legislature to the Governor provides no guarantee that the incompetent patient's
right to withdraw life-prolonging procedures will in fact be honored. [T]he
Act does not even require that the Governor consider the patient's wishes in
deciding whether to issue a stay, and instead allows a unilateral decision by
the Governor to stay the withholding of life-prolonging procedures without
affording any procedural process to the patient.

We recognize that the tragic circumstances underlying this case make it
difficult to put emotions aside and focus solely on the legal issue presented.
However, we are a nation of laws and we must govern our decisions by the
rule of law and not by our own emotions. Our hearts can fully comprehend
the grief so fully demonstrated by Theresa's family members on this record.
But our hearts are not the law. What is in the Constitution always must prevail over emotion.

The continuing vitality of our system of separation of powers precludes
the other two branches from nullifying the judicial branch's final orders. If
the Legislature with the assent of the Governor can do what was attempted
here, the judicial branch would be subordinated to the final directive of the
other branches. Also subordinated would be the rights of individuals,
including the well established privacy right to self determination. No court
judgment could ever be considered truly final and no constitutional right
truly secure, because the precedent of this case would hold to the contrary.
Vested rights could be stripped away based on popular clamor. The essential core of what the Founding Fathers sought to change from their experience with English rule would be lost, especially their belief that our courts
exist precisely to preserve the rights of individuals, even when doing so is
contrary to popular will.

## DISCUSSION QUESTIONS

(1) Compare and contrast the physical condition and presumed consent
of Theresa Schiavo with that of Karen Quinlan and Nancy Cruzan, and the
reasoning of these three courts compare.

(2) If the U.S. Supreme Court in *Cruzan* considered the *Schiavo* case,
what would be their likely conclusion, concerning both Terry and the
legislation passed in Florida? Should legislatures be permitted to intervene
when they do not approve of the court decisions in their state?

## BOUVIA v. GLENCHUR
### 179 Cal. App. 3d 1127 (Court of Appeal of California, 1986)

Elizabeth Bouvia, a patient in a public hospital, seeks the removal from her
body of a nasogastric tube inserted and maintained against her will and
without her consent by physicians who so placed it for the purpose of

keeping her alive through involuntary forced feeding. We [grant] Elizabeth Bouvia the relief for which she prayed.

Petitioner is a 28-year-old woman. Since birth she has suffered from severe cerebral palsy. She is quadriplegic. She is now a patient at a public hospital. Other parties are physicians, nurses and the medical and support staff employed by the County of Los Angeles. Petitioner's physical handicaps of palsy and quadriplegia have progressed to the point where she is completely bedridden. Except for a few fingers of one hand and some slight head and facial movements, she is immobile. She is physically helpless and wholly unable to care for herself. She is totally dependent upon others for all of her needs. These include feeding, washing, cleaning, toileting, turning, and helping her with elimination and other bodily functions. She cannot stand or sit upright in bed or in a wheelchair. She lies flat in bed and must do so the rest of her life. She suffers also from degenerative and severely crippling arthritis. She is in continual pain. Another tube permanently attached to her chest automatically injects her with periodic doses of morphine which relieves some, but not all of her physical pain and discomfort.

She is intelligent, very mentally competent. She earned a college degree. She was married but her husband has left her. She suffered a miscarriage. She lived with her parents until her father told her that they could no longer care for her. She has stayed intermittently with friends and at public facilities. A search for a permanent place to live where she might receive the constant care which she needs has been unsuccessful. She is without financial means to support herself and, therefore, must accept public assistance for medical and other care.

She has on several occasions expressed the desire to die. Petitioner must be spoon fed in order to eat. Her present medical and dietary staff have determined that she is not consuming a sufficient amount of nutrients. Petitioner stops eating when she feels she cannot orally swallow more, without nausea and vomiting. As she cannot now retain solids, she is fed soft liquid-like food. Because of her previously announced resolve to starve herself, the medical staff feared her weight loss might reach a life-threatening. Her weight seems to hover between 65 and 70 pounds. Accordingly, they inserted the tube against her will and contrary to her express written instructions. [Note: Her instructions were dictated to her lawyers, written by them and signed by her by means of her making a feeble "x" on the paper with a pen which she held in her mouth.]

[A] patient has the right to refuse any medical treatment or medical service, even when such treatment is labelled "furnishing nourishment and hydration." This right exists even if its exercise creates a "life threatening condition." The right to refuse medical treatment is basic and fundamental. It is recognized as a part of the right of privacy protected by both the state and federal constitutions. Its exercise requires no one's approval. It is not merely one vote subject to being overridden by medical opinion.

Moreover, there is no practical or logical reason to limit the exercise of this right to "terminal" patients. The right to refuse treatment does not need the sanction or approval by any legislative act, directing how and when it shall be exercised. It is indisputable that petitioner is mentally competent. She is not comatose. She is quite intelligent, alert, and understands the risks

17

involved.

A county hospital, its physicians and administrators, urge that the interests of the state should prevail over the rights of Elizabeth Bouvia to refuse treatment. The state's interests [are] (1) preserving life, (2) preventing suicide, (3) protecting innocent third parties, and (4) maintaining the ethical standards of the medical profession.

Who shall say what the minimum amount of available life must be? Does it matter if it be 15 to 20 years, 15 to 20 months, or 15 to 20 days, if such life has been physically destroyed and its quality, dignity and purpose gone? As in all matters lines must be drawn at some point, somewhere, but that decision must ultimately belong to the one whose life is in issue.

Here Elizabeth Bouvia's decision to forego medical treatment or life-support through a mechanical means belongs to her. It is not a medical decision for her physicians to make. Neither is it a legal question whose soundness is to be resolved by lawyers or judges. It is not a conditional right subject to approval by ethics committees or courts of law. It is a moral and philosophical decision that, being a competent adult, is her's alone.

Here, if force fed, petitioner faces 15 to 20 years of a painful existence, endurable only by the constant administrations of morphine. Her condition is irreversible. There is no cure for her palsy or arthritis. Petitioner would have to be fed, cleaned, turned, bedded, toileted by others for 15 to 20 years! Although alert, bright, sensitive, perhaps even brave and feisty, she must lie immobile, unable to exist except through physical acts of others. Her mind and spirit may be free to take great flights but she herself is imprisoned and must lie physically helpless subject to the ignominy, embarrassment, humiliation and dehumanizing aspects created by her helplessness. We do not believe it is the policy of this state that all and every life must be preserved against the will of the sufferer. It is incongruous, if not monstrous, for medical practitioners to assert their right to preserve a life that someone else must live, or, more accurately, endure, for "15 to 20 years." We cannot conceive it to be the policy of this state to inflict such an ordeal upon anyone.

It is, therefore, immaterial that the removal of the nasogastric tube will hasten or cause Bouvia's eventual death. Being competent she has the right to live out the remainder of her natural life in dignity and peace. It is precisely the aim and purpose of the many decisions upholding the withdrawal of life-support systems to accord and provide as large a measure of dignity, respect and comfort as possible to every patient for the remainder of his days, whatever be their number. This goal is not to hasten death, though its earlier arrival may be an expected and understood likelihood.

[A] desire to terminate one's life is probably the ultimate exercise of one's right to privacy. Her decision to allow nature to take its course is not equivalent to an election to commit suicide with real parties aiding and abetting therein.

It is not necessary to here define or dwell at length upon what constitutes suicide. No criminal or civil liability attaches to honoring a competent, informed patient's refusal of medical service.

We hold only that her right to refuse medical treatment, even of the life-sustaining variety, entitles her to the immediate removal of the nasogas-

18

tric tube that has been involuntarily inserted into her body. The hospital and medical staff are still free to perform a substantial if not the greater part of their duty, i.e., that of trying to alleviate Bouvia's pain and suffering.

It Is Ordered: (1) directing [the hospital] to remove the nasogastric tube from petitioner, Elizabeth Bouvia's body, and (2) prohibiting any[one] from replacing or aiding in replacing said tube or any other or similar device in or on petitioner without her consent.

CONCUR: The right to die is an integral part of our right to control our own destinies so long as the rights of others are not affected. That right should include the ability to enlist assistance from others, including the medical profession, in making death as painless and quick as possible.

Whatever choice Elizabeth Bouvia may ultimately make, I can only hope that her courage, persistence and example will cause our society to deal realistically with the plight of those unfortunate individuals to whom death beckons as a welcome respite from suffering. If there is ever a time when we ought to be able to get the "government off our backs" it is when we face death -- either by choice or otherwise.

## DISCUSSION QUESTIONS

(1) Is Bouvia attempting to commit "suicide"? Does she have a right to do so? If so, from what rights, if any, is it derived? If not, why not?

(2) What rights and obligations should health professionals have when presented with a request for assistance that will result in death?

## WASHINGTON v. GLUCKSBERG
### 521 U.S. 702 (U.S. Supreme Court, 1997)

The question presented in this case is whether Washington's prohibition against "causing" or "aiding" a suicide offends the Fourteenth Amendment to the United States Constitution. We hold that it does not.

It has always been a crime to assist a suicide in the State of Washington. Petitioners in this case are the State of Washington and its Attorney General. Respondents are physicians who practice in Washington. These doctors occasionally treat terminally ill, suffering patients, and declare that they would assist these patients in ending their lives if not for Washington's assisted-suicide ban. In January 1994, respondents, along with three gravely ill, pseudonymous plaintiffs who have since died and Compassion in Dying, a nonprofit organization that counsels people considering physician-assisted suicide, sued in District Court, seeking a declaration that [Washington's assisted-suicide ban] is, on its face, unconstitutional.

In almost every State--indeed, in almost every western democracy--it is a crime to assist a suicide. The States' assisted-suicide bans are not innovations. Rather, they are longstanding expressions of the States' commitment to the protection and preservation of all human life. Indeed, opposition to and condemnation of suicide--and, therefore, of assisting suicide --are consistent and enduring themes of our philosophical, legal, and cultural heritages.

Though deeply rooted, the States' assisted-suicide bans have in recent years been reexamined and, generally, reaffirmed. Because of advances in medicine and technology, Americans today are increasingly likely to die in institutions, from chronic illnesses. Public concern and democratic action are therefore sharply focused on how best to protect dignity and independence at the end of life, with the result that there have been many significant changes in state laws and in the attitudes these laws reflect.

Attitudes toward suicide itself have changed, but our laws have consistently condemned, and continue to prohibit, assisting suicide. Despite changes in medical technology and notwithstanding an increased emphasis on the importance of end-of-life decisionmaking, we have not retreated from this prohibition.

The Due Process Clause guarantees more than fair process, and the "liberty" it protects includes more than the absence of physical restraint. The Clause also provides heightened protection against government interference with certain fundamental rights and liberty interests.

Our established method of substantive-due-process analysis has two primary features: First, we have regularly observed that the Due Process Clause specially protects those fundamental rights and liberties which are, objectively, "deeply rooted in this Nation's history and tradition," and "implicit in the concept of ordered liberty," such that "neither liberty nor justice would exist if they were sacrificed." Second, we have required in substantive-due-process cases a "careful description" of the asserted fundamental liberty interest. Our Nation's history, legal traditions, and practices thus provide the crucial "guideposts for responsible decisionmaking," that direct and restrain our exposition of the Due Process Clause.

[W]e are confronted with a consistent and almost universal tradition that has long rejected the asserted right, and continues explicitly to reject it today, even for terminally ill, mentally competent adults. To hold for respondents, we would have to reverse centuries of legal doctrine and practice, and strike down the considered policy choice of almost every State.

[T]he asserted "right" to assistance in committing suicide is not a fundamental liberty interest protected by the Due Process Clause. The Constitution also requires, however, that Washington's assisted-suicide ban be rationally related to legitimate government interests. This requirement is unquestionably met here.

First, Washington has an "unqualified interest in the preservation of human life." The State's prohibition on assisted suicide, like all homicide laws, both reflects and advances its commitment to this interest.

Those who attempt suicide--terminally ill or not--often suffer from depression or other mental disorders. Thus, legal physician-assisted suicide could make it more difficult for the State to protect depressed or mentally ill persons, or those who are suffering from untreated pain, from suicidal impulses.

The State also has an interest in protecting the integrity and ethics of the medical profession.

Next, the State has an interest in protecting vulnerable groups--including the poor, the elderly, and disabled persons--from abuse, neglect, and mistakes. We have recognized the real risk of subtle coercion and undue influence in end-of-life situations. If physician-assisted suicide were permitted, many might resort to it to spare their families the substantial financial burden of end-of-life health-care costs.

The State's interest here goes beyond protecting the vulnerable from coercion; it extends to protecting disabled and terminally ill people from prejudice, negative and inaccurate stereotypes, and "societal indifference." The State's assisted-suicide ban reflects and reinforces its policy that the lives of terminally ill, disabled, and elderly people must be no less valued than the lives of the young and healthy, and that a seriously disabled person's suicidal impulses should be interpreted and treated the same way as anyone else's.

Finally, the State may fear that permitting assisted suicide will start it down the path to voluntary and perhaps even involuntary euthanasia.

We need not weigh exactingly the relative strengths of these various interests. They are unquestionably important and legitimate, and Washington's ban on assisted suicide is at least reasonably related to their promotion and protection. We therefore hold that [the Washington ban] does not violate the Fourteenth Amendment.

Throughout the Nation, Americans are engaged in an earnest and profound debate about the morality, legality, and practicality of physician-assisted suicide. Our holding permits this debate to continue, as it should in a democratic society.

## DISCUSSION QUESTIONS

(1) Should the constitutional right to liberty protect the right of an individual to determine the manner and time of one's death?

(2) Are there any precautions against exploitation of vulnerable groups that would satisfy the Court here? How significant is this concern in the continuing assisted suicide debate?

## VACCO v. QUILL
521 U.S. 793 (U.S. Supreme Court, 1997)

In New York, as in most States, it is a crime to aid another to commit or attempt suicide, but patients may refuse even lifesaving medical treatment. The question presented by this case is whether New York's prohibition on assisting suicide therefore violates the Equal Protection Clause of the Fourteenth Amendment. We hold that it does not.

Petitioners are various New York public officials. Respondents are physicians who practice in New York. Respondents, and three gravely ill patients who have since died, sued the State's Attorney General. They urged that because New York permits a competent person to refuse life-sustaining medical treatment, and because the refusal of such treatment is "essentially the same thing" as physician-assisted suicide, New York's assisted-suicide ban violates the Equal Protection Clause.

The Equal Protection Clause commands that no State shall "deny to any person within its jurisdiction the equal protection of the laws." This embodies a general rule that States must treat like cases alike but may treat unlike cases accordingly. If a legislative classification or distinction "neither burdens a fundamental right nor targets a suspect class, we will uphold [it] so long as it bears a rational relation to some legitimate end."

New York's statutes outlawing assisting suicide affect and address matters of profound significance to all New Yorkers alike. They neither infringe fundamental rights nor involve suspect classifications.

[N]either New York's ban on assisting suicide nor its statutes permitting patients to refuse medical treatment treat anyone differently than anyone else or draw any distinctions between persons. Everyone, regardless of physical condition, is entitled, if competent, to refuse unwanted lifesaving medical treatment; no one is permitted to assist a suicide.

[W]e think the distinction between assisting suicide and withdrawing life-sustaining treatment is both important and logical. The distinction comports with fundamental legal principles of causation and intent. First, when a patient refuses life-sustaining medical treatment, he dies from an underlying fatal disease or pathology; but if a patient ingests lethal medication prescribed by a physician, he is killed by that medication.

Furthermore, a physician who withdraws, or honors a patient's refusal to begin, life-sustaining medical treatment purposefully intends only to respect his patient's wishes. The same is true when a doctor provides aggressive palliative care; in some cases, painkilling drugs may hasten a patient's death, but the physician's purpose and intent is, or may be, only to ease his patient's pain. A doctor who assists a suicide, however, "must, necessarily and indubitably, intend primarily that the patient be made dead." Similarly, a patient who commits suicide with a doctor's aid necessarily has the specific intent to end his or her own life, while a patient who refuses or discontinues treatment might not.

The law has long used actors' intent or purpose to distinguish between two acts that may have the same result. Put differently, the law distinguishes actions taken "because of" a given end from actions taken "in spite of" their unintended but foreseen consequences.

New York has neither endorsed a general right to "hasten death" nor approved physician-assisted suicide. Quite the opposite: The State has reaffirmed the line between "killing" and "letting die."

Logic and contemporary practice support New York's judgment that the two acts are different, and New York may therefore, consistent with the Constitution, treat them differently. By permitting everyone to refuse unwanted medical treatment while prohibiting anyone from assisting a suicide, New York law follows a longstanding and rational distinction.

## DISCUSSION QUESTIONS

(1) Does the Court's reliance on "intent" protect doctors from being accused of murder and patients from being accused of attempted suicide?

(2) Is the distinction between "killing" and "letting die" defensible?

# CHAPTER 2. PRIVATE LIVES

## Educating Children

## WISCONSIN v. YODER
### 406 U.S. 205 (U.S. Supreme Court, 1972)

[W]e granted *certiorari* to review a decision of the Wisconsin Supreme Court holding that respondents' convictions of violating the State's compulsory school-attendance law were invalid under the Free Exercise Clause of the First Amendment to the United States Constitution. [W]e affirm.

Respondents are members of the Amish religion. Wisconsin's compulsory school-attendance law required them to cause their children to attend public or private school until reaching age 16 but the respondents declined to send their children, ages 14 and 15, to public school after they completed the eighth grade. The children were not enrolled in any private school, or within any recognized exception to the compulsory-attendance law. [R]espondents were charged, tried, and convicted of violating the compulsory-attendance law and were fined the sum of $5 each.

Formal high school education beyond the eighth grade is contrary to Amish beliefs, not only because it places Amish children in an environment hostile to Amish beliefs with increasing emphasis on competition in class work and sports and with pressure to conform to the styles, manners, and ways of the peer group, but also because it takes them away from their community, physically and emotionally, during the crucial and formative adolescent period of life. During this period, the children must acquire Amish attitudes favoring manual work and self-reliance and the specific skills needed to perform the adult role of an Amish farmer or housewife. They must learn to enjoy physical labor. Once a child has learned basic reading, writing, and elementary mathematics, these traits, skills, and attitudes admittedly fall within the category of those best learned through example and "doing" rather than in a classroom. And, at this time in life, the Amish child must also grow in his faith and his relationship to the Amish community if he is to be prepared to accept the heavy obligations imposed by adult baptism. In short, high school attendance with teachers who are not of the Amish faith -- and may even be hostile to it -- interposes a serious barrier to the integration of the Amish child into the Amish religious community.

There is no doubt as to the power of a State, having a high responsibility for education of its citizens, to impose reasonable regulations for the control and duration of basic education.[T]he values of parental direction of the religious upbringing and education of their children in their early and formative years [also] have a high place in our society. Thus, a State's interest in universal education is not totally free from a balancing process when it impinges on fundamental rights and interests. It follows that in order for Wisconsin to compel school attendance beyond the eighth grade against a claim that such attendance interferes with the practice of a legitimate religious belief, it must appear either that the State does not deny the free exercise of religious belief by its requirement, or that there is a state interest of sufficient magnitude to override the interest claiming protection.

[H]owever strong the State's interest in universal compulsory education, it is by no means absolute to the exclusion or subordination of all other interests.

[W]e must be careful to determine whether the Amish religious faith and their mode of life are, as they claim, inseparable and interdependent. A way of life, however virtuous and admirable, may not be interposed as a barrier to reasonable state regulation of education if it is based on purely secular considerations; to have the protection of the Religion Clauses, the claims must be rooted in religious belief. Thus, if the Amish asserted their claims because of their subjective evaluation and rejection of the contemporary secular values accepted by the majority, much as Thoreau rejected the social values of his time and isolated himself at Walden Pond, their claims would not rest on a religious basis. Thoreau's choice was philosophical and personal rather than religious, and such belief does not rise to the demands of the Religion Clauses.

[T]he record in this case abundantly supports the claim that the traditional way of life of the Amish is not merely a matter of personal preference, but one of deep religious conviction, shared by an organized group, and intimately related to daily living.

[T]he unchallenged testimony of acknowledged experts in education and religious history, almost 300 years of consistent practice, and strong evidence of a sustained faith pervading and regulating respondents' entire mode of life support the claim that enforcement of the State's requirement of compulsory formal education after the eighth grade would gravely endanger if not destroy the free exercise of respondents' religious beliefs.

Wisconsin concedes that under the Religion Clauses religious beliefs are absolutely free from the State's control, but it argues that "actions," even though religiously grounded, are outside the protection of the First Amendment. But our decisions have rejected the idea that religiously grounded conduct is always outside the protection of the Free Exercise Clause.

Nor can this case be disposed of on the grounds that Wisconsin's requirement for school attendance to age 16 applies uniformly to all citizens of the State and does not, on its face, discriminate against religions or a particular religion, or that it is motivated by legitimate secular concerns. A regulation neutral on its face may, in its application, nonetheless offend the constitutional requirement for governmental neutrality if it unduly burdens the free exercise of religion.

The State notes that some degree of education is necessary to prepare citizens to participate effectively and intelligently in our open political system if we are to preserve freedom and independence. Further, education prepares individuals to be self-reliant and self-sufficient participants in society. We accept these propositions.

There is nothing in this record to suggest that the Amish qualities of reliability, self-reliance, and dedication to work would fail to find ready markets in today's society. [W]e are unwilling to assume that persons possessing such valuable vocational skills and habits are doomed to become burdens on society should they determine to leave the Amish faith, nor is there any basis in the record to warrant a finding that an additional one or two years of formal school education beyond the eighth grade would serve to eliminate any such problem that might exist.

Finally, the State argues that a decision exempting Amish children from the State's requirement fails to recognize the substantive right of the Amish child to a secondary education, and fails to give due regard to the power of the State to extend the benefit of secondary education to children regardless of the wishes of their parents.

In the face of our consistent emphasis on the central values underlying the Religion Clauses in our constitutional scheme of government, we cannot accept a claim of such all-encompassing scope and with such sweeping potential for broad and unforeseeable application as that urged by the State.

[W]e hold that the First and Fourteenth Amendments prevent the State from compelling respondents to cause their children to attend formal high school to age 16.

DISSENT: The Court's analysis assumes that the only interests at stake in the case are those of the Amish parents on the one hand, and those of the State on the other.

Our opinions are full of talk about the power of the parents over the child's education. Recent cases, however, have clearly held that the children themselves have constitutionally protectible interests. These children are "persons" within the meaning of the Bill of Rights.

It is the future of the student, not the future of the parents, that is imperiled by today's decision. If a parent keeps his child out of school beyond the grade school, then the child will be forever barred from entry into the new and amazing world of diversity that we have today. The child may decide that that is the preferred course, or he may rebel. It is the student's judgment, not his parents', that is essential if we are to give full meaning to what we have said about the Bill of Rights and of the right of students to be masters of their own destiny. If he is harnessed to the Amish way of life by those in authority over him and if his education is truncated, his entire life may be stunted and deformed. The child should be given an opportunity to be heard before the State gives the exemption which we honor today.

## DISCUSSION QUESTIONS

(1) Has the Court appropriately addressed the rights of the Amish children in this decision?

(2) If a religious group refused to send its female children to school, on the grounds that educating females violated their religious beliefs, should this practice be permitted as a free exercise of religion protected by the Constitution?

## PLYLER v. DOE
### 457 U.S. 202 (U.S. Supreme Court, 1982)

The question presented is whether, consistent with the Equal Protection Clause of the Fourteenth Amendment, Texas may deny to undocumented school-age children the free public education that it provides to children who are citizens of the United States or legally admitted aliens.

Since the late 19th century, the United States has restricted immigration into this country. Unsanctioned entry into the United States is a crime, and those who have entered unlawfully are subject to deportation. But despite the existence of these legal restrictions, a substantial number of persons have succeeded in unlawfully entering the United States, and now live within various States, including the State of Texas.

In 1975, the Texas Legislature revised its education laws to withhold from local school districts any state funds for the education of children who were not "legally admitted" into the United States. The revision also authorized local school districts to deny enrollment in their public schools to children not "legally admitted" to the country.

This is a class action, filed on behalf of certain school-age children of Mexican origin residing in Smith County, Tex., who could not establish that they had been legally admitted into the United States. The action complained of the exclusion of plaintiff children from the public schools of the Tyler Independent School District.

The Fourteenth Amendment provides that "[no] State shall . . . deprive any person of life, liberty, or property, without due process of law; nor deny to any person within its jurisdiction the equal protection of the laws." Whatever his status under the immigration laws, an alien is surely a "person" in any ordinary sense of that term. Aliens, even aliens whose presence in this country is unlawful, have long been recognized as "persons" guaranteed due process of law by the Fifth and Fourteenth Amendments.

Indeed, it appears that Congress, by using the phrase "person within its jurisdiction," sought expressly to ensure that the equal protection of the laws was provided to the alien population.

That a person's initial entry into a State, or into the United States, was unlawful, and that he may for that reason be expelled, cannot negate the simple fact of his presence within the State's territorial perimeter. And until he leaves the jurisdiction -- either voluntarily, or involuntarily in accordance with the Constitution and laws of the United States -- he is entitled to the equal protection of the laws that a State may choose to establish.

The Equal Protection Clause directs that "all persons similarly circumstanced shall be treated alike." But so too, "[the] Constitution does not require things which are different in fact or opinion to be treated in law as though they were the same."

Sheer incapability or lax enforcement of the laws barring entry into this country, coupled with the failure to establish an effective bar to the employment of undocumented aliens, has resulted in the creation of a substantial "shadow population" of illegal migrants -- numbering in the millions -- within our borders. This situation raises the specter of a permanent caste of undocumented resident aliens, encouraged by some to remain here as a source of cheap labor, but nevertheless denied the benefits that our society makes available to citizens and lawful residents. The existence of such an underclass presents most difficult problems for a Nation that prides itself on adherence to principles of equality under law.

[U]ndocumented status is not irrelevant to any proper legislative goal. Nor is undocumented status an absolutely immutable characteristic since it is the product of conscious, indeed unlawful, action. But [the Texas statute] is directed against children, and imposes its discriminatory burden on the basis of a legal characteristic over which children can have little control. It is thus difficult to conceive of a rational justification for penalizing these children for their presence within the United States. Yet that appears to be precisely the effect of [the Texas statute].

Public education is not a "right" granted to individuals by the Constitution. But neither is it merely some governmental "benefit" indistinguishable from other forms of social welfare legislation. Both the importance of education in maintaining our basic institutions, and the lasting impact of its deprivation on the life of the child, mark the distinction. In addition, education provides the basic tools by which individuals might lead economically productive lives to the benefit of us all. In sum, education has a fundamental role in maintaining the fabric of our society. We cannot ignore the significant social costs borne by our Nation when select groups are denied the means to absorb the values and skills upon which our social order rests.

[The Texas statute] imposes a lifetime hardship on a discrete class of children not accountable for their disabling status. The stigma of illiteracy will mark them for the rest of their lives. By denying these children a basic education, we deny them the ability to live within the structure of our civic institutions, and foreclose any realistic possibility that they will contribute in even the smallest way to the progress of our Nation. In determining the rationality of [the Texas statute], we may appropriately take into account its costs to the Nation and to the innocent children who are its victims. In light of these countervailing costs, the discrimination [here] can hardly be considered rational unless it furthers some substantial goal of the State.

To be sure, like all persons who have entered the United States unlawfully, these children are subject to deportation. But there is no assurance that a child subject to deportation will ever be deported. An illegal entrant might be granted federal permission to continue to reside in this country, or even to become a citizen. [A] State cannot realistically determine that any particular undocumented child will in fact be deported until after deportation proceedings have been completed.

There is no evidence in the record suggesting that illegal entrants impose any significant burden on the State's economy. To the contrary, the available evidence suggests that illegal aliens underutilize public services, while contributing their labor to the local economy and tax money to the state. The dominant incentive for illegal entry into Texas is the availability of employment; few if any illegal immigrants come to this country, or presumably to Texas, in order to avail themselves of a free education. Thus, even making the doubtful assumption that the net impact of illegal aliens on the economy of the State is negative, we think it clear that "[charging] tuition to undocumented children constitutes a ludicrously ineffectual attempt to stem the tide of illegal immigration," at least when compared with the alternative of prohibiting the employment of illegal aliens.

It is difficult to understand precisely what the State hopes to achieve by promoting the creation and perpetuation of a subclass of illiterates within our boundaries, surely adding to the problems and costs of unemployment, welfare, and crime. It is thus clear that whatever savings might be achieved by denying these children an education, they are wholly insubstantial in light of the costs involved to these children, the State, and the Nation.

If the State is to deny a discrete group of innocent children the free public education that it offers to other children residing within its borders, that denial must be justified by a showing that it furthers some substantial state interest. No such showing was made here. Accordingly, the judgment [holding the Texas statute unconstitutional] is Affirmed.

DISSENT: Were it our business to set the Nation's social policy, I would agree without hesitation that it is senseless for an enlightened society to deprive any children -- including illegal aliens -- of an elementary education. I fully agree that it would be folly -- and wrong -- to tolerate creation of a segment of society made up of illiterate persons, many having a limited or no command of our language. However, the Constitution does not constitute us as "Platonic Guardians" nor does it vest in this Court the authority to strike down laws because they do not meet our standards of desirable social policy, "wisdom," or "common sense." We trespass on the assigned function of the political branches under our structure of limited and separated powers when we assume a policymaking role as the Court does today.

## DISCUSSION QUESTIONS

(1) Which arguments here rely on the rights of the children? Which arguments appeal to consequences to society in general?
(2) What other benefits might illegal aliens claim based on the reasoning here?

## VERNONIA SCHOOL DISTRICT v. ACTON
### 515 U.S. 646 (U.S. Supreme Court, 1995)

The Student Athlete Drug Policy adopted by School District 47J in Vernonia, Oregon, authorizes random urinalysis drug testing of students who participate in the District's school athletics programs. We granted *certiorari* to decide whether this violates the United States Constitution.

Petitioner operates one high school and three grade schools in the logging community of Vernonia, Oregon. As elsewhere in small-town America school sports play a prominent role in the town's life, and student athletes are admired in their schools and in the community.

In the mid-to-late 1980's, teachers and administrators observed a sharp increase in drug use. Students began to speak out about their attraction to the drug culture, and to boast that there was nothing the school could do about it. Along with more drugs came more disciplinary problems. Between 1988 and 1989 the number of disciplinary referrals in Vernonia schools rose to more than twice the number reported in the early 1980's, and several students were suspended. Students became increasingly rude during class; outbursts of profane language became common.

Not only were student athletes included among the drug users but athletes were the leaders of the drug culture. This caused the District's administrators particular concern, since drug use increases the risk of sports-related injury.

Initially, the District responded to the problem by offering special clas-

28

ses, speakers, and presentations designed to deter drug use. It even brought in a specially trained dog to detect drugs, but the drug problem persisted.

At that point, District officials began considering a drug-testing program. They held a parent "input night" to discuss the proposed Student Athlete Drug Policy, and the parents in attendance gave their unanimous approval. The school board approved the Policy for implementation in the fall of 1989. Its purpose is to prevent student athletes from using drugs, to protect their health and safety, and to provide drug users with assistance programs.

The Policy applies to all students participating in interscholastic athletics. Students must sign a form consenting to the testing and must obtain the written consent of their parents. Athletes are tested at the beginning of the season for their sport. In addition, once each week of the season the names of the athletes are placed in a "pool" from which a student, with the supervision of two adults, blindly draws the names of 10% of the athletes for random testing. The Policy states that a second offense results in [suspension for the current and next season]; a third offense in suspension for the remainder of the current season and the next two athletic seasons.

In the fall of 1991, respondent James Acton, then a seventh grader, signed up to play football at one of the District's grade schools. He was denied participation, however, because he and his parents refused to sign the testing consent forms. The Actons filed suit, seeking declaratory and injunctive relief from enforcement of the Policy on the grounds that it violated the United States Constitution and the Oregon Constitution.

The Fourth Amendment to the United States Constitution provides that the Federal Government shall not violate "the right of the people to be secure in their persons, houses, papers, and effects, against unreasonable searches and seizures." [T]he Fourteenth Amendment extends this constitutional guarantee to searches and seizures by state officers, including public school officials. [S]tate-compelled collection and testing of urine, such as that required by the Policy, constitutes a "search" subject to the demands of the Fourth Amendment.

[T]he ultimate measure of the constitutionality of a governmental search is "reasonableness." The first factor to be considered is the nature of the privacy interest upon which the search at issue intrudes. The Fourth Amendment does not protect all subjective expectations of privacy, but only those that society recognizes as "legitimate." What expectations are legitimate varies with context, depending, for example, upon whether the individual asserting the privacy interest is at home, at work, in a car, or in a public park. In addition, the legitimacy of certain privacy expectations *vis-a-vis* the State may depend upon the individual's legal relationship with the State. Central to the present case is the fact that the subjects of the Policy are (1) children, who (2) have been committed to the temporary custody of the State as schoolmaster.

Fourth Amendment rights are different in public schools than elsewhere; the "reasonableness" inquiry cannot disregard the schools' custodial and tutelary responsibility for children. For their own good and that of their classmates, public school children are routinely required to submit to various physical examinations.

Legitimate privacy expectations are even less with regard to student athletes. School sports are not for the bashful. They require "suiting up" before each practice or event, and showering and changing afterwards. Public school locker rooms, the usual sites for these activities, are not notable for the privacy they afford.

There is an additional respect in which school athletes have a reduced expectation of privacy. By choosing to "go out for the team," they voluntarily subject themselves to a degree of regulation higher than that imposed on students generally. [S]tudents who voluntarily participate in school athletics have reason to expect intrusions upon normal rights, including privacy.

The tests at issue here look only for drugs, and not for whether the student is, for example, epileptic, pregnant, or diabetic. Moreover, the drugs for which the samples are screened are standard, and do not vary according to the identity of the student. And finally, the results of the tests are disclosed only to a limited class of school personnel who have a need to know; and they are not turned over to law enforcement authorities or used for any internal disciplinary function.

[W]e turn to consider the nature and immediacy of the governmental concern at issue here, and the efficacy of this means for meeting it. That the nature of the concern is important--indeed, perhaps compelling --can hardly be doubted. Deterring drug use by our Nation's schoolchildren is at least as important as enhancing efficient enforcement of the Nation's laws against the importation of drugs, or deterring drug use by engineers and trainmen. [I]t must not be lost sight of that this program is directed more narrowly to drug use by school athletes, where the risk of immediate physical harm to the drug user or those with whom he is playing his sport is particularly high.

As to the efficacy of this means for addressing the problem: It seems to us self-evident that a drug problem largely fueled by the "role model" effect of athletes' drug use, and of particular danger to athletes, is effectively addressed by making sure that athletes do not use drugs.

Taking into account all the factors we have considered above--the decreased expectation of privacy, the relative unobtrusiveness of the search, and the severity of the need met by the search--we conclude Vernonia's Policy is reasonable and hence constitutional.

DISSENT: [T]he millions of students who participate in interscholastic sports, an overwhelming majority of whom have given school officials no reason whatsoever to suspect they use drugs at school, are open to an intrusive bodily search. In justifying this result, the Court dispenses with a requirement of individualized suspicion on considered policy grounds.

The view that mass, suspicionless searches, however evenhanded, are generally unreasonable remains inviolate in the criminal law enforcement context. Thus, it remains the law that the police cannot, say, subject to drug testing every person entering or leaving a certain drug-ridden neighborhood in order to find evidence of crime. And this is true even though it is hard to think of a more compelling government interest than the need to fight the scourge of drugs on our streets and in our neighborhoods.

[T]he far more reasonable choice would have been to focus on the class of students found to have violated school rules against severe disruption in class and around campus, disruption that had a strong nexus to drug use.

It cannot be too often stated that the greatest threats to our constitutional freedoms come in times of crisis. [T]he District's suspicionless policy of testing all student athletes sweeps too broadly, and too imprecisely, to be reasonable under the Fourth Amendment.

## DISCUSSION QUESTIONS

(1) Does the rationale here for testing high school athletes also support random drug testing of college athletes?

(2) What searches in the high schools would be unreasonable, based on the reasoning here?

## OWASSAO v. FALVO
### 534 U.S. 426 (U.S. Supreme Court, 2002)

Teachers sometimes ask students to score each other's tests, papers, and assignments as the teacher explains the correct answers to the entire class. Respondent contends this practice, which the parties refer to as peer grading, violates the Family Educational Rights and Privacy Act of 1974 (FERPA or Act). We took this case to resolve the issue.

Under FERPA, schools and educational agencies receiving federal financial assistance must comply with certain conditions. One condition is that sensitive information about students may not be released without parental consent. The Act states that federal funds are to be withheld from school districts that have "a policy or practice of permitting the release of education records (or personally identifiable information contained therein . . . ) of students without the written consent of their parents." The phrase "education records" is defined, under the Act, as "records, files, documents, and other materials" containing information directly related to a student, which "are maintained by an educational agency or institution or by a person acting for such agency or institution." The precise question for us is whether peer-graded classroom work and assignments are education records.

Three of respondent Falvo's children are enrolled in Owasso Independent School District, in a suburb of Tulsa, Oklahoma. The children's teachers, like many in this country, use peer grading. In a typical case, the students exchange papers with each other and score them according to the teacher's instructions, then return the work to the student who prepared it. In this case it appears the student could either call out the score or walk to the teacher's desk and reveal it in confidence, though by that stage, of course, the score was known at least to the one other student who did the grading. Both the grading and the system of calling out the scores are in contention here.

Respondent claimed the peer grading embarrassed her children. She asked the school district to adopt a uniform policy banning peer grading and requiring teachers either to grade assignments themselves or at least to forbid students from grading papers other than their own. The school district declined to do so, and respondent brought a class action. The United States District Court granted summary judgment in favor of the school district's position. The Court of Appeals for the Tenth Circuit reversed. We granted *certiorari* to decide whether peer grading violates FERPA. Finding no violation of the Act, we reverse.

First, the student papers are not, at that stage, "maintained" within the meaning of [FERPA]. Even assuming the teacher's grade book is an education record, the score on a student-graded assignment is not "contained therein," until the teacher records it. The teacher does not maintain the grade while students correct their peers' assignments or call out their own marks. Nor do the student graders maintain the grades within the meaning of [FERPA]. The word "maintain" suggests FERPA records will be kept in a filing cabinet in a records room at the school or on a permanent secure database, perhaps even after the student is no longer enrolled. The student graders only handle assignments for a few moments as the teacher calls out the answers.

The phrase "acting for" connotes agents of the school, such as teachers, administrators, and other school employees. Just as it does not accord with our usual understanding to say students are "acting for" an educational institution when they follow their teacher's direction to take a quiz, it is equally awkward to say students are "acting for" an educational institution when they follow their teacher's direction to score it. Correcting a classmate's work can be as much a part of the assignment as taking the test itself. It is a way to teach material again in a new context, and it helps show students how to assist and respect fellow pupils. By explaining the answers to the class as the students correct the papers, the teacher not only reinforces the lesson but also discovers whether the students have understood the material and are ready to move on. We do not think FERPA prohibits these educational techniques.

Respondent's construction of "education records" to cover student homework or classroom work would impose substantial burdens on teachers across the country. It would force all instructors to take time, which otherwise could be spent teaching and in preparation, to correct an assortment of daily student assignments. The interpretation respondent urges would force teachers to abandon other customary practices, such as group grading of team assignments. Indeed, the logical consequences of respondent's view are all but unbounded. Counsel for respondent seemed to agree that if a teacher puts a happy face, a gold star, or a disapproving remark on a classroom assignment, federal law does not allow other students to see it.

We doubt Congress meant to intervene in this drastic fashion with traditional state functions. The Congress is not likely to have mandated this result, and we do not interpret the statute to require it.

[T]he grades on students' papers would not be covered under FERPA at least until the teacher has collected them and recorded them in his or her grade book. We limit our holding to this narrow point, and do not decide the broader question whether the grades on individual student assignments, once they are turned in to teachers, are protected by the Act.

## DISCUSSION QUESTIONS

(1) Many professors use electronic tools for peer review of written work, group projects, and other graded work in college courses. Are any of these grading practices problematic under FERPA?

(2) This decision rests on an analysis of the meaning of the FERPA statute. Should a student have a right to privacy in education based on more fundamental rights under the Constitution?

## Sex and Marriage

## GRISWOLD v. CONNECTICUT
### 381 U.S. 479 (U.S. Supreme Court, 1965)

Appellant Griswold is Executive Director of the Planned Parenthood League of Connecticut. Appellant Buxton is a licensed physician and a professor at the Yale Medical School who served as Medical Director for the League at its Center in New Haven -- a center open and operating when appellants were arrested.

They gave information, instruction, and medical advice to married persons as to the means of preventing conception. They examined the wife and prescribed the best contraceptive device or material for her use.

The statutes whose constitutionality is involved in this appeal [provide] "Any person who uses any drug, medicinal article or instrument for the purpose of preventing conception shall be fined not less than fifty dollars or imprisoned not less than sixty days nor more than one year or be both fined and imprisoned." "Any person who assists, abets, counsels, causes, hires or commands another to commit any offense may be prosecuted and punished as if he were the principal offender."

The appellants were found guilty as accessories and fined $100 each.

[W]e are met with a wide range of questions that implicate the Due Process Clause of the Fourteenth Amendment. We do not sit as a super-legislature to determine the wisdom, need, and propriety of laws that touch economic problems, business affairs, or social conditions. This law, however, operates directly on an intimate relation of husband and wife and their physician's role in one aspect of that relation.

[S]pecific guarantees in the Bill of Rights have penumbras, formed by emanations from those guarantees that help give them life and substance. Various guarantees create zones of privacy. The right of association contained in the penumbra of the First Amendment is one. The Third Amendment in its prohibition against the quartering of soldiers "in any house" in time of peace without the consent of the owner is another facet of that privacy. The Fourth Amendment explicitly affirms the "right of the people to be secure in their persons, houses, papers, and effects, against unreasonable searches and seizures." The Fifth Amendment in its Self-Incrimination Clause enables the citizen to create a zone of privacy which government may not force him to surrender to his detriment. The Ninth Amendment provides: "The enumeration in the Constitution, of certain rights, shall not be construed to deny or disparage others retained by the people." The Fourth and Fifth Amendments [guarantee] protection against all governmental invasions "of the sanctity of a man's home and the privacies of life."

The present case concerns a relationship lying within the zone of privacy created by several fundamental constitutional guarantees. And it concerns a law which, in forbidding the use of contraceptives, seeks to achieve its goals by means having a destructive impact upon that relationship. Would we allow the police to search the sacred precincts of marital bedrooms for telltale signs of the use of contraceptives? The very idea is repulsive to the notions of privacy surrounding the marriage relationship.

We deal with a right of privacy older than the Bill of Rights -- older than our political parties, older than our school system. Marriage is a coming together for better or for worse, hopefully enduring, and intimate to the degree of being sacred. It is an association that promotes a way of life, not causes; a harmony in living, not political faiths; a bilateral loyalty, not commercial or social projects. Yet it is an association for as noble a purpose as any involved in our prior decisions. [The decisions upholding the convictions are] Reversed.

CONCUR: I agree with the Court that Connecticut's birth-control law unconstitutionally intrudes upon the right of marital privacy. The Ninth Amendment reads, "The enumeration in the Constitution, of certain rights, shall not be construed to deny or disparage others retained by the people." Although the Constitution does not speak in so many words of the right of privacy in marriage, I cannot believe that it offers these fundamental rights no protection. The fact that no particular provision of the Constitution explicitly forbids the State from disrupting the traditional relation of the family -- a relation as old and as fundamental as our entire civilization -- surely does not show that the Government was meant to have the power to do so. Rather, as the Ninth Amendment expressly recognizes, there are fundamental personal rights such as this one, which are protected from abridgment by the Government though not specifically mentioned in the Constitution.

DISSENT: Since 1879 Connecticut has had on its books a law which forbids the use of contraceptives by anyone. I think this is an uncommonly silly law. As a practical matter, the law is obviously unenforceable, except in the oblique context of the present case. As a philosophical matter, I believe the use of contraceptives in the relationship of marriage should be left to personal and private choice, based upon each individual's moral, ethical, and religious beliefs. As a matter of social policy, I think professional counsel about methods of birth control should be available to all, so that each individual's choice can be meaningfully made. But we are not asked in this case to say whether we think this law is unwise, or even asinine. We are asked to hold that it violates the United States Constitution. And that I cannot do.

What provision of the Constitution, then, does make this state law invalid? The Court says it is the right of privacy "created by several fundamental constitutional guarantees." With all deference, I can find no such general right of privacy in the Bill of Rights, in any other part of the Constitution, or in any case ever before decided by this Court.

It is the essence of judicial duty to subordinate our own personal views, our own ideas of what legislation is wise and what is not. If, as I should surely hope, the law before us does not reflect the standards of the people of Connecticut, the people of Connecticut can freely exercise their true Ninth and Tenth Amendment rights to persuade their elected representatives to repeal it. That is the constitutional way to take this law off the books.

# DISCUSSION QUESTIONS

(1) Should the Court uphold a right to privacy, even though the word "privacy" never appears in the U.S. Constitution?

(2) Are the philosophical and moral views of the justices relevant in deciding important cases the Court hears?

## CAREY v. POPULATION SERVICES INTERNATIONAL
### 431 U.S. 678 (U.S. Supreme Court, 1977)

Under New York Law it is a crime (1) for any person to sell or distribute any contraceptive of any kind to a minor under the age of 16 years; (2) for anyone other than a licensed pharmacist to distribute contraceptives to persons 16 or over; and (3) for anyone, including licensed pharmacists, to advertise or display contraceptives. A District Court for the Southern District of New York declared [this statute] unconstitutional in its entirety under the First and Fourteenth Amendments of the Federal Constitution insofar as it applies to nonprescription contraceptives, and enjoined its enforcement as so applied. We affirm.

PPA is a corporation primarily engaged in the mail-order retail sale of nomedical contraceptive devices from its offices in North Carolina. PPA regularly advertises its products in periodicals published or circulated in New York, accepts orders from New York residents, and fills orders by mailing contraceptives to New York purchasers. Neither the advertisements nor the order forms accompanying them limit availability of PPA's products to persons of any particular age. Various New York officials have advised PPA that its activities violate New York law.

Although "[t]he Constitution does not explicitly mention any right of privacy," the Court has recognized that one aspect of the "liberty" protected by the Due Process Clause of the Fourteenth Amendment is "a right of personal privacy, or a guarantee of certain areas or zones of privacy." While the outer limits of this aspect of privacy have not been marked by the Court, it is clear that among the decisions that an individual may make without unjustified government interference are personal decisions "relating to marriage, procreation, contraception, family relationships; and child rearing and education." The decision whether or not to beget or bear a child is at the very heart of this cluster of constitutionally protected choices.

That the constitutionally protected right of privacy extends to an individual's liberty to make choices regarding contraception does not automatically invalidate every state regulation in this area. The business of manufacturing and selling contraceptives may be regulated in ways that do not infringe protected individual choices. And even a burdensome regulation may be validated by a sufficiently compelling state interest. [W]here a decision as fundamental as that whether to bear or beget a child is involved, regulations imposing a burden on it may be justified only by compelling state interests, and must be narrowly drawn to express only those interests.

Restrictions on the distribution of contraceptives clearly burden the freedom to make such decisions. A total prohibition against sale of contraceptives, for example, would intrude upon individual decisions in matters of procreation and contraception as harshly as a direct ban on their use.

Limiting the distribution of nonprescription contraceptives to licensed pharmacists clearly imposes a significant burden on the right of the individuals to use contraceptives if they choose to do so. The burden is, of course, not as great as that under a total ban on distribution. Nevertheless, the restriction of distribution channels to a small fraction of the total number of possible retail outlets renders contraceptive devices considerably less accessible to the public, reduces the opportunity for privacy of selection and purchase, and lessens the possibility of price competition.

There remains the inquiry whether the provision serves a compelling state interest. Insofar as [the statute] applies to nonhazardous contraceptives, it bears no relation to the State's interest in protecting health. Nor is the interest in protecting potential life implicated in regulation of contraceptives.

The question of the extent of state power to regulate conduct of minors not constitutionally regulable when committed by adults is a vexing one, perhaps not susceptible of precise answer. Appellants argue that significant state interests are served by restricting minors' access to contraceptives, because free availability to minors of contraceptives would lead to increased sexual activity among the young, in violation of the policy of New York to discourage such behavior.

[T]here is substantial reason for doubt whether limiting access to contraceptives will in fact substantially discourage early sexual behavior. [W]ith or without access to contraceptives, the incidence of sexual activity among minors is high, and the consequences of such activity are frequently devastating.

Appellants argue that such a restriction serves to emphasize to young people the seriousness with which the State views the decision to engage in sexual intercourse at an early age. But this is only another form of the argument that juvenile sexual conduct will be deterred by making contraceptives more difficult to obtain.

Appellants contend that advertisements of contraceptive products would be offensive and embarrassing to those exposed to them, and that permitting them would legitimize sexual activity of young people. But these are classically not justifications validating the suppression of expression protected by the First Amendment. At least where obscenity is not involved, we have consistently held that the fact that protected speech may be offensive to some does not justify its suppression. As for the possible "legitimation" of illicit sexual behavior, whatever might be the case if the advertisements directly incited illicit sexual activity among the young, none of the advertisements in this record can even remotely be characterized as "directed to inciting or producing imminent lawless action and... likely to incite or produce such action." They merely state the availability of products and services that are not only entirely legal, but constitutionally protected. These arguments therefore do not justify the total suppression of advertising concerning contraceptives. Affirmed.

DISSENT: The majority of New York's citizens are in effect told that however deeply they may be concerned about the problem of promiscuous sex and intercourse among unmarried teenagers, they may not adopt this

36

means of dealing with it. The Court holds that New York may not use its police power to legislate in the interests of its concept of the public morality as it pertains to minors. I would reverse the judgment.

## DISCUSSION QUESTIONS

(1) Did the New York legislature impose morality through the law in passing this statute? Does the Court impose its personal moral views in this decision? Is it ever appropriate to legislate or adjudicate morality through the power of the legal system?

### LOVING v. VIRGINIA
388 U.S. 1 (U.S. Supreme Court, 1967)

This case presents a constitutional question never addressed by this Court: whether a statutory scheme adopted by the State of Virginia to prevent marriages between persons solely on the basis of racial classifications violates the Equal Protection and Due Process Clauses of the Fourteenth Amendment. [W]e conclude that these statutes cannot stand consistently with the Fourteenth Amendment.

In June 1958, two residents of Virginia, Mildred Jeter, a Negro woman, and Richard Loving, a white man, were married in the District of Columbia. Shortly after, the Lovings returned to Virginia and established their marital abode. [In October] 1958, a grand jury issued an indictment charging the Lovings with violating Virginia's ban on interracial marriages. [T]he Lovings pleaded guilty and were sentenced to one year in jail; the trial judge suspended the sentence on the condition that the Lovings leave the State and not return to Virginia together for 25 years. He stated that: "Almighty God created the races white, black, yellow, malay and red, and he placed them on separate continents. And but for the interference with his arrangement there would be no cause for such marriages. The fact that he separated the races shows that he did not intend for the races to mix."

[T]he Lovings took up residence in the District of Columbia. [I]n 1963, they filed a motion to vacate the judgment and set aside the sentence on the ground that the statutes were repugnant to the Fourteenth Amendment. The Supreme Court of Appeals [of Virginia] upheld the constitutionality of the antimiscegenation statutes and affirmed the convictions.

Virginia is one of 16 States which prohibit and punish marriages on the basis of racial classifications. Penalties for miscegenation arose as an incident to slavery and have been common in Virginia since the colonial period. The present statutory scheme dates from the adoption of the Racial Integrity Act of 1924. The central features of this Act are the absolute prohibition of a "white person" marrying other than another "white person" [and] a prohibition against issuing marriage licenses until the issuing official is satisfied that the applicants' statements as to race are correct.

[T]he state court concluded that the State's legitimate purposes were "to preserve the racial integrity of its citizens," and to prevent "the corruption of blood," "a mongrel breed of citizens," and "the obliteration of racial pride," obviously an endorsement of the doctrine of White Supremacy. [T]he State contends that, because its miscegenation statutes punish equally both the white and the Negro participants in an interracial marriage, these statutes, despite their reliance on racial classifications, do not constitute an invidious discrimination based upon race.

[W]e reject the notion that the "equal application" of a statute containing racial classifications is enough to remove the classifications from the Fourteenth Amendment's proscription of all invidious racial discriminations.

[T]he Equal Protection Clause requires the consideration of whether the classifications drawn by any statute constitute an arbitrary and invidious discrimination. The clear and central purpose of the Fourteenth Amendment was to eliminate all official state sources of invidious racial discrimination.

Virginia's miscegenation statutes rest solely upon distinctions drawn according to race. The statutes proscribe generally accepted conduct if engaged in by members of different races. [T]his Court has consistently repudiated "distinctions between citizens solely because of their ancestry" as being "odious to a free people whose institutions are founded upon the doctrine of equality." There is no legitimate overriding purpose independent of invidious racial discrimination which justifies this classification. The fact that Virginia prohibits only interracial marriages involving white persons demonstrates that the racial classifications [are] measures designed to maintain White Supremacy. We have consistently denied the constitutionality of measures which restrict the rights of citizens on account of race. There can be no doubt that restricting the freedom to marry solely because of racial classifications violates the central meaning of the Equal Protection Clause.

These statutes also deprive the Lovings of liberty without due process of law in violation of the Due Process Clause of the Fourteenth Amendment. The freedom to marry has long been recognized as one of the vital personal rights essential to the orderly pursuit of happiness by free men.

Marriage is one of the "basic civil rights of man," fundamental to our very existence and survival. To deny this fundamental freedom on so unsupportable a basis as the racial classifications embodied in these statutes, classifications so directly subversive of the principle of equality at the heart of the Fourteenth Amendment, is surely to deprive all the State's citizens of liberty without due process of law. The Fourteenth Amendment requires that the freedom of choice to marry not be restricted by invidious racial discriminations. Under our Constitution, the freedom to marry, or not marry, a person of another race resides with the individual and cannot be infringed by the State. These convictions must be reversed.

## DISCUSSION QUESTIONS

(1) What other restrictions on marriage might a state impose which would be upheld, under the reasoning here?

(2) None of the justices who sometimes object to imposition of moral codes dissented from this decision. What might explain this?

# IN THE MATTER OF BABY M
## 109 N.J. 396 (Supreme Court of New Jersey, 1988)

[T]he Court is asked to determine the validity of a contract that purports to provide a new way of bringing children into a family. For a fee of $10,000, a woman agrees to be artificially inseminated with the semen of another woman's husband; she is to conceive a child, carry it to term, and after its birth surrender it to the natural father and his wife. The intent of the contract is that the child's natural mother will thereafter be forever separated from her child. The wife is to adopt the child, and she and the natural father are to be regarded as its parents for all purposes. [T]his is called a "surrogacy contract," the natural mother inappropriately called the "surrogate mother."

We invalidate the surrogacy contract because it conflicts with the law and public policy of this State. While we recognize the depth of the yearning of infertile couples to have their own children, we find the payment of money to a "surrogate" mother illegal, perhaps criminal, and potentially degrading to women. Although in this case we grant custody to the natural father, the evidence having clearly proved such custody to be in the best interests of the infant, we void both the termination of the surrogate mother's parental rights and the adoption of the child by the wife/stepparent. We thus restore the "surrogate" as the mother of the child.

We find no offense to our present laws where a woman voluntarily and without payment agrees to act as a "surrogate" mother, provided that she is not subject to a binding agreement to surrender her child. Moreover, our holding today does not preclude the Legislature from altering the current statutory scheme so as to permit surrogacy contracts. Under current law, however, the surrogacy agreement before us is illegal and invalid.

In 1985, William Stern and Mary Beth Whitehead entered into a surrogacy contract. It recited that Stern's wife, Elizabeth, was infertile, that they wanted a child, and that Mrs. Whitehead was willing to provide that child as the mother with Mr. Stern as the father.

The contract provided that through artificial insemination using Mr. Stern's sperm, Mrs. Whitehead would become pregnant, carry the child to term, bear it, deliver it to the Sterns, and thereafter do whatever was necessary to terminate her maternal rights so that Mrs. Stern could thereafter adopt the child. Mrs. Whitehead's husband, Richard, was also a party to the contract; Mrs. Stern was not. Mr. Whitehead promised to do all acts necessary to rebut the presumption of paternity under the Parentage Act. Although Mrs. Stern was not a party to the surrogacy agreement, the contract gave her sole custody of the child in the event of Mr. Stern's death. Mrs. Stern's status as a nonparty to the surrogate parenting agreement presumably was to avoid the application of the baby-selling statute to this arrangement. Mr. Stern agreed to attempt the artificial insemination and to pay Mrs. Whitehead $10,000 after the child's birth, on its delivery to him.

Mrs. Whitehead realized, almost from the moment of birth, that she could not part with this child. Some indication of the attachment was conveyed to the Sterns at the hospital when they told Mrs. Whitehead what they were going to name the baby. She apparently broke into tears and indicated that she did not know if she could give up the child.

Nonetheless, Mrs. Whitehead was, for the moment, true to her word. Despite powerful inclinations to the contrary, she turned her child over to the Sterns at the Whiteheads' home. Later in the evening, Mrs. Whitehead became deeply disturbed, disconsolate, stricken with unbearable sadness. She had to have her child. She could not eat, sleep, or concentrate on anything other than her need for her baby. The next day she went to the Sterns' home and told them how much she was suffering.

The depth of Mrs. Whitehead's despair surprised and frightened the Sterns. She told them that she could not live without her baby, that she must have her, even if only for one week, that thereafter she would surrender her child. The Sterns, concerned that Mrs. Whitehead might indeed commit suicide, turned the child over to her. It was not until four months later, after a series of attempts to regain possession of the child, that Melissa was returned to the Sterns, having been forcibly removed from the home where she was then living with Mr. and Mrs. Whitehead, the home in Florida owned by Mary Beth Whitehead's parents.

The struggle over Baby M began when it became apparent that Mrs. Whitehead could not return the child to Mr. Stern. Due to Mrs. Whitehead's refusal to relinquish the baby, Mr. Stern filed a complaint seeking enforcement of the surrogacy contract. We have concluded that this surrogacy contract is invalid. Our conclusion has two bases: direct conflict with existing statutes and conflict with the public policies of this State.

One of the surrogacy contract's basic purposes, to achieve the adoption of a child through private placement, though permitted in New Jersey "is very much disfavored." Its use of money for this purpose -- and we have no doubt whatsoever that the money is being paid to obtain an adoption and not, as the Sterns argue, for the personal services of Mary Beth Whitehead -- is illegal and perhaps criminal. In addition to the inducement of money, there is the coercion of contract: the natural mother's irrevocable agreement, prior to birth, even prior to conception, to surrender the child to the adoptive couple. Such an agreement is totally unenforceable in private placement adoption. Integral to these invalid provisions of the contract is the related agreement, equally invalid, on the part of the natural mother to cooperate with proceedings to terminate her parental rights, as well as her contractual concession, in aid of the adoption, that the child's best interests would be served by awarding custody to the natural father and his wife.

The contract's basic premise, that the natural parents can decide in advance of birth which one is to have custody of the child, bears no relationship to the settled law that the child's best interests shall determine custody.

This is the sale of a child, or, at the very least, the sale of a mother's right to her child, the only mitigating factor being that one of the purchasers is the father. Almost every evil that prompted the prohibition on the payment of money in connection with adoptions exists here.

Intimated, but disputed, is the assertion that surrogacy will be used for the benefit of the rich at the expense of the poor. [I]t is clear to us that it is unlikely that surrogate mothers will be as proportionately numerous among those women in the top twenty percent income bracket as among those in the bottom twenty percent.

Mrs. Whitehead agreed to the surrogacy arrangement, supposedly fully understanding the consequences. Putting aside the issue of how compelling her need for money may have been, and how significant her understanding of the consequences, we suggest that her consent is irrelevant. There are, in a civilized society, some things that money cannot buy. There are, in short, values that society deems more important than granting to wealth whatever it can buy, be it labor, love, or life.

Both parties argue that the Constitutions -- state and federal -- mandate approval of their basic claims. The source of their constitutional arguments is essentially the same: the right of privacy, the right to procreate, the right to the companionship of one's child. They are the rights of personal intimacy, of marriage, of sex, of family, of procreation.

The right to procreate very simply is the right to have natural children, whether through sexual intercourse or artificial insemination. Mr. Stern has not been deprived of that right. Through artificial insemination of Mrs. Whitehead, Baby M is his child. The custody, care, companionship, and nurturing that follow birth are not parts of the right to procreation; they are rights that may also be constitutionally protected, but that involve many considerations other than the right of procreation.

If the Legislature decides to address surrogacy, consideration of this case will highlight many of its potential harms. In addition to the inevitable confrontation with the ethical and moral issues involved, there is the question of the wisdom and effectiveness of regulating a matter so private, yet of such public interest. Legislative consideration of surrogacy may also provide the opportunity to begin to focus on the overall implications of the new reproductive biotechnology -- *in vitro* fertilization, preservation of sperm and eggs, embryo implantation and the like. The problem is how to enjoy the benefits of the technology while minimizing the risk of abuse. The problem can be addressed only when society decides what its values and objectives are in this troubling, yet promising, area.

## DISCUSSION QUESTIONS

(1) What provisions should a state legislature include in determining appropriate laws concerning surrogate motherhood? What values and objectives of society should be taken into account in legislating?

(2) Should the renting of wombs by women be analyzed in the same way in which we consider prostitution?

### Gay Rights

### LAWRENCE v. TEXAS
539 U.S. 558 (U.S. Supreme Court, 2003)

Liberty protects the person from unwarranted government intrusions into a dwelling or other private places. And there are other spheres of our lives and existence, outside the home, where the State should not be a dominant presence. Freedom extends beyond spatial bounds. Liberty presumes an autonomy of self that includes freedom of thought, belief, expression, and

41

certain intimate conduct. The instant case involves liberty of the person both in its spatial and more transcendent dimensions.

The question before the Court is the validity of a Texas statute making it a crime for two persons of the same sex to engage in certain intimate sexual conduct.

In Houston, Texas, officers of the Police Department were dispatched to a private residence in response to a weapons disturbance. The officers observed Lawrence and another man engaging in a sexual act. The petitioners were arrested, held in custody over night, and charged and convicted.

The complaints described their crime as "deviate sexual intercourse, namely anal sex, with a member of the same sex (man)." The applicable state law defines "deviate sexual intercourse" as follows: "(A) any contact between any part of the genitals of one person and the mouth or anus of another person; or (B) the penetration of the genitals or the anus of another person with an object."

The petitioners challenged the statute as a violation of the Equal Protection Clause of the Fourteenth Amendment and of a like provision of the Texas Constitution. The Court of Appeals affirmed the convictions. The majority opinion indicates that the Court considered our decision in *Bowers v. Hardwick* (1986) to be controlling. We granted *certiorari*, to consider three questions:

1. Whether Petitioners' criminal convictions under the Texas "Homosexual Conduct" law--which criminalizes sexual intimacy by same-sex couples, but not identical behavior by different-sex couples--violate the Fourteenth Amendment guarantee of equal protection of laws?

2. Whether Petitioners' criminal convictions for adult consensual sexual intimacy in the home violate their vital interests in liberty and privacy protected by the Due Process Clause of the Fourteenth Amendment?

3. Whether *Bowers v. Hardwick* should be overruled?"

The petitioners were adults at the time of the alleged offense. Their conduct was in private and consensual. The facts in *Bowers* had some similarities to the instant case.

The Court began its substantive discussion in *Bowers*: "The issue presented is whether the Federal Constitution confers a fundamental right upon homosexuals to engage in sodomy and hence invalidates the laws of the many States that still make such conduct illegal and have done so for a very long time." That statement discloses the Court's own failure to appreciate the extent of the liberty at stake. To say that the issue in *Bowers* was simply the right to engage in certain sexual conduct demeans the claim the individual put forward, just as it would demean a married couple were it to be said marriage is simply about the right to have sexual intercourse. The laws involved in *Bowers* and here are, to be sure, statutes that purport to do no more than prohibit a particular sexual act. Their penalties and purposes, though, have more far-reaching consequences, touching upon the most private human conduct, sexual behavior, and in the most private of places, the home. The statutes do seek to control a personal relationship that, whether or not entitled to formal recognition in the law, is within the liberty of persons to choose without being punished as criminals.

It suffices to acknowledge that adults may choose to enter upon this relationship in the confines of their homes and their own private lives and still retain their dignity as free persons. When sexuality finds overt expression in intimate conduct with another person, the conduct can be but one element in a personal bond that is more enduring. The liberty protected by the Constitution allows homosexual persons the right to make this choice.

[I]t should be noted that there is no longstanding history in this country of laws directed at homosexual conduct as a distinct matter. It was not until the 1970's that any State singled out same-sex relations for criminal prosecution, and only nine States have done so. Over the last decades, States with same-sex prohibitions have moved toward abolishing them.[T]he historical grounds relied upon in *Bowers* are more complex than the majority opinion indicate[s]. Their historical premises are not without doubt and, at the very least, are overstated.

It must be acknowledged that the Court in *Bowers* was making the broader point that for centuries there have been powerful voices to condemn homosexual conduct as immoral. The condemnation has been shaped by religious beliefs, conceptions of right and acceptable behavior, and respect for the traditional family. For many persons these are not trivial concerns but profound and deep convictions accepted as ethical and moral principles to which they aspire and which thus determine the course of their lives. These considerations do not answer the question before us, however. The issue is whether the majority may use the power of the State to enforce these views on the whole society through operation of the criminal law.

The doctrine of *stare decisis* is essential to the respect accorded to the judgments of the Court and to the stability of the law. It is not, however, an inexorable command. The holding in *Bowers* has not induced detrimental reliance comparable to some instances where recognized individual rights are involved. Indeed, there has been no individual or societal reliance on *Bowers* of the sort that could counsel against overturning its holding once there are compelling reasons to do so.

*Bowers* was not correct when it was decided, and it is not correct today. It ought not to remain binding precedent. *Bowers v. Hardwick* should be and now is overruled.

The present case does not involve minors. It does not involve persons who might be injured or coerced or who are situated in relationships where consent might not easily be refused. It does not involve public conduct or prostitution. It does not involve whether the government must give formal recognition to any relationship that homosexual persons seek to enter. The case does involve two adults who, with full and mutual consent from each other, engaged in sexual practices common to a homosexual lifestyle. The petitioners are entitled to respect for their private lives. The State cannot demean their existence or control their destiny by making their private sexual conduct a crime. Their right to liberty under the Due Process Clause gives them the full right to engage in their conduct without intervention of the government. The Texas statute furthers no legitimate state interest which can justify its intrusion into the personal and private life of the individual.

CONCUR: The Equal Protection Clause of the Fourteenth Amendment "is essentially a direction that all persons similarly situated should be treated alike." The statute at issue here makes sodomy a crime only if a person "engages in deviate sexual intercourse with another individual of the same sex." Sodomy between opposite-sex partners is not a crime in Texas. That is, Texas treats the same conduct differently based solely on the participants.

A law branding one class of persons as criminal solely based on the State's moral disapproval of that class and the conduct associated with that class runs contrary to the values of the Constitution and the Equal Protection Clause. I therefore concur in the Court's judgment that Texas' sodomy law banning "deviate sexual intercourse" between consenting adults of the same sex, but not between consenting adults of different sexes, is unconstitutional.

DISSENT: "Liberty finds no refuge in a jurisprudence of doubt." That was the Court's sententious response, barely more than a decade ago, to those seeking to overrule *Roe v. Wade*. The Court's response today, to those who have engaged in a 17-year crusade to overrule *Bowers v. Hardwick* is very different. The need for stability and certainty presents no barrier.

I do not myself believe in rigid adherence to *stare decisis* in constitutional cases; but I do believe that we should be consistent rather than manipulative in invoking the doctrine. Today, the widespread opposition to *Bowers*, a decision resolving an issue as "intensely divisive" as the issue in *Roe*, is offered as a reason in favor of overruling it.

Today's approach to *stare decisis* invites us to overrule an erroneously decided precedent if: (1) its foundations have been "eroded" by subsequent decisions, (2) it has been subject to "substantial and continuing" criticism; and (3) it has not induced "individual or societal reliance" that counsels against overturning. The problem is that *Roe* itself satisfies these conditions to at least the same degree as *Bowers*.

Having decided that it need not adhere to *stare decisis*, the Court still must establish that *Bowers* was wrongly decided and that the Texas statute, as applied to petitioners, is unconstitutional.

[The] Texas Penal Code undoubtedly imposes constraints on liberty. So do laws prohibiting prostitution, recreational use of heroin, and, for that matter, working more than 60 hours per week in a bakery. But there is no right to "liberty" under the Due Process Clause, though today's opinion repeatedly makes that claim.

The Texas statute undeniably seeks to further the belief of its citizens that certain forms of sexual behavior are "immoral and unacceptable" --the same interest furthered by criminal laws against fornication, bigamy, adultery, adult incest, bestiality, and obscenity. *Bowers* held that this was a legitimate state interest. The Court today reaches the opposite conclusion. This effectively decrees the end of all morals legislation. If the promotion of majoritarian sexual morality is not even a legitimate state interest, none of the above-mentioned laws can survive rational-basis review.

To be sure, [the statute] does distinguish between the sexes insofar as concerns the partner with whom the sexual acts are performed: men can violate the law only with other men, and women only with other women. But this cannot itself be a denial of equal protection, since it is precisely the same distinction regarding partner that is drawn in state laws prohibiting marriage with someone of the same sex while permitting marriage with someone of the opposite sex.

[T]he Court has taken sides in the culture war, departing from its role of assuring, as neutral observer, that the democratic rules of engagement are observed. Many Americans do not want persons who openly engage in homosexual conduct as partners in their business, as scoutmasters for their children, as teachers in their children's schools, or as boarders in their home. They view this as protecting themselves and their families from a lifestyle that they believe to be immoral and destructive. The Court views it as "discrimination" which it is the function of our judgments to deter.

The people may feel that their disapprobation of homosexual conduct is strong enough to disallow homosexual marriage, but not strong enough to criminalize private homosexual acts--and may legislate accordingly. The Court today pretends that it possesses a similar freedom of action, so that we need not fear judicial imposition of homosexual marriage, as has recently occurred in Canada. [T]he Court says that the present case "does not involve whether the government must give formal recognition to any relationship that homosexual persons seek to enter." Do not believe it. [A]n earlier passage declares that "persons in a homosexual relationship may seek autonomy for these purposes, just as heterosexual persons do." Today's opinion dismantles the structure of constitutional law that has permitted a distinction to be made between heterosexual and homosexual unions, insofar as formal recognition in marriage is concerned. If moral disapprobation of homosexual conduct is "no legitimate state interest" for purposes of proscribing that conduct; and if, as the Court coos, "when sexuality finds overt expression in intimate conduct with another person, the conduct can be but one element in a personal bond that is more enduring;" what justification could there possibly be for denying the benefits of marriage to homosexual couples exercising "the liberty protected by the Constitution"? Surely not the encouragement of procreation, since the sterile and the elderly are allowed to marry. This case "does not involve" the issue of homosexual marriage only if one entertains the belief that principle and logic have nothing to do with the decisions of this Court. Many will hope that, as the Court comfortingly assures us, this is so.

## DISCUSSION QUESTIONS

(1) If our right to liberty protects private homosexual conduct, should it also protect prostitution, recreational use of heroin, fornication, bigamy, adultery, adult incest, bestiality, obscenity, and same-sex marriage?

(2) To what extent are we justified in using the coercive power of the law to restrict individual liberty? To prevent harm to others? To prevent harm to the actor himself or herself?

(3) Are we ever justified in using the law to enforce moral principles?

## WATKINS v. UNITED STATES ARMY
### 847 F.2d 1329 (9th Cir., 1987)

In August 1967, Perry Watkins enlisted in the United States Army. In filling out the Army's pre-induction medical form, he candidly marked "yes" in response to a question whether he had homosexual tendencies. The Army nonetheless considered Watkins "qualified for admission" and inducted him into its ranks. Watkins became, in the words of his commanding officer, "one of our most respected and trusted soldiers." Even though Watkins' homosexuality was common knowledge, the Army never claimed that his sexual orientation or behavior interfered in any way with military functions.

In 1981 the Army promulgated new regulations which mandated the disqualification of all homosexuals from the Army without regard to the length or quality of their military service. [T]he Army notified Watkins that he would be discharged and denied reenlistment because of his homosexuality. In this court action, Watkins challenges the Army's actions and new regulations on various statutory and constitutional grounds.

Watkins claim[s] that the Army's regulations deny him equal protection of the laws in violation of the Fifth Amendment. Specifically, Watkins argues that the Army's regulations constitute an invidious discrimination based on sexual orientation.

We conclude that these regulations discriminate against homosexuals on the basis of their sexual orientation. Under the Army's regulations, "homosexuality," not sexual conduct, is the operative trait for disqualification. In short, the regulations do not penalize all statements of sexual desire, or even only statements of homosexual desire; they penalize only homosexuals who declare their homosexual orientation.

If a straight soldier and a gay soldier of the same sex engage in homosexual acts because they are drunk, immature or curious, the straight soldier may remain in the Army while the gay soldier is automatically terminated. In short, the regulations do not penalize soldiers for engaging in homosexual acts; they penalize soldiers who have engaged in homosexual acts only when the Army decides that those soldiers are actually gay.

[T]he discrimination against homosexual orientation is about as complete as one could imagine. The regulations make any act or statement that might conceivably indicate a homosexual orientation evidence of homosexuality; that evidence is in turn weighed against any evidence of a heterosexual orientation. It is thus clear that the regulations directly burden the class consisting of persons of homosexual orientation.

We now address the merits of Watkins' claim that we must subject the Army's regulations to strict scrutiny because homosexuals constitute a suspect class under equal protection jurisprudence. [T]he discrimination faced by homosexuals in our society is plainly no less pernicious or intense than the discrimination faced by other groups already treated as suspect classes, such as aliens or people of a particular national origin.

[W]e have no trouble concluding that sexual orientation is immutable for the purposes of equal protection doctrine. Although the causes of homosexuality are not fully understood, scientific research indicates that we have little control over our sexual orientation and that, once acquired, our sexual orientation is largely impervious to change.

In sum, our analysis of the relevant factors in determining whether a given group should be considered a suspect class for the purposes of equal protection doctrine ineluctably leads us to the conclusion that homosexuals constitute such a suspect class.

[E]ven granting special deference to the policy choices of the military, we must reject many of the Army's asserted justifications because they illegitimately cater to private biases.

These concerns strike a familiar chord. For much of our history, the military's fear of racial tension kept black soldiers separated from whites. As recently as World War II both the Army chief of staff and the Secretary of the Navy justified racial segregation in the ranks as necessary to maintain efficiency, discipline, and morale. Indeed, the Supreme Court has decisively rejected the notion that private prejudice against minorities can ever justify official discrimination, even when those private prejudices create real and legitimate problems.

[T]he Army believes that its ban against homosexuals simply codifies society's moral consensus that homosexuality is evil. Yet, even accepting *arguendo* this proposition that anti-homosexual animus is grounded in morality (as opposed to prejudice masking as morality), equal protection doctrine does not permit notions of majoritarian morality to serve as compelling justification for laws that discriminate against suspect classes.

We hold that the Army's regulations violate the constitutional guarantee of equal protection of the laws because they discriminate against persons of homosexual orientation, a suspect class, and because the regulations are not necessary to promote a legitimate compelling governmental interest. We thus enter an injunction requiring the Army to consider Watkins' reenlistment application without regard to his sexual orientation.

## DISCUSSION QUESTIONS

(1) Has the majority imposed its personal moral views on this decision or is it based clearly on the law alone?

(2) Should the rights of homosexuals in the military be the same as the rights of racial minorities?

## BOY SCOUTS OF AMERICA v. DALE
### 530 U.S. 64 (U.S. Supreme Court, 2000)

The Boy Scouts is a private, not-for-profit organization engaged in instilling its system of values in young people. The Boy Scouts asserts that homosexual conduct is inconsistent with the values it seeks to instill. James Dale [is] a former Eagle Scout whose adult membership in the Boy Scouts was revoked when the Boy Scouts learned that he is an avowed homosexual and gay rights activist. The New Jersey Supreme Court held that New Jersey's public accommodations law requires that the Boy Scouts admit Dale. This case presents the question whether applying New Jersey's public accommodations law in this way violates the Boy Scouts' First Amendment right of expressive association. We hold that it does.

Dale applied for adult membership in the Boy Scouts in 1989. The Boy Scouts approved his application for the position of assistant scoutmaster. Around the same time, Dale left home to attend Rutgers University. After arriving at Rutgers, Dale first acknowledged to himself and others that he is gay. He became involved with, and eventually became the copresident of, the Rutgers University Lesbian/Gay Alliance. Dale attended a seminar addressing the psychological and health needs of lesbian and gay teenagers.

A newspaper covering the event interviewed Dale about his advocacy of homosexual teenagers' need for gay role models. [T]he newspaper published the interview and Dale's photograph over a caption identifying him as the copresident of the Lesbian/Gay Alliance.

Later, Dale received a letter from Monmouth Council Executive James Kay revoking his adult membership. Dale wrote to Kay requesting the reason for Monmouth Council's decision. Kay responded that the Boy Scouts "specifically forbid membership to homosexuals."

The forced inclusion of an unwanted person in a group infringes the group's freedom of expressive association if the presence of that person affects in a significant way the group's ability to advocate public or private viewpoints. To determine whether a group is protected by the First Amendment's expressive associational right, we must determine whether the group engages in "expressive association."

[T]he general mission of the Boy Scouts is clear: "To instill values in young people." The Boy Scouts seeks to instill these values by having its adult leaders spend time with the youth members, instructing and engaging them in activities like camping, archery, and fishing. During the time spent with the youth members, the scoutmasters and assistant scoutmasters inculcate them with the Boy Scouts' values -- both expressly and by example. It seems indisputable that an association that seeks to transmit such a system of values engages in expressive activity.

Given that the Boy Scouts engages in expressive activity, we must determine whether the forced inclusion of Dale as an assistant scoutmaster would significantly affect the Boy Scouts' ability to advocate public or private viewpoints.

The Boy Scouts asserts that homosexual conduct is inconsistent with the values embodied in the Scout Oath and Law, particularly with the values represented by the terms "morally straight" and "clean."

Obviously, the Oath and Law do not expressly mention sexuality or sexual orientation. And the terms "morally straight" and "clean" are by no means self-defining. Different people would attribute to those terms very different meanings. [S]ome people may believe that engaging in homosexual conduct is not at odds with being "morally straight" and "clean." And others may believe that engaging in homosexual conduct is contrary to being "morally straight" and "clean." The Boy Scouts says it falls within the latter.

We must then determine whether Dale's presence as an assistant scoutmaster would significantly burden the Boy Scouts' desire to not "promote homosexual conduct as a legitimate form of behavior." As we give deference to an association's assertions regarding the nature of its expression, we must also give deference to an association's view of what would impair its expression. Dale is one of a group of gay Scouts who have "become leaders in their community and are open and honest about their sexual orientation."

We recognized in [other] cases that States have a compelling interest in eliminating discrimination against women in public accommodations. But in each of these cases we went on to conclude that the enforcement of these statutes would not materially interfere with the ideas that the organization sought to express.

We are not guided by our views of whether the Boy Scouts' teachings with respect to homosexual conduct are right or wrong; public or judicial disapproval of a tenet of an organization's expression does not justify the State's effort to compel the organization to accept members where such acceptance would derogate from the organization's expressive message.

DISSENT: The majority holds that New Jersey's law violates BSA's right to associate and its right to free speech. But that law does not "impose any serious burdens" on BSA's "collective effort on behalf of [its] shared goals," nor does it force BSA to communicate any message that it does not wish to endorse.

It is plain as the light of day that neither one of these principles – "morally straight" and "clean" -- says the slightest thing about homosexuality. Indeed, neither term in the Boy   Scouts' Law and Oath expresses any position whatsoever on sexual matters.

The only apparent explanation for the majority's holding, is that homosexuals are simply so different from the rest of society that their presence alone -- unlike any other individual's -- should be singled out for special First Amendment treatment. Under the majority's reasoning, an openly gay male is irreversibly affixed with the label "homosexual." That label, even though unseen, communicates a message that permits his exclusion wherever he goes. His openness is the sole and sufficient justification for his ostracism. Though unintended, reliance on such a justification is tantamount to a constitutionally prescribed symbol of inferiority.

## DISCUSSION QUESTIONS

(1) Is the Court consistent in requiring the Jaycees and Rotary clubs to admit women, but not to require the Boy Scouts to admit homosexuals?

(2) Should the right to association extend to groups which want to exclude certain races? Ages? Religions?

(3) Is the court's conclusion here consistent with its analysis in *Lawrence v. Texas*?

## BAKER v. VERMONT
### 744 A.2d 864 (Supreme Court of Vermont, 1999)

May the State of Vermont exclude same-sex couples from the benefits and protections that its laws provide to opposite-sex married couples? That is the fundamental question we address in this appeal, a question that the Court well knows arouses deeply-felt religious, moral, and political beliefs. The issue before the Court, moreover, does not turn on the religious or moral debate over intimate same-sex relationships, but rather on the statutory and constitutional basis for the exclusion of same-sex couples from the secular benefits and protections offered married couples.

We conclude that under the Common Benefits Clause of the Vermont Constitution, which, in part, reads, "That government is, or ought to be, instituted for the common benefit, protection, and security of the people, nation, or community, and not for the particular emolument or advantage of any single person, family, or set of persons, who are a part only of that community," plaintiffs may not be deprived of the statutory benefits and protections afforded persons of the opposite sex who choose to marry. We hold that the State is constitutionally required to extend to same-sex couples the common benefits and protections that flow from marriage under Vermont law. Whether this ultimately takes the form of inclusion within the marriage laws themselves or a parallel "domestic partnership" system or some equivalent statutory alternative, rests with the Legislature.

Plaintiffs are three same-sex couples who have lived together in committed relationships for periods ranging from four to twenty-five years. Each couple applied for a marriage license from their respective town clerk, and each was refused a license as ineligible under the applicable state marriage laws. Plaintiffs thereupon filed this lawsuit seeking a declaratory judgment that the refusal to issue them a license violated the marriage statutes and the Vermont Constitution.

[P]laintiffs contend that the exclusion violates their right to the common benefit and protection of the law guaranteed by the Vermont Constitution. They note that in denying them access to a civil marriage license, the law effectively excludes them from a broad array of legal benefits and protections incident to the marital relation, including access to a spouse's medical, life, and disability insurance, hospital visitation and other medical decision-making privileges, spousal support, intestate succession, homestead protections, and many other statutory protections.

[I]t is important to emphasize that it is the Common Benefits Clause of the Vermont Constitution we are construing, rather than its counterpart, the Equal Protection Clause of the Fourteenth Amendment to the United States Constitution.

We must ultimately ascertain whether the omission of a part of the community from the benefit, protection and security of the challenged law bears a reasonable and just relation to the governmental purpose.

[T]he State has a legitimate and long-standing interest in promoting a permanent commitment between couples for the security of their children. It is equally undeniable that the State's interest has been advanced by extending formal public sanction and protection to the union of those couples considered capable of having children, i.e., men and women. And there is no doubt that the overwhelming majority of births today continue to result from natural conception between one man and one woman.

It is equally undisputed that many opposite-sex couples marry for reasons unrelated to procreation, that some of these couples never intend to have children, and that others are incapable of having children. The law extends the benefits and protections of marriage to many persons with no logical connection to the stated governmental goal.

Furthermore, there is no dispute that a significant number of children today are actually being raised by same-sex parents, and that increasing numbers of children are being conceived by such parents through a variety of assisted-reproductive techniques.

[T]o the extent that the State's purpose in licensing civil marriage was, and is, to legitimize children and provide for their security, the statutes plainly exclude many same-sex couples who are no different from opposite-sex couples with respect to these objectives. If anything, the exclusion of same-sex couples from the legal protections incident to marriage exposes their children to the precise risks that the State argues the marriage laws are designed to secure against. In short, the marital exclusion treats persons who are similarly situated for purposes of the law, differently.

[T]he marriage laws transform a private agreement into a source of significant public benefits and protections. The legal benefits and protections flowing from a marriage license are of such significance that any statutory exclusion must necessarily be grounded on public concerns of sufficient weight, cogency, and authority that the justice of the deprivation cannot seriously be questioned.

In 1996, the Vermont General Assembly enacted a law removing all prior legal barriers to the adoption of children by same-sex couples. In light of these express policy choices, the State's arguments that Vermont public policy favors opposite-sex over same-sex parents or disfavors the use of artificial reproductive technologies, are patently without substance.

[W]e conclude that none of the interests asserted by the State provides a reasonable and just basis for the continued exclusion of same-sex couples from the benefits incident to a civil marriage license under Vermont law.

We hold only that plaintiffs are entitled under the Vermont Constitution to obtain the same benefits and protections afforded by Vermont law to married opposite-sex couples. We do not purport to infringe upon the prerogatives of the Legislature to craft an appropriate means of addressing this constitutional mandate, other than to note that the record here refers to a number of potentially constitutional statutory schemes from other jurisdictions. These include what are typically referred to as "domestic partnership" or "registered partnership" acts, which generally establish an alternative legal status to marriage for same-sex couples, impose similar formal requirements and limitations, create a parallel licensing or registration scheme, and extend all or most of the same rights and obligations provided by the law to married partners.

DISSENT: I concur with the majority's holding, but I respectfully dissent from its novel and truncated remedy, which in my view abdicates this Court's constitutional duty to redress violations of constitutional rights. I would grant the requested relief and enjoin defendants from denying plaintiffs a marriage license based solely on the sex of the applicants.

## DISCUSSION QUESTIONS

(1) Is marriage primarily a religious covenant or a legal agreement? What are the implications of each?

(2) Although this decision was based on the Vermont state constitution, is any of the reasoning applicable to marriage laws in other states?

## GOODRIDGE v. DEPT. OF PUBLIC HEALTH
440 Mass. 309 (Supreme Judicial Court of Massachusetts, 2003)

Marriage is a vital social institution. The exclusive commitment of two individuals to each other nurtures love and mutual support; it brings stability to our society. For those who choose to marry, and for their children, marriage provides an abundance of legal, financial, and social benefits. In return it imposes weighty legal, financial, and social obligations. The question before us is whether the Commonwealth may deny the protections, benefits, and obligations conferred by civil marriage to two individuals of the same sex who wish to marry. We conclude that it may not. The Massachusetts Constitution affirms the dignity and equality of all individuals. It forbids the creation of second-class citizens.

We are mindful that our decision marks a change in the history of our marriage law. Many people hold deep-seated religious, moral, and ethical convictions that marriage should be limited to the union of one man and one woman, and that homosexual conduct is immoral. Many hold equally strong religious, moral, and ethical convictions that same-sex couples are entitled to be married, and that homosexual persons should be treated no differently than their heterosexual neighbors. Neither view answers the question before us.

Barred access to the protections, benefits, and obligations of civil marriage, a person who enters into an intimate, exclusive union with another of the same sex is arbitrarily deprived of membership in one of our community's most rewarding and cherished institutions. That exclusion is incompatible with the constitutional principles of respect for individual autonomy and equality under law.

The plaintiffs include business executives, lawyers, an investment banker, educators, therapists, and a computer engineer. Many are active in church, community, and school groups. They have employed such legal means as are available to them -- for example, joint adoption, powers of attorney, and joint ownership of real property -- to secure aspects of their relationships. Each plaintiff attests a desire to marry his or her partner in order to affirm publicly their commitment to each other and to secure the legal protections and benefits afforded to married couples and their children.

The plaintiffs' claim that the marriage restriction violates the Massachusetts Constitution can be analyzed in two ways. Does it offend the Constitution's guarantees of equality before the law? Or do the liberty and due process provisions of the Massachusetts Constitution secure the plaintiffs' right to marry their chosen partner?

We begin by considering the nature of civil marriage itself. Simply put, the government creates civil marriage. In Massachusetts, civil marriage is precisely what its name implies: a wholly secular institution. No religious ceremony has ever been required to validate a Massachusetts marriage.

Without the right to choose to marry, one is excluded from the full range of human experience and denied full protection of the laws for one's "avowed commitment to an intimate and lasting human relationship." Because civil marriage is central to the lives of individuals and the welfare of the community, our laws assiduously protect the individual's right to marry against undue government incursion.

For decades, indeed centuries, in much of this country no lawful marriage was possible between white and black Americans. That long history availed not when the United States Supreme Court held that a statutory bar to interracial marriage violated the Fourteenth Amendment.

The individual liberty and equality safeguards of the Massachusetts

52

Constitution protect both "freedom from" unwarranted government intrusion into protected spheres of life and "freedom to" partake in benefits created by the State for the common good. Both freedoms are involved here. Whether and whom to marry, how to express sexual intimacy, and whether and how to establish a family -- these are among the most basic of every individual's liberty and due process rights. And central to personal freedom and security is the assurance that the laws will apply equally to persons in similar situations. The liberty interest in choosing whether and whom to marry would be hollow if the Commonwealth could, without sufficient justification, foreclose an individual from freely choosing the person with whom to share an exclusive commitment in the unique institution of civil marriage.

Our laws of civil marriage do not privilege procreative heterosexual intercourse between married people above every other form of adult intimacy and every other means of creating a family. Fertility is not a condition of marriage, nor is it grounds for divorce. People who have never consummated their marriage, and never plan to, may be and stay married. People who cannot stir from their deathbed may marry. While it is true that many, perhaps most, married couples have children together, it is the exclusive and permanent commitment of the marriage partners to one another, not the begetting of children, that is the *sine qua non* of civil marriage.

No one disputes that the plaintiff couples are families, that many are parents, and that the children they are raising, like all children, need and should have the fullest opportunity to grow up in a secure, protected family unit. Similarly, no one disputes that, under the rubric of marriage, the State provides a cornucopia of substantial benefits to married parents and their children.

[W]e are confronted with an entire, sizeable class of parents raising children who have absolutely no access to civil marriage and its protections because they are forbidden from procuring a marriage license. It cannot be rational to penalize children by depriving them of State benefits because the State disapproves of their parents' sexual orientation.

An absolute statutory ban on same-sex marriage bears no rational relationship to the goal of economy. First, the conclusory generalization -- that same-sex couples are less financially dependent on each other than opposite-sex couples – ignores that many same-sex couples have children and other dependents (here, aged parents) in their care. The department does not contend, nor could it, that these dependents are less needy or deserving than the dependents of married couples. Second, Massachusetts marriage laws do not condition receipt of public and private financial benefits to married individuals on a demonstration of financial dependence on each other; the benefits are available to married couples regardless of whether they mingle their finances or actually depend on each other for support.

We also reject the argument that expanding the institution of civil marriage in Massachusetts to include same-sex couples will lead to interstate conflict. We would not presume to dictate how another State should respond to today's decision. But neither should considerations of comity prevent us from according Massachusetts residents the full measure of protection available under the Massachusetts Constitution. The genius of our Federal system is that each State's Constitution has vitality specific to its own traditions, and that, subject to the minimum requirements of the Fourteenth Amendment, each State is free to address difficult issues of individual liberty in the manner its own Constitution demands.

Here, no one argues that striking down the marriage laws is an appropriate form of relief. Eliminating civil marriage would be wholly inconsistent with the Legislature's deep commitment to fostering stable families and would dismantle a vital organizing principle of our society.

We declare that barring an individual from the protections, benefits, and obligations of civil marriage solely because that person would marry a person of the same sex violates the Massachusetts Constitution. Entry of judgment shall be stayed for 180 days to permit the Legislature to take such action as it may deem appropriate in light of this opinion. reasoning in the court's opinion.

DISSENT [SPINA]: A claim of gender discrimination will lie where it is shown that differential treatment disadvantages one sex over the other. [Massachusetts laws] creates no distinction between the sexes, but applies to men and women in precisely the same way. It does not create any disadvantage identified with gender, as both men and women are similarly limited to marrying a person of the opposite sex.

The marriage statutes do not impermissibly burden a right protected by our constitutional guarantee of due process. There is no restriction on the right of any plaintiff to enter into marriage. Each is free to marry a willing person of the opposite sex.

The remedy that the court has fashioned amounts to a statutory revision that replaces the intent of the Legislature with that of the court. Here, the alteration of the gender-specific language alters precisely what the Legislature unambiguously intended to preserve, the marital rights of single men and women. Such a dramatic change in social institutions must remain at the behest of the people through the democratic process.

DISSENT [SOSMAN]: Reduced to its essence, the court's opinion concludes that, because same-sex couples are now raising children, and withholding the benefits of civil marriage from their union makes it harder for them to raise those children, the State must therefore provide the benefits of civil marriage to same-sex couples just as it does to opposite-sex couples. Of course, many people are raising children outside the confines of traditional marriage, and, by definition, those children are being deprived of the various benefits that would flow if they were being raised in a household with married parents. That does not mean that the Legislature must accord the full benefits of marital status on every household raising children.

## DISCUSSION QUESTIONS

(1) Should the laws on "marriage" be decided entirely by the legislature, without interference from the courts? If yes, was the court unjustified in striking down the ban on interracial marriage in *Loving v. Virginia*?

(2) Is it possible to separate civil marriage regulated by the state from religious marriage governed by religious dictates?

(3) If most people in a state believe that same-sex marriage is immoral, should that be sufficient reason to prohibit it in the eyes of the law?

# CHAPTER 3. WAR, PEACE, AND PACIFISM

## UNITED STATES v. O'BRIEN
### 391 U.S. 367 (U.S. Supreme Court, 1968)

On the morning of March 31, 1966, David Paul O'Brien and three companions burned their Selective Service registration certificates on the steps of the South Boston Courthouse. A sizable crowd, including several agents of the Federal Bureau of Investigation, witnessed the event. After he was advised of his right to counsel and to silence, O'Brien stated to FBI agents that he had burned his registration certificate because of his beliefs, knowing that he was violating federal law.

For this act, O'Brien was indicted, tried, convicted, and sentenced in the United States District Court for the District of Massachusetts. [The] Universal Military Training and Service Act was amended by Congress in 1965, so that at the time O'Brien burned his certificate an offense was committed by any person, "who forges, alters, knowingly destroys, knowingly mutilates, or in any manner changes any such certificate . . . ."

O'Brien argued that the [statute] prohibiting the knowing destruction or mutilation of certificates was unconstitutional because it was enacted to abridge free speech, and because it served no legitimate legislative purpose.

We hold that the 1965 Amendment is constitutional. We therefore reinstate the judgment and sentence of the District Court.

When a male reaches the age of 18, he is required by the Universal Military Training and Service Act to register with a local draft board. Both the registration and classification certificates are small white cards. The registration certificate specifies the name of the registrant, the date of registration, and the number and address of the local board with which he is registered. Also inscribed upon it are the date and place of the registrant's birth, his residence at registration, his physical description, his signature, and his Selective Service number. The Selective Service number itself indicates his State of registration, his local board, his year of birth, and his chronological position in the local board's classification record.

The classification certificate shows the registrant's name, Selective Service number, signature, and eligibility classification. It specifies whether he was so classified by his local board, an appeal board, or the President. It contains the address of his local board and the date the certificate was mailed.

We cannot accept the view that an apparently limitless variety of conduct can be labeled "speech" whenever the person engaging in the conduct intends thereby to express an idea. However, even on the assumption that the alleged communicative element in O'Brien's conduct is sufficient to bring into play the First Amendment, it does not necessarily follow that the destruction of a registration certificate is constitutionally protected activity. This Court has held that when "speech" and "nonspeech" elements are combined in the same course of conduct, a sufficiently important governmental interest in regulating the nonspeech element can justify incidental limitations on First Amendment freedoms. [A] government regulation is sufficiently justified if it is within the constitutional power of the Government; if it furthers an important or substantial governmental interest; if the governmental interest is unrelated to the suppression of free expression; and if the incidental restriction on alleged First Amendment freedoms is no greater than is essential to the furtherance of that interest. We find that the 1965 Amendment to the Universal Military Training and Service Act meets all of these requirements, and consequently that O'Brien can be constitutionally convicted for violating it.

We think it apparent that the continuing availability to each registrant of his Selective Service certificates substantially furthers the smooth and proper functioning of the system that Congress has established to raise armies. We think it also apparent that the Nation has a vital interest in having a system for raising armies that functions with maximum efficiency and is capable of easily and quickly responding to continually changing circumstances. For these reasons, the Government has a substantial interest in assuring the continuing availability of issued Selective Service certificates.

It is equally clear that the 1965 Amendment specifically protects this substantial governmental interest. We perceive no alternative means that would more precisely and narrowly assure the continuing availability of issued Selective Service certificates than a law which prohibits their wilful mutilation or destruction. The 1965 Amendment prohibits such conduct and does nothing more. The governmental interest and the scope of the 1965 Amendment are limited to preventing harm to the smooth and efficient functioning of the Selective Service System. When O'Brien deliberately rendered unavailable his registration certificate, he wilfully frustrated this governmental interest. For this noncommunicative impact of his conduct, and for nothing else, he was convicted.

## DISCUSSION QUESTIONS

(1) Should burning your draft card in a public demonstration be considered a constitutionally protected exercise of free speech?

(2) Does the statute at issue here set forth the only reasonable way of maintaining the smooth functioning of the Selective Service?

### WELSH v. UNITED STATES
398 U.S. 333 (U.S. Supreme Court, 1970)

The petitioner, Elliott Ashton Welsh II, was convicted of refusing to submit to induction into the Armed Forces, and was sentenced to imprisonment for three years. One of petitioner's defenses to the prosecution was that the Universal Military Training and Service Act exempted him from combat and noncombat service because he was "by reason of religious training and belief . . . conscientiously opposed to participation in war in any form." We granted *certiorari* chiefly to review the contention that Welsh's conviction should be set aside. [W]e vote to reverse.

In filling out exemption applications Welsh [was] unable to sign the statement that stated "I am, by reason of my religious training and belief, conscientiously opposed to participation in war in any form." Welsh could sign only after striking the words "my religious training and." On those same applications, [he] could [not] definitely affirm or deny that he believed in a "Supreme Being," stating that [he] preferred to leave the question open. But Welsh affirmed on [that] application that [he] held deep conscientious scruples against taking part in wars where people were killed. [He] strongly believed that killing in war was wrong, unethical, and immoral, and [his conscience] forbade [him] to take part in such an evil practice. [His] objection to participating in war in any form could not be said to come from a "still, small voice of conscience"; rather, that voice was so loud and insistent that [he] preferred to go to jail rather than serve in the Armed Forces. There was never any question about the sincerity and depth of [his] convictions as a conscientious objector. But the Selective Service System concluded that the beliefs were in some sense insufficiently "religious" to qualify for conscientious objector exemptions. Welsh was denied the exemption because his Appeal Board and the Department of Justice hearing officer "could find no religious basis for the registrant's beliefs, opinions and convictions." Welsh subsequently refused to submit to induction into the military and [was] convicted of that offense.

Most of the great religions of today and of the past have embodied the idea of a Supreme Being or a Supreme Reality -- a God -- who communicates to man in some way a consciousness of what is right and should be done, of what is wrong and therefore should be shunned. If an individual deeply and sincerely holds beliefs that are purely ethical or moral in source and content but that nevertheless impose upon him a duty of conscience to refrain from participating in any war at any time, those beliefs certainly occupy in the life of that individual "a place parallel to that filled by . . . God" in traditionally religious persons. Because his beliefs function as a religion in his life, such an individual is as much entitled to a "religious" conscientious objector exemption as is someone who derives his conscientious opposition to war from traditional religious convictions.

When a registrant states that his objections to war are "religious," that information is highly relevant to the question of the function his beliefs have in his life. But very few registrants are fully aware of the broad scope of the word "religious", and accordingly a registrant's statement that his beliefs are nonreligious is a highly unreliable guide for those charged with administering the exemption. Welsh himself presents a case in point. Although he originally characterized his beliefs as nonreligious, he later upon reflection wrote a long and thoughtful letter to his Appeal Board in which he declared that his beliefs were "certainly religious in the ethical sense of the word."

. We certainly do not think that exclusion of those persons with "essentially political, sociological, or philosophical views or a merely personal moral code" should be read to exclude those who hold strong beliefs about our domestic and foreign affairs or even those whose conscientious objection to participation in all wars is founded to a substantial extent upon considerations of public policy.

Welsh stated that he "believe[d] the taking of life -- anyone's life -- to be morally wrong." In his original conscientious objector application he wrote the following: "I believe that human life is valuable in and of itself; in its living; therefore I will not injure or kill another human being. This belief

57

(and the corresponding 'duty' to abstain from violence toward another person) is not 'superior to those arising from any human relation.' On the contrary: *it is essential to every human relation.* I cannot, therefore, conscientiously comply with the Government's insistence that I assume duties which I feel are immoral and totally repugnant."

On the basis of these beliefs and the conclusion of the Court of Appeals that he held them "with the strength of more traditional religious convictions," we think Welsh was clearly entitled to a conscientious objector exemption. [The act] exempts from military service all those whose consciences, spurred by deeply held moral, ethical, or religious beliefs, would give them no rest or peace if they allowed themselves to become a part of an instrument of war.

CONCUR: The constitutional question that must be faced in this case is whether a statute that defers to the individual's conscience only when his views emanate from adherence to theistic religious beliefs is within the power of Congress. Congress, of course, could, entirely consistently with the requirements of the Constitution, eliminate *all* exemptions for conscientious objectors. However, having chosen to exempt, it cannot draw the line between theistic or nontheistic religious beliefs on the one hand and secular beliefs on the other. Any such distinctions are not, in my view, compatible with the Establishment Clause of the First Amendment.

DISSENT: I cannot join today's construction extending draft exemption to those who disclaim religious objections to war and whose views about war represent a purely personal code arising not from religious training and belief as the statute requires but from readings in philosophy, history, and sociology. Our obligation in statutory construction cases is to enforce the will of Congress, not our own.

## DISCUSSION QUESTIONS

(1) What should "religious" mean, for purposes of obtaining conscientious objector status? Should it be restricted to those who believe in a Supreme Being?

(2) Does this decision unfairly favor those who are sufficiently well-educated to articulate their moral views in such a way as to avoid being drafted to serve in an unpopular war?

## ROSTKER v. GOLDBERG
### 453 U.S. 57 (U.S. Supreme Court, 1981)

The question presented is whether the Military Selective Service Act violates the Fifth Amendment to the United States Constitution in authorizing the President to require the registration of males and not females.

Congress is given the power under the Constitution "To raise and support Armies," "To provide and maintain a Navy," and "To make Rules for the Government and Regulation of the land and naval Forces." Congress has enacted the Military Selective Service Act (MSSA), [which] empowers the President to require the registration of "every male citizen" and male resident aliens between the ages of 18 and 26. The registration provision serves no other purpose beyond providing a pool for subsequent induction.

Registration for the draft was discontinued in 1975. In early 1980, President Carter determined that it was necessary to reactivate the draft registration process. The immediate impetus for this decision was the Soviet armed invasion of Afghanistan.

Congress agreed that it was necessary to reactivate the registration process, and allocated funds for that purpose. Although Congress considered the question at great length, it declined to amend the MSSA to permit the registration of women.

These events of last year breathed new life into a lawsuit which had been essentially dormant in the lower courts for nearly a decade. It began in 1971 when several men subject to registration for the draft and subsequent induction into the Armed Services filed a complaint in the United States District Court challenging the MSSA on several grounds. On July 1, 1980, the court certified a plaintiff class of "all male persons who are registered or subject to registration or are liable for training and service in the armed forces of the United States."

Whenever called upon to judge the constitutionality of an Act of Congress the Court accords "great weight to the decisions of Congress." This is not, however, merely a case involving the customary deference accorded congressional decisions. The case arises in the context of Congress' authority over national defense and military affairs, and perhaps in no other area has the Court accorded Congress greater deference.

None of this is to say that Congress is free to disregard the Constitution when it acts in the area of military affairs. Congress remains subject to the limitations of the Due Process Clause, but the tests and limitations to be applied may differ because of the military context.

Congress and its Committees carefully considered and debated two alternative means of furthering that interest: the first was to register only males for potential conscription, and the other was to register both sexes. Congress chose the former alternative. When that decision is challenged, the question a court must decide is not which alternative it would have chosen, but whether that chosen by Congress denies equal protection of the laws.

The purpose of registration was to prepare for a draft of combat troops. Women as a group, however, unlike men as a group, are not eligible for combat. Congress specifically recognized and endorsed the exclusion of women from combat in exempting women from registration.

The existence of the combat restrictions clearly indicates the basis for Congress' decision to exempt women from registration. Since women are excluded from combat, Congress concluded that they would not be needed in the event of a draft, and therefore decided not to register them.

This is not a case of Congress arbitrarily choosing to burden one of two similarly situated groups, such as would be the case with an all-black or all-white, or an all-Catholic or all-Lutheran, or an all-Republican or all-Democratic registration. Men and women, because of the combat restrictions on women, are simply not similarly situated for purposes of a draft or registration for a draft. Congress' decision to authorize the registration of only men, therefore, does not violate the Due Process Clause. The Constitution requires that Congress treat similarly situated persons similarly, not that it engage in gestures of superficial equality.

In light of the foregoing, we conclude that Congress acted well within its constitutional authority when it authorized the registration of men, and not women, under the Military Selective Service Act.

DISSENT: The Court today places its imprimatur on one of the most potent remaining public expressions of "ancient canards about the proper role of women." It upholds a statute that requires males but not females to register for the draft, and which thereby categorically excludes women from a fundamental civic obligation. Because I believe the Court's decision is inconsistent with the Constitution's guarantee of equal protection of the laws, I dissent.

[S]tatutes which discriminate on the basis of gender, must be examined under "heightened" scrutiny. Under this test, a genderbased classification cannot withstand constitutional challenge unless the classification is substantially related to the achievement of an important governmental objective. [T]here is no basis for concluding that excluding women from registration is substantially related to the achievement of a concededly important governmental interest in maintaining an effective defense.

This analysis, however, focuses on the wrong question. The relevant inquiry is not whether a gender-neutral classification would substantially advance important governmental interests. Rather, the question is whether the gender-based classification is itself substantially related to the achievement of the asserted governmental interest. Thus, the Government must show that registering women would substantially impede its efforts to prepare for such a draft.

By "considerations of equity," the military experts acknowledged that female conscripts can perform as well as male conscripts in certain positions, and that there is therefore no reason why one group should be totally excluded from registration and a draft. Thus, what the majority so blithely dismisses as "equity" is nothing less than the Fifth Amendment's guarantee of equal protection of the laws.

## DISCUSSION QUESTIONS

(1) If the nation re-institutes a military draft, should it include women as well as men?

(2) Should women be permitted to serve in combat in the military? Should they be required to serve in combat?

## FEDORENKO v. UNITED STATES
449 U.S. 490 (U.S. Supreme Court, 1981)

[T]he Immigration and Nationality Act requires revocation of United States citizenship that was "illegally procured or . . . procured by concealment of a material fact or by willful misrepresentation." The Government brought this denaturalization action, alleging that petitioner procured his citizenship illegally or by willfully misrepresenting a material fact.

Petitioner was born in the Ukraine in 1907. He was drafted into the Russian Army in June 1941, but was captured by the Germans shortly thereafter. After being held in a series of prisoner-of-war camps, petitioner was selected to go to the German camp at Travnicki in Poland, where he received training as a concentration camp guard. In September 1942, he was assigned to the Nazi concentration camp at Treblinka in Poland, where he was issued a uniform and rifle and where he served as a guard during 1942 and 1943. The infamous Treblinka concentration camp was described by the District Court as a "human abattoir" at which several hundred thousand Jewish civilians were murdered. After an armed uprising by the inmates at Treblinka led to the closure of the camp in August 1943, petitioner was transferred to a German labor camp at Danzig and then to the German prisoner-of-war camp at Poelitz, where he continued to serve as an armed guard. Petitioner was eventually transferred to Hamburg where he served as a warehouse guard. Shortly before the British forces entered that city in 1945, petitioner discarded his uniform and was able to pass as civilian. For the next four years, he worked in Germany as a laborer.

In 1948, Congress enacted the Displaced Persons Act (DPA), to enable European refugees driven from their homelands by the war to emigrate to the United States. The Act's definition of "displaced persons" eligible for immigration to this country specifically excluded individuals who had "assisted the enemy in persecuting [civilians]" or had "voluntarily assisted the enemy forces . . . in their operations." [T]he DPA placed the burden of proving eligibility on the person seeking admission and provided that "[any] person who shall willfully make a misrepresentation for the purpose of gaining admission into the United States as an eligible displaced person shall thereafter not be admissible into the United States."

In October 1949, petitioner applied for admission to the United States as a displaced person. Petitioner falsified his visa application by lying about his wartime activities. He told the investigators from the Displaced Persons Commission that he had been a farmer in Sarny, Poland, from 1937 until March 1942, and that he had then been deported to Germany and forced to work in a factory in Poelitz until the end of the war, when he fled to Hamburg. Petitioner's false statements were not discovered at the time and he was issued a DPA visa, and sailed to the United States where he was admitted for permanent residence. He took up residence in Connecticut and for three decades led an uneventful and law-abiding life as a factory worker.

In 1969, petitioner applied for naturalization at the INS office in Hartford, Conn. Petitioner did not disclose his wartime service as a concentration camp armed guard in his application, and he did not mention it in his sworn testimony to INS naturalization examiners. The INS examiners took petitioner's visa papers at face value and recommended that his citizenship application be granted. On this recommendation, the Superior Court of New Haven County granted his petition for naturalization and he became an American citizen on April 23, 1970.

Seven years later, after petitioner had moved to Miami Beach, the Government filed this action in the United States District Court for the Southern District of Florida to revoke petitioner's citizenship. The complaint alleged that petitioner should have been deemed ineligible for a DPA visa because he had served as an armed guard at Treblinka and had committed crimes or atrocities against inmates of the camp because they were Jewish. The Government charged that petitioner had willfully concealed this information both in applying for a DPA visa and in applying for citizenship, and that therefore petitioner had procured his naturalization illegally or by willfully misrepresenting material facts.

The Government's witnesses at trial included six survivors of Treblinka who claimed that they had seen petitioner commit specific acts of violence against inmates of the camp. Each witness made a pretrial identification of petitioner from a photo array that included his 1949 visa photograph, and three of the witnesses made courtroom identifications.

Petitioner admitted his service as an armed guard at Treblinka and that he had known that thousands of Jewish inmates were being murdered there. Petitioner claimed that he was forced to serve as a guard and denied any personal involvement in the atrocities committed at the camp; he insisted that he had merely been a perimeter guard. Petitioner admitted, however, that he had followed orders and shot in the general direction of escaping inmates during the August 1943 uprising that led to closure of the camp. Petitioner maintained that he was a prisoner of war at Treblinka, although he admitted that the Russian armed guards significantly outnumbered the German soldiers at the camp, that he was paid a stipend and received a good service stripe from the Germans, and that he was allowed to leave the camp regularly but never tried to escape. Finally, petitioner conceded that he deliberately gave false statements about his wartime activities.

On the one hand, our decisions have recognized that the right to acquire American citizenship is a precious one, and that once citizenship has been acquired, its loss can have severe and unsettling consequences. The evidence justifying revocation of citizenship must be "clear, unequivocal, and convincing" and not leave "the issue in doubt." Any less exacting standard would be inconsistent with the importance of the right that is at stake in a denaturalization proceeding.

At the same time, our cases have also recognized that there must be strict compliance with all the congressionally imposed prerequisites to the acquisition of citizenship.

The plain language of the [DPA] mandates [a] literal interpretation: an individual's service as a concentration camp armed guard -- whether voluntary or involuntary -- made him ineligible for a visa. That Congress was perfectly capable of adopting a "voluntariness" limitation where it felt that one was necessary is plain.

In sum, we hold that petitioner's citizenship must be revoked because it was illegally procured.

DISSENT: I cannot accept the view that any citizen's past involuntary conduct can provide the basis for stripping him of his American citizenship. Every person who entered the United States pursuant to the authority granted by that statute, who subsequently acquired American citizenship, and who can be shown "to have assisted the enemy in persecuting civil populations" -- even under the most severe duress -- has no right to retain his or her citizenship.

The Court's resolution of this issue is particularly unpersuasive when applied to the "kapos," the Jewish prisoners who supervised the Jewish workers at the camp. According to witnesses who survived Treblinka, the kapos were commanded by the SS to administer beatings to the prisoners, and they did so with just enough force to make the beating appear realistic yet avoid injury to the prisoner. Even if we assume that the kapos were completely successful in deceiving the SS guards and that the beatings caused no injury to other inmates, I believe their conduct would have to be characterized as assisting in the persecution of other prisoners. In my view, the reason that such conduct should not make the kapos ineligible for citizenship is that it surely was not voluntary. The fact that the Court's interpretation of the DPA would exclude a group whose actions were uniformly defended by survivors of Treblinka merely underscores the strained reading the Court has given the statute.

## DISCUSSION QUESTIONS

(1) From the facts here, did Fedorenko "voluntarily" assist the enemy?

(2) Should assistance to the enemy, whether voluntary or involuntary, in all cases make a person ineligible for United States citizenship?

## RASUL v. BUSH
No. 03-334 (U.S. Supreme Court, 2004)

These cases present the narrow but important question whether United States courts lack jurisdiction to consider challenges to the legality of the detention of foreign nationals captured abroad in connection with hostilities and incarcerated at the Guantanamo Bay Naval Base, Cuba.

On September 11, 2001, agents of the al Qaeda terrorist network hijacked four commercial airliners and used them as missiles to attack American targets. While one of the four attacks was foiled by the heroism of the plane's passengers, the other three killed approximately 3,000 innocent civilians, destroyed hundreds of millions of dollars of property, and severely damaged the U. S. economy. Congress passed a joint resolution authorizing the President to use "all necessary and appropriate force against those nations, organizations, or persons he determines planned, authorized, committed, or aided the terrorist attacks . . . or harbored such organizations or persons." [T]he President sent Armed Forces into Afghanistan to wage a military campaign against al Qaeda and the Taliban regime that supported it.

Petitioners are 2 Australian citizens and 12 Kuwaiti citizens who were captured abroad during hostilities between the United States and the Taliban. Since early 2002, the U. S. military has held them--along with approximately 640 other non-Americans captured abroad--at the Naval Base at Guantanamo Bay. The United States occupies the Base, which comprises 45 square miles of land and water along the southeast coast of Cuba, pursuant to a 1903 Lease Agreement executed with the newly independent Republic of Cuba. Under the Agreement, "the Republic of Cuba consents that during the period of the occupation by the United States . . . the United States shall exercise complete jurisdiction and control over and within said areas."

In 2002, petitioners, through relatives, filed actions in the U. S. District Court for the District of Columbia challenging the legality of their detention at the Base. All alleged that none of the petitioners has ever been a combatant against the United States or has been engaged in any terrorist acts. They also alleged that none has been charged with any wrongdoing, permitted to consult with counsel, or provided access to the courts or any other tribunal.

The two Australians each filed a petition for writ of *habeas corpus*, seeking release from custody, access to counsel, freedom from interrogations, and other relief. [T]he Kuwaiti detainees filed a complaint seeking to be informed of the charges against them, to be allowed to meet with their families and with counsel, and to have access to the courts or some other impartial tribunal. They claimed that denial of these rights violates the Constitution, international law, and treaties of the United States. Invoking the court's jurisdiction, they asserted causes of action under the general federal *habeas corpus* statute.

The question now before us is whether the *habeas* statute confers a right to judicial review of the legality of Executive detention of aliens in a territory over which the United States exercises plenary and exclusive jurisdiction, but not "ultimate sovereignty."

Petitioners in these cases are not nationals of countries at war with the United States, and they deny that they have engaged in or plotted acts of aggression against the United States; they have never been afforded access to any tribunal, much less charged with and convicted of wrongdoing; and for more than two years they have been imprisoned in territory over which the United States exercises exclusive jurisdiction and control.

[T]he United States exercises "complete jurisdiction and control" over the Guantanamo Bay Naval Base, and may continue to exercise such control permanently if it so chooses. Respondents themselves concede that the *habeas* statute would create federal-court jurisdiction over the claims of an American citizen held at the base. Aliens held at the base, no less than American citizens, are entitled to invoke the federal courts' authority.

What is presently at stake is only whether the federal courts have jurisdiction to determine the legality of the Executive's potentially indefinite detention of individuals who claim to be wholly innocent of wrongdoing. Answering that question in the affirmative, we remand for the District Court to consider in the first instance the merits of petitioners' claims.

CONCUR: The Court is correct to conclude that federal courts have jurisdiction to consider challenges to the legality of the detention of foreign nationals held at the Guantanamo Bay Naval Base in Cuba.

Guantanamo Bay is in every practical respect a United States territory, and it is one far removed from any hostilities. The detainees at Guantanamo Bay are being held indefinitely, and without benefit of any legal proceeding to determine their status. Indefinite detention without trial or other proceeding allows friends and foes alike to remain in detention. Perhaps, where detainees are taken from a zone of hostilities, detention without proceedings or trial would be justified by military necessity for a matter of weeks; but as the period of detention stretches from months to years, the case for continued detention to meet military exigencies becomes weaker.

DISSENT: The reality is this: Today's opinion extends the *habeas* statute, for the first time, to aliens held beyond the sovereign territory of the United States and beyond the territorial jurisdiction of its courts. No reasons are given for this result; no acknowledgment of its consequences made. Today, the Court springs a trap on the Executive, subjecting Guantanamo Bay to the oversight of the federal courts even though it has never before been thought to be within their jurisdiction--and thus making it a foolish place to have housed alien wartime detainees.

The consequence of this holding, as applied to aliens outside the country, is breathtaking. It permits an alien captured in a foreign theater of active combat to bring a petition against the Secretary of Defense. Over the course of the last century, the United States has held millions of alien prisoners abroad. A great many of these prisoners would no doubt have complained about the circumstances of their capture and the terms of their confinement. The military is currently detaining over 600 prisoners at Guantanamo Bay alone; each detainee undoubtedly has complaints--real or contrived--about those terms and circumstances. The Court's unheralded expansion of federal-court jurisdiction is not even mitigated by a comforting assurance that the legion of ensuing claims will be easily resolved on the merits. To the contrary, the Court says that the "[p]etitioners' allegations . . . unquestionably describe 'custody in violation of the Constitution or laws or treaties of the United States.'" From this point forward, federal courts will entertain petitions from these prisoners, and others like them around the world, challenging actions and events far away, and forcing the courts to oversee one aspect of the Executive's conduct of a foreign war.

The Court does not explain how "complete jurisdiction and control" without sovereignty causes an enclave to be part of the United States for purposes of its domestic laws. Since "jurisdiction and control" obtained through a lease is no different in effect from "jurisdiction and control" acquired by lawful force of arms, parts of Afghanistan and Iraq should logically be regarded as subject to our domestic laws.

The Commander in Chief and his subordinates had every reason to expect that the internment of combatants at Guantanamo Bay would not have the consequence of bringing the cumbersome machinery of our domestic courts into military affairs. For this Court to create such a monstrous scheme in time of war, and in frustration of our military commanders' reliance upon clearly stated law, is judicial adventurism of the worst sort.

## DISCUSSION QUESTIONS

(1) Should the constitutional rights and principles of the United States apply to everyone in the custody of the U.S., even if they are not citizens?

(2) Should the interest in principles of human rights embodied in the Constitution yield to military necessity in a time of war?

# CHAPTER 4. THE ENVIRONMENT:
# PROTECTING NATURE AND ANIMALS


## TENNESSEE VALLEY AUTHORITY v. HILL
### 437 U.S. 153 (U.S. Supreme Court, 1978)

The questions presented in this case are (a) whether the Endangered Species Act of 1973 requires a court to enjoin the operation of a virtually completed federal dam -- which had been authorized prior to 1973 -- when the Secretary of the Interior has determined that operation of the dam would eradicate an endangered species; and (b) whether continued congressional appropriations for the dam after 1973 constituted an implied repeal of the Endangered Species Act, at least as to the particular dam.

The Little Tennessee River originates in the mountains of northern Georgia and flows through the national forest lands of North Carolina into Tennessee, where it converges with the Big Tennessee River near Knoxville.

In this area of the Little Tennessee River the Tennessee Valley Authority, a wholly owned public corporation of the United States, began constructing the Tellico Dam and Reservoir Project in 1967, shortly after Congress appropriated initial funds for its development. Tellico is a multipurpose regional development project designed principally to stimulate shoreline development, generate sufficient electric current to heat 20,000 homes, and provide flatwater recreation and flood control, as well as improve economic conditions. Of particular relevance to this case is one aspect of the project, a dam which TVA determined to place on the Little Tennessee. When fully operational, the dam would impound water covering some 16,500 acres -- much of which represents valuable and productive farmland -- thereby converting the river's shallow, fast-flowing waters into a deep reservoir over 30 miles in length.

The Tellico Dam has never opened, however, despite the fact that construction has been virtually completed and the dam is essentially ready for operation. Although Congress has appropriated monies for Tellico every year since 1967, progress was delayed, and ultimately stopped, by a tangle of lawsuits and administrative proceedings.

[In 1973] a discovery was made in the waters of the Little Tennessee which would profoundly affect the Tellico Project. Exploring the area around Coytee Springs, which is about seven miles from the mouth of the river, a University of Tennessee ichthyologist found a previously unknown species of perch, the snail darter, or Percina (Imostoma) tanasi. This three--inch, tannish-colored fish, whose numbers are estimated to be in the range of 10,000 to 15,000, would soon engage the attention of environmentalists, the TVA, the Department of the Interior, the Congress of the United States, and ultimately the federal courts, as a new and additional basis to halt construction of the dam.

The moving force behind the snail darter's sudden fame came some four months after its discovery, when the Congress passed the Endangered Species Act of 1973 (Act). This legislation, among other things, authorizes the Secretary of the Interior to declare species of animal life "endangered" and to identify the "critical habitat" of these creatures.

[T]he Secretary formally listed the snail darter as an endangered species on October 8, 1975. More important for the purposes of this case, the Secretary determined that the snail darter apparently lives only in that portion of the Little Tennessee River which would be completely inundated by the reservoir created as a consequence of the Tellico Dam's completion.

In February 1976, respondents filed the case now under review, seeking to enjoin completion of the dam and impoundment of the reservoir on the ground that those actions would violate the Act by directly causing the extinction of the species Percina (Imostoma) tanasi.

[T]he Court of Appeals ruled that the District Court had erred by not issuing an injunction. While recognizing the irretrievable loss of millions of dollars of public funds which would accompany injunctive relief, the court nonetheless decided that the Act explicitly commanded precisely that result. We granted *certiorari* to review the judgment of the Court of Appeals.

We begin with the premise that operation of the Tellico Dam will either eradicate the known population of snail darters or destroy their critical habitat. [T]wo questions are presented: (a) would TVA be in violation of the Act if it completed and operated the Tellico Dam as planned? (b) if TVA's actions would offend the Act, is an injunction the appropriate remedy for the violation? For the reasons stated hereinafter, we hold that both questions must be answered in the affirmative.

It may seem curious to some that the survival of a relatively small number of three-inch fish among all the countless millions of species extant would require the permanent halting of a virtually completed dam for which Congress has expended more than $100 million. The paradox is not minimized by the fact that Congress continued to appropriate large sums of public money for the project, even after congressional Appropriations Committees were apprised of its apparent impact upon the survival of the snail darter. We conclude, however, that the explicit provisions of the Endangered Species Act require precisely that result. One would be hard pressed to find a statutory provision whose terms were any plainer than those in the Endangered Species Act. Its very words affirmatively command all federal agencies "to insure that actions authorized, funded, or carried out by them do not jeopardize the continued existence" of an endangered species or "result in the destruction or modification of habitat of such species." This language admits of no exception.

[T]his view of the Act will produce results requiring the sacrifice of the anticipated benefits of the project and of many millions of dollars in public funds. But examination of the language, history, and structure of the legislation under review here indicates beyond doubt that Congress intended endangered species to be afforded the highest of priorities.

As it was finally passed, the Endangered Species Act of 1973 represented the most comprehensive legislation for the preservation of endangered species ever enacted by any nation.

One might dispute the applicability of these examples to the Tellico Dam by saying that in this case the burden on the public through the loss of millions of unrecoverable dollars would greatly outweigh the loss of the snail darter. But neither the Endangered Species Act nor the Constitution provides federal courts with authority to make such fine utilitarian calculations. On the contrary, the plain language of the Act, buttressed by its legislative history, shows clearly that Congress viewed the value of endangered species as "incalculable." Quite obviously, it would be difficult for a court to balance the loss of a sum certain -- even $100 million -- against a congressionally declared "incalculable" value, even assuming we had the power to engage in such a weighing process, which we emphatically do not.

We agree with the Court of Appeals that in our constitutional system the commitment to the separation of powers is too fundamental for us to pre-empt congressional action by judicially decreeing what accords with "common sense and the public weal." Our Constitution vests such responsibilities in the political branches. Affirmed.

DISSENT: Today the Court, like the Court of Appeals below, adopts a reading of the [Endangered Species] Act that gives it a retroactive effect and disregards 12 years of consistently expressed congressional intent to complete the Tellico Project. With all due respect, I view this result as an extreme example of a literalist construction, not required by the language of the Act and adopted without regard to its manifest purpose.

But more far reaching than the adverse effect on the people of this economically depressed area is the continuing threat to the operation of every federal project, no matter how important to the Nation.

## DISCUSSION QUESTIONS

(1) Should economic consequences be irrelevant in implementation of the Endangered Species Act?

(2) Should the Court interpret the language of statutes loosely and pay more attention to the overall impact of its decisions on the country?

## SIERRA CLUB v. MORTON
### 405 U.S. 727 (U.S. Supreme Court, 1972)

The Mineral King Valley is an area of great natural beauty nestled in the Sierra Nevada Mountains in Tulare County, California, adjacent to Sequoia National Park. It has been part of the Sequoia National Forest since 1926, and is designated as a national game refuge by special Act of Congress. Though once the site of extensive mining activity, Mineral King is now used almost exclusively for recreational purposes. Its relative inaccessibility and lack of development have limited the number of visitors each year, and at the same time have preserved the valley's quality as a quasi- wilderness area largely uncluttered by the products of civilization.

The United States Forest Service, which is entrusted with the maintenance and administration of national forests, began in the late 1940's to give consideration to Mineral King as a potential site for recreational development. Prodded by a rapidly increasing demand for skiing facilities, the Forest Service published a prospectus in 1965, inviting bids from private developers for the construction and operation of a ski resort that would also serve as a summer recreation area. The proposal of Walt Disney Enterprises, Inc., was chosen from those of six bidders.

The final Disney plan, approved by the Forest Service in January 1969, outlines a $35 million complex of motels, restaurants, swimming pools, parking lots, and other structures designed to accommodate 14,000 visitors daily. This complex is to be constructed on 80 acres of the valley floor under a 30-year use permit from the Forest Service. Other facilities, including ski lifts, ski trails, a cog-assisted railway, and utility installations, are to be constructed on the mountain slopes and in other parts of the valley under a revocable special-use permit.

Representatives of the Sierra Club, who favor maintaining Mineral King largely in its present state, followed the progress of recreational planning for the valley with close attention and increasing dismay. In June 1969 the Club filed the present suit in the United States District Court for the Northern District of California, seeking a declaratory judgment that various aspects of the proposed development contravene federal laws and regulations governing the preservation of national parks, forests, and game refuges, and also seeking preliminary and permanent injunctions restraining the federal officials involved from granting their approval or issuing permits in connection with the Mineral King project. The petitioner Sierra Club sued as a membership corporation with "a special interest in the conservation and the sound maintenance of the national parks, game refuges and forests of the country."

The first question presented is whether the Sierra Club has alleged facts that entitle it to obtain judicial review of the challenged action. Whether a party has a sufficient stake in [a] controversy to obtain judicial resolution of that controversy is what has traditionally been referred to as the question of standing to sue.

The injury alleged by the Sierra Club will be incurred entirely by reason of the change in the uses to which Mineral King will be put, and the attendant change in the aesthetics and ecology of the area. Aesthetic and environmental well-being, like economic well-being, are important ingredients of the quality of life in our society, and the fact that particular environmental interests are shared by the many rather than the few does not make them less deserving of legal protection through the judicial process. But the "injury in fact" test requires more than an injury to a cognizable interest. It requires that the party seeking review be himself among the injured. The impact of the proposed changes in the environment of Mineral King will not fall indiscriminately upon every citizen. The alleged injury will be felt directly only by those who use Mineral King and Sequoia National Park, and for whom the aesthetic and recreational values of the area will be lessened by the highway and ski resort. The Sierra Club failed to allege that it or its members would be affected in any of their activities or pastimes by the Disney development. Nowhere did the Club state that its members use Mineral King for any purpose, much less that they use it in any way that would be significantly affected by the proposed actions of the respondents.

[W]e conclude that the Sierra Club lacked standing to maintain this action.

DISSENT [DOUGLAS]: The critical question of "standing" would be simplified and also put neatly in focus if we fashioned a federal rule that allowed environmental issues to be litigated before federal agencies or federal courts in the name of the inanimate object about to be despoiled, defaced, or invaded by roads and bulldozers and where injury is the subject of public outrage. Contemporary public concern for protecting nature's ecological equilibrium should lead to the conferral of standing upon environmental objects to sue for their own preservation. This suit would therefore be more properly labeled as Mineral King v. Morton.

Inanimate objects are sometimes parties in litigation. So it should be as respects valleys, alpine meadows, rivers, lakes, estuaries, beaches, ridges, groves of trees, swampland, or even air that feels the destructive pressures of modern technology and modern life. The river, for example, is the living symbol of all the life it sustains or nourishes -- fish, aquatic insects, water ouzels, otter, fisher, deer, elk, bear, and all other animals, including man, who are dependent on it or who enjoy it for its sight, its sound, or its life. The river as plaintiff speaks for the ecological unit of life that is part of it. Those people who have a meaningful relation to that body of water -- whether it be a fisherman, a canoeist, a zoologist, or a logger -- must be able to speak for the values which the river represents and which are threatened with destruction.

Mineral King is doubtless like other wonders of the Sierra Nevada such as Tuolumne Meadows and the John Muir Trail. Those who hike it, fish it, hunt it, camp in it, frequent it, or visit it merely to sit in solitude and wonderment are legitimate spokesmen for it, whether they may be few or many. Those who have that intimate relation with the inanimate object about to be injured, polluted, or otherwise despoiled are its legitimate spokesmen.

The voice of the inanimate object, therefore, should not be stilled. Ecology reflects the land ethic; and Aldo Leopold wrote in A Sand County Almanac (1949), "The land ethic simply enlarges the boundaries of the community to include soils, waters, plants, and animals, or collectively: the land." That, as I see it, is the issue of "standing" in the present case.

DISSENT [BLACKMUN]: [T]his is not ordinary, run-of-the-mill litigation. The case poses -- if only we choose to acknowledge and reach them -- significant aspects of a wide, growing, and disturbing problem, that is, the Nation's and the world's deteriorating environment with its resulting ecological disturbances.

I would permit an imaginative expansion of our traditional concepts of standing in order to enable an organization such as the Sierra Club, possessed, as it is, of pertinent, bona fide, and well-recognized attributes and purposes in the area of environment, to litigate environmental issues. This incursion upon tradition need not be very extensive. Certainly, it should be no cause for alarm. It need only recognize the interest of one who has a provable, sincere, dedicated, and established status. We need not fear that Pandora's box will be opened or that there will be no limit to the number of those who desire to participate in environmental litigation. The courts will exercise appropriate restraints just as they have exercised them in the past.

## DISCUSSION QUESTIONS

(1) Who, or what, should have a right to be heard in our courts to claim environmental protection?

(2) Who should be authorized to represent environmental interests in the courts on behalf of the general public?

## CHURCH OF THE LUKUMI BABALU AYE v. CITY OF HIALEAH
### 508 U.S. 520 (U.S. Supreme Court, 1993)

The principle that government may not enact laws that suppress religious belief or practice is so well understood that few violations are recorded in our opinions. Concerned that this fundamental nonpersecution principle of the First Amendment was implicated here, however, we granted *certiorari*.

This case involves practices of the Santeria religion, which originated in the 19th century. When hundreds of thousands of members of the Yoruba people were brought as slaves from western Africa to Cuba, their traditional African religion absorbed significant elements of Roman Catholicism. The resulting fusion is Santeria, "the way of the saints." The Cuban Yoruba express their devotion to spirits, called orishas, through the iconography of Catholic saints, Catholic symbols are often present at Santeria rites, and Santeria devotees attend the Catholic sacraments.

The Santeria faith teaches that every individual has a destiny from God, a destiny fulfilled with the aid and energy of the orishas. The basis of the Santeria religion is the nurture of a personal relation with the orishas, and one of the principal forms of devotion is an animal sacrifice.

According to Santeria teaching, the orishas are powerful but not immortal. They depend for survival on the sacrifice. Animals sacrificed in Santeria rituals include chickens, pigeons, doves, ducks, guinea pigs, goats, sheep, and turtles. The animals are killed by the cutting of the carotid arteries in the neck. The sacrificed animal is cooked and eaten.

Petitioner Church of the Lukumi Babalu Aye, Inc. (Church), and its congregants practice the Santeria religion. In April 1987, the Church leased land in the city of Hialeah, Florida, and announced plans to establish a house of worship as well as a school, cultural center, and museum.

The prospect of a Santeria church in their midst was distressing to many members of the Hialeah community, and the announcement of the plans to open a Santeria church in Hialeah prompted the city council to hold an emergency public session on June 9, 1987.

First, the city council adopted [a] Resolution, which noted the "concern" expressed by residents of the city "that certain religions may propose to engage in practices which are inconsistent with public morals, peace or safety," and declared that "the City reiterates its commitment to a prohibition against any and all acts of any and all religious groups which are inconsistent with public morals, peace or safety."

In September 1987, the city council adopted three substantive ordinances addressing the issue of religious animal sacrifice. [One] defined "sacrifice" as "to unnecessarily kill, torment, torture, or mutilate an animal in a public or private ritual or ceremony not for the primary purpose of food consumption," and prohibited owning or possessing an animal "intending to use such animal for food purposes." It restricted application of this prohibition, however, to any individual or group that "kills, slaughters or sacrifices animals for any type of ritual, regardless of whether or not the flesh or blood of the animal is to be consumed." The ordinance contained an exemption for slaughtering by "licensed establishment[s]" of animals "specifically raised for food purposes."

Declaring, moreover, that the city council "has determined that the sacrificing of animals within the city limits is contrary to the public health, safety, welfare and morals of the community," the city council adopted [an] ordinance [that] provided that "it shall be unlawful for any person, persons, corporations or associations to sacrifice any animal within the corporate limits of the City of Hialeah, Florida." The final Ordinance, defined "slaughter" as "the killing of animals for food" and prohibited slaughter outside of areas zoned for slaughterhouse use.

Following enactment of these ordinances, the Church filed this action in the United States District Court for the Southern District of Florida.

The Free Exercise Clause of the First Amendment, which has been applied to the States through the Fourteenth Amendment, provides that "Congress shall make no law respecting an establishment of religion, or prohibiting the free exercise thereof . . . ." The city does not argue that Santeria is not a "religion" within the meaning of the First Amendment. Nor could it. Although the practice of animal sacrifice may seem abhorrent to some, "religious beliefs need not be acceptable, logical, consistent, or comprehensible to others in order to merit First Amendment protection." Given the historical association between animal sacrifice and religious worship, petitioners' assertion that animal sacrifice is an integral part of their religion "cannot be deemed bizarre or incredible."

In addressing the constitutional protection for free exercise of religion, our cases establish the general proposition that a law that is neutral and of general applicability need not be justified by a compelling governmental interest even if the law has the incidental effect of burdening a particular religious practice. The record in this case compels the conclusion that suppression of the central element of the Santeria worship service was the object of the ordinances.

It becomes evident that these ordinances target Santeria sacrifice when the ordinances' operation is considered. [F]ew if any killings of animals are prohibited other than Santeria sacrifice. Indeed, careful drafting ensured that, although Santeria sacrifice is prohibited, killings that are no more necessary or humane in almost all other circumstances are unpunished.

Killings for religious reasons are deemed unnecessary, whereas most other killings fall outside the prohibition. The city deems hunting, slaughter of animals for food, eradication of insects and pests, and euthanasia as necessary. Respondent's application of the ordinance's test of necessity devalues religious reasons for killing by judging them to be of lesser import than nonreligious reasons. Thus, religious practice is being singled out for discriminatory treatment.

The legitimate governmental interests in protecting the public health and preventing cruelty to animals could be addressed by restrictions stopping far short of a flat prohibition of all Santeria sacrificial practice. If improper disposal, not the sacrifice itself, is the harm to be prevented, the city could have imposed a general regulation on the disposal of organic garbage. It did not do so.

Under similar analysis, narrower regulation would achieve the city's interest in preventing cruelty to animals. With regard to the city's interest in ensuring the adequate care of animals, regulation of conditions and treatment, regardless of why an animal is kept, is the logical response to the city's concern, not a prohibition on possession for the purpose of sacrifice. The same is true for the city's interest in prohibiting cruel methods of killing. If the city has a real concern that other methods are less humane, however, the subject of the regulation should be the method of slaughter itself, not a religious classification.

In sum, the neutrality inquiry leads to one conclusion: The ordinances had as their object the suppression of religion. The pattern we have recited discloses animosity to Santeria adherents and their religious practices; the ordinances by their own terms target this religious exercise; the texts of the ordinances were gerrymandered with care to proscribe religious killings of animals but to exclude almost all secular killings; and the ordinances suppress much more religious conduct than is necessary in order to achieve the legitimate ends asserted in their defense. These ordinances are not neutral.

The Free Exercise Clause commits government itself to religious tolerance, and upon even slight suspicion that proposals for state intervention stem from animosity to religion or distrust of its practices, all officials must pause to remember their own high duty to the Constitution and to the rights it secures. Legislators may not devise mechanisms, overt or disguised, designed to persecute or oppress a religion or its practices. The laws here in question were enacted contrary to these constitutional principles, and they are void.

## DISCUSSION QUESTIONS

(1) If you were an animal rights activist supporting the city's attempt to ban animal sacrifice, how would you assess the court's arguments and conclusions?

(2) If a religious group practiced the sacrifice of human infants as part of its religion, should the First Amendment protect that practice? Should animals be treated with the same respect as human infants?

## CHAPTER 5.  FREEDOM OF EXPRESSION

### Symbolic Speech

### COHEN v. CALIFORNIA
403 U.S. 15 (U.S. Supreme Court, 1971)

Appellant Paul Robert Cohen was convicted of violating that part of California Penal Code which prohibits "maliciously and willfully disturb[ing] the peace or quiet of any neighborhood or person . . . by . . . offensive conduct . . . ." He was given 30 days' imprisonment. The facts upon which his conviction rests are as follows:

On April 26, 1968, the defendant was observed in the Los Angeles County Courthouse in the corridor outside of division 20 of the municipal court wearing a jacket bearing the words 'Fuck the Draft' which were plainly visible. There were women and children present in the corridor. The defendant was arrested. The defendant testified that he wore the jacket knowing that the words were on the jacket as a means of informing the public of the depth of his feelings against the Vietnam War and the draft.

The conviction quite clearly rests upon the asserted offensiveness of the words Cohen used to convey his message to the public. The only "conduct" which the State sought to punish is the fact of communication. Thus, we deal here with a conviction resting solely upon "speech," not upon any separately identifiable conduct which allegedly was intended by Cohen to be perceived by others as expressive of particular views but which, on its face, does not necessarily convey any message and hence arguably could be regulated without effectively repressing Cohen's ability to express himself. [T]he State lacks power to punish Cohen for the underlying content of the message the inscription conveyed. [S]o long as there is no showing of an intent to incite disobedience to or disruption of the draft, Cohen could not, consistently with the First and Fourteenth Amendments, be punished for asserting the position on the inutility or immorality of the draft his jacket reflected.

Appellant's conviction rests squarely upon his exercise of the "freedom of speech" protected from arbitrary governmental interference by the Constitution and can be justified, if at all, only as a valid regulation of the manner in which he exercised that freedom, not as a permissible prohibition on the substantive message it conveys. This does not end the inquiry, of course, for the First and Fourteenth Amendments have never been thought to give absolute protection to every individual to speak whenever or wherever he pleases, or to use any form of address in any circumstances that he chooses. Any attempt to support this conviction on the ground that the statute seeks to preserve an appropriately decorous atmosphere in the courthouse where Cohen was arrested must fail in the absence of any language in the statute that would have put appellant on notice that certain kinds of otherwise permissible speech or conduct would nevertheless, under California law, not be tolerated in certain places.

This is not an obscenity case. It cannot plausibly be maintained that this vulgar allusion to the Selective Service System would conjure up such psychic stimulation in anyone likely to be confronted with Cohen's crudely defaced jacket.

This Court has held that the States are free to ban the simple use of so-called "fighting words," those personally abusive epithets which, when addressed to the ordinary citizen, are inherently likely to provoke violent reaction. While the four-letter word displayed by Cohen in relation to the draft is not uncommonly employed in a personally provocative fashion, in this instance it was clearly not "directed to the person of the hearer." No individual actually or likely to be present could reasonably have regarded the words on appellant's jacket as a direct personal insult. Nor do we have here an instance of the exercise of the State's police power to prevent a speaker from intentionally provoking a given group to hostile reaction. There is no showing that anyone who saw Cohen was in fact violently aroused or that appellant intended such a result.

Finally, much has been made of the claim that Cohen's distasteful mode of expression was thrust upon unwilling or unsuspecting viewers, and that the State might therefore legitimately act to protect the sensitive from otherwise unavoidable exposure to appellant's crude form of protest. Of course, the mere presumed presence of unwitting listeners or viewers does not automatically justify curtailing all speech capable of giving offense. While this Court has recognized that government may properly act in many situations to prohibit intrusion into the privacy of the home of unwelcome views and ideas which cannot be totally banned from the public dialogue, we have at the same time consistently stressed that "we are often 'captives' outside the sanctuary of the home and subject to objectionable speech." The ability of government, consonant with the Constitution, to shut off discourse solely to protect others from hearing it is dependent upon a showing that substantial privacy interests are being invaded in an essentially intolerable manner. Any broader view of this authority would effectively empower a majority to silence dissidents simply as a matter of personal predilections. Those in the Los Angeles courthouse could effectively avoid further bombardment of their sensibilities simply by averting their eyes. [I]f Cohen's "speech" was otherwise entitled to constitutional protection, we do not think the fact that some unwilling "listeners" in a public building may have been briefly exposed to it can serve to justify this breach of the peace conviction.

Against this background, the issue flushed by this case stands out in bold relief. It is whether California can excise, as "offensive conduct," one particular scurrilous epithet from the public discourse, either upon the theory that its use is inherently likely to cause violent reaction or upon a more general assertion that the States, acting as guardians of public morality, may properly remove this offensive word from the public vocabulary.

The constitutional right of free expression is powerful medicine in a society as diverse and populous as ours. It is designed and intended to remove governmental restraints from public discussion, putting the decision as to what views shall be voiced largely into the hands of each of us, in the hope that use of such freedom will ultimately produce a more capable citizenry and more perfect polity and in the belief that no other approach would comport with the premise of individual dignity and choice upon which our political system rests. To many, the immediate consequence of this freedom may often appear to be only verbal tumult, discord, and even offensive utterance. These are, however, within established limits, in truth necessary side effects of the broader enduring values which the process of open debate permits us to achieve. We cannot lose sight of the fact that, in what otherwise might seem a trifling and annoying instance of individual distasteful abuse of a privilege, these fundamental societal values are truly implicated.

[W]hile the particular four-letter word here is perhaps more distasteful than most others of its genre, it is nevertheless often true that one man's vulgarity is another's lyric. [W]e think it is largely because governmental officials cannot make principled distinctions in this area that the Constitution leaves matters of taste and style so largely to the individual.

[W]e cannot overlook the fact that much linguistic expression serves a dual communicative function: it conveys not only ideas capable of relatively precise, detached explication, but otherwise inexpressible emotions as well. In fact, words are often chosen as much for their emotive as their cognitive force. We cannot sanction the view that the Constitution, while solicitous of the cognitive content of individual speech, has little or no regard for that emotive function which, practically speaking, may often be the more important element of the overall message sought to be communicated.

Finally, we cannot indulge the facile assumption that one can forbid particular words without also running a substantial risk of suppressing ideas in the process. It is, in sum, our judgment that, absent a more particularized and compelling reason for its actions, the State may not, consistently with the First and Fourteenth Amendments, make the simple public display here involved of this single four-letter expletive a criminal offense.

DISSENT: Cohen's absurd and immature antic, in my view, was mainly conduct and little speech. As a consequence, this Court's agonizing over First Amendment values seems misplaced and unnecessary.

## DISCUSSION QUESTIONS

(1) What is the difference between "conduct," "speech," and "symbolic speech"?

(2) In what circumstances should the offensive word here be censored?

## IN THE MATTER OF GEORGE T.
### 33 Cal. 4th 620 (Supreme Court of California, 2004)

We consider whether a high school student made a criminal threat by giving two classmates a poem labeled "Dark Poetry," which recites in part, "I am Dark, Destructive, & Dangerous. I slap on my face of happiness but inside I am evil!! For I can be the next kid to bring guns to kill students at school. So parents watch your children cuz I'm BACK!!" [W]e conclude that the ambiguous nature of the poem, along with the circumstances surrounding its dissemination, fail to establish that the poem constituted a criminal threat.

Fifteen-year-old George T. (minor) had been a student at Santa Teresa High School when he approached fellow student Mary S., handed Mary three sheets of paper and told her, "[r]ead these." The first sheet of paper contained a note stating, "These poems describe me and my feelings. Tell me if they describe you and your feelings." The two other sheets of paper contained poems. Mary read only one of the poems, which was labeled "Dark Poetry" and entitled "Faces."

Mary became frightened, handed the poems back to minor, and immediately left the campus in fear. Asked why she felt the poem was a threat, Mary responded: "It's obvious he thought of himself as a dark, destructive, and dangerous person. And if he was willing to admit that about himself and then also state that he could be the next person to bring guns and kill students, then I'd say that he was threatening." She understood the term "dark poetry" to mean "angry threats; any thoughts that aren't positive."

Minor testified the poem "Faces" was not intended to be a threat. He thought of poetry as art and stated that he was very much interested in the subject, particularly as a medium to describe "emotions instead of acting them out." Minor and his friends would jokingly say, "I'm going to be the next Columbine kid." Minor testified that he and some of his friends had joked about Columbine, with someone stating that "I'll probably be the next Columbine killer," and indicating who would be killed and who would be spared.

[N]ot all threats are criminal. The prosecution must prove "(1) that the defendant 'willfully threaten[ed] to commit a crime which will result in death or great bodily injury to another person,' (2) that the defendant made the threat 'with the specific intent that the statement ... is to be taken as a threat, even if there is no intent of actually carrying it out,' (3) that the threat was 'on its face and under the circumstances in which it [was] made, ... so unequivocal, unconditional, immediate, and specific as to convey to the person threatened, a gravity of purpose and an immediate prospect of execution of the threat,' (4) that the threat actually caused the person threatened 'to be in sustained fear for his or her own safety or for his or her immediate family's safety,' and (5) that the threatened person's fear was 'reasonabl[e]' under the circumstances."

A communication that is ambiguous on its face may nonetheless be found to be a criminal threat if the surrounding circumstances clarify the communication's meaning.

What is readily apparent is that much of the poem plainly does not constitute a threat. "Faces" begins by describing the protagonist's feelings about the "faces" that surround him: "Where did they come from? They would probably become the next doctors or loirs or something. All really intelligent and ahead in their game. I wish I had a choice on what I want to be like they do. All so happy and vagrant. Each origonal in their own way. They make me want to puke." There is no doubt this portion of the poem fails to convey a criminal threat as no violent conduct whatsoever is expressed or intimated. Neither do the next two lines of the poem convey a threat: "For I am Dark, Destructive, & Dangerous. I slap on my face of happiness but inside I am evil!!" These lines amount to an introspective description of the protagonist, disclosing that he is "destructive," "dangerous," and "evil." But again, such divulgence threatens no action.

Only the final two lines of the poem could arguably be construed to be a criminal threat: "For I can be the next kid to bring guns to kill students at school. So parents watch your children cuz I'm BACK!!" Mary believed this was a threat, but her testimony reveals that her conclusion rested upon a considerable amount of interpretation: "I feel that when he said, 'I can be the next person,' that he meant that he will be, because also he says that he's dark, destructive, and dangerous person. And I'd describe a dangerous person as someone who has something in mind of killing someone or multiple people." The court's finding that minor threatened to kill turned primarily on its interpretation of the words, "For I can be the next kid to bring guns to kill students at school" to mean not only that minor could do so, but that he would do so. In other words, the court construed the word "can" to mean "will." But that is not what the poem recites. However the poem was interpreted, the fact remains that "can" does not mean "will." While the protagonist in "Faces" declares that he has the potential or capacity to kill students given his dark and hidden feelings, he does not actually threaten to do so. While perhaps discomforting and unsettling, in this unique context this disclosure simply does not constitute an actual threat to kill or inflict harm.

As is evident, the poem "Faces" is ambiguous and plainly equivocal. It does not describe or threaten future conduct since it does not state that the protagonist plans to kill students.

Of course, exactly what the poem means is open to varying interpretations because a poem may mean different things to different readers. As a medium of expression, a poem is inherently ambiguous.

In short, viewed in isolation the poem is not "so unequivocal" as to have conveyed a gravity of purpose and an immediate prospect that minor would bring guns to school and kill them. Ambiguity, however, is not necessarily sufficient to immunize the poem from being deemed a criminal threat because the surrounding circumstances may clarify facial ambiguity. When the words are vague, context takes on added significance, but care must be taken not to diminish the requirements that the communicator have the specific intent to convey a threat and that the threat convey a gravity of purpose and immediate prospect of the threat's execution.

[I]ncriminating circumstances in this case are noticeably lacking: there was no history of animosity or conflict between the students, no threatening gestures or mannerisms accompanied the poem, and no conduct suggested that there was an immediate prospect of execution of a threat to kill. Thus the circumstances surrounding the poem's dissemination fail to show that, as a threat, it was sufficiently unequivocal to convey an immediate prospect that minor would bring guns to school and shoot students.

[W]e hold the poem entitled "Faces" and the circumstances surrounding its dissemination fail to establish that it was a criminal threat because the text of the poem, understood in light of the surrounding circumstances, was not "so unequivocal, unconditional, immediate, and specific as to convey a gravity of purpose and an immediate prospect of execution of the threat."

This case implicates two apparently competing interests: a school administration's interest in ensuring the safety of its students and faculty versus students' right to engage in creative expression. Following Columbine, Santee, and other notorious school shootings, there is a heightened sensitivity on school campuses to latent signs that a student may undertake to bring guns to school and embark on a shooting rampage. Such signs may include violence-laden student writings. For example, the two student killers in Columbine had written poems for their English classes containing "extremely violent imagery." Ensuring a safe school environment and protecting freedom of expression, however, are not necessarily antagonistic goals.

Minor's reference to school shootings and his dissemination of his poem in close proximity to the Santee school shooting no doubt reasonably heightened the school's concern that minor might emulate the actions of previous school shooters. Certainly, school personnel were amply justified in taking action but that is not the issue before us. We decide here only that minor's poem did not constitute a criminal threat.

## DISCUSSION QUESTIONS

(1) Should symbolic artistic expression be taken more seriously to protect the safety of students, especially after Columbine and Santee?

(2) Should a painting graphically depicting a student shooting a police officer in the back of the head be protected as symbolic speech, on the grounds that it is ambiguous art, subject to interpretation?

## TEXAS v. JOHNSON
### 491 U.S. 397 (U.S. Supreme Court, 1989)

After publicly burning an American flag as a means of political protest, Gregory Lee Johnson was convicted of desecrating a flag in violation of Texas law. This case presents the question whether his conviction is consistent with the First Amendment. We hold that it is not.

While the Republican National Convention was taking place in Dallas in 1984, Johnson participated in a political demonstration dubbed the "Republican War Chest Tour." [T]he purpose of this event was to protest the policies of the Reagan administration and of certain Dallas-based corporations. The demonstration ended in front of Dallas City Hall, where Johnson unfurled the American flag, doused it with kerosene, and set it on fire. No one was physically injured or threatened with injury, though several witnesses testified that they had been seriously offended by the flag burning.

Of the approximately 100 demonstrators, Johnson alone was charged with a crime, the desecration of a venerated object in violation of [Texas law]. [H]e was convicted, sentenced to one year in prison, and fined $2,000.

Johnson was convicted of flag desecration for burning the flag rather than for uttering insulting words. We must first determine whether Johnson's burning of the flag constituted expressive conduct, permitting him to invoke the First Amendment in challenging his conviction. If his conduct was expressive, we next decide whether the State's regulation is related to the suppression of free expression.

The First Amendment literally forbids the abridgment only of "speech," but we have long recognized that its protection does not end at the spoken or written word. [W]e have acknowledged that conduct may be "sufficiently imbued with elements of communication to fall within the scope of the First and Fourteenth Amendments."

In deciding whether particular conduct possesses sufficient communicative elements to bring the First Amendment into play, we have asked whether "[a]n intent to convey a particularized message was present, and [whether] the likelihood was great that the message would be understood by those who viewed it."

That we have had little difficulty identifying an expressive element in conduct relating to flags should not be surprising. The very purpose of a national flag is to serve as a symbol of our country. Pregnant with expressive content, the flag as readily signifies this Nation as does the combination of letters found in "America."

We have not automatically concluded, however, that any action taken with respect to our flag is expressive. Instead, in characterizing such action for First Amendment purposes, we have considered the context in which it occurred. Johnson burned an American flag as part -- indeed, as the culmination -- of a political demonstration that coincided with the convening of the Republican Party and its renomination of Ronald Reagan for President. The expressive, overtly political nature of this conduct was both intentional and overwhelmingly apparent. In these circumstances, Johnson's burning of the flag was conduct "sufficiently imbued with elements of communication" to implicate the First Amendment.

The government generally has a freer hand in restricting expressive conduct than it has in restricting the written or spoken word. It may not, however, proscribe particular conduct because it has expressive elements.

The State offers two separate interests to justify this conviction: preventing breaches of the peace and preserving the flag as a symbol of nationhood and national unity.

We conclude that the State's interest in maintaining order is not implicated on these facts. And, in fact, Texas already has a statute specifically prohibiting breaches of the peace, which tends to confirm that Texas need not punish this flag desecration in order to keep the peace.

The State also asserts an interest in preserving the flag as a symbol of nationhood and national unity. We are persuaded that this interest is related to expression in the case of Johnson's burning of the flag. The State, apparently, is concerned that such conduct will lead people to believe either that the flag does not stand for nationhood and national unity, but instead reflects other, less positive concepts, or that the concepts reflected in the flag do not in fact exist, that is, that we do not enjoy unity as a Nation.

It remains to consider whether the State's interest in preserving the flag as a symbol of nationhood and national unity justifies Johnson's conviction. Johnson was not, we add, prosecuted for the expression of just any idea; he was prosecuted for his expression of dissatisfaction with the policies of this country, expression situated at the core of our First Amendment values.

Moreover, Johnson was prosecuted because he knew that his politically charged expression would cause "serious offense." If he had burned the flag as a means of disposing of it because it was dirty or torn, he would not have been convicted of flag desecration under this Texas law: federal law designates burning as the preferred means of disposing of a flag "when it is in such condition that it is no longer a fitting emblem for display," and Texas has no quarrel with this means of disposal. The Texas law is thus not aimed at protecting the physical integrity of the flag in all circumstances, but is designed instead to protect it only against impairments that would cause serious offense to others.

If there is a bedrock principle underlying the First Amendment, it is that the government may not prohibit the expression of an idea simply because society finds the idea itself offensive or disagreeable. We have not recognized an exception to this principle even where our flag has been involved.

To conclude that the government may permit designated symbols to be used to communicate only a limited set of messages would be to enter territory having no discernible or defensible boundaries. Could the government, on this theory, prohibit the burning of state flags? Of copies of the Presidential seal? Of the Constitution? In evaluating these choices under the First Amendment, how would we decide which symbols were sufficiently special to warrant this unique status? To do so, we would be forced to consult our own political preferences, and impose them on the citizenry, in the very way that the First Amendment forbids us to do.

We are tempted to say that the flag's deservedly cherished place in our community will be strengthened, not weakened, by our holding today. Our decision is a reaffirmation of the principles of freedom and inclusiveness that the flag best reflects, and of the conviction that our toleration of criticism such as Johnson's is a sign and source of our strength.

The way to preserve the flag's special role is not to punish those who feel differently about these matters. It is to persuade them that they are wrong. We do not consecrate the flag by punishing its desecration, for in doing so we dilute the freedom that this cherished emblem represents.

DISSENT: The result of the Texas statute is obviously to deny one in Johnson's frame of mind one of many means of "symbolic speech." [F]lag burning is the equivalent of an inarticulate grunt or roar that is most likely to be indulged in not to express any particular idea, but to antagonize others. The Texas statute deprived Johnson of only one rather inarticulate symbolic form of protest -- a form of protest that was profoundly offensive to many -- and left him with a full panoply of other symbols and every conceivable form of verbal expression to express his deep disapproval of national policy. Thus, in no way can it be said that Texas is punishing him because his hearers -- or any other group of people -- were profoundly opposed to the message that he sought to convey. Such opposition is no proper basis for restricting speech or expression under the First Amendment. It was Johnson's use of this particular symbol, and not the idea that he sought to convey by it or by his many other expressions, for which he was punished.

## DISCUSSION QUESTIONS

(1) Should the American flag have special protection against desecration not enjoyed by other national symbols?

(2) Was Johnson's flag-burning "symbolic speech" or only an "inarticulate grunt" not protected by the First Amendment?

(3) Would any laws regulating the American flag be permissible, consistently with the First Amendment?

# R. A. V. v. CITY OF ST. PAUL
## 505 U.S. 377 (U.S. Supreme Court, 1992)

In the predawn hours of June 21, 1990, petitioner and several other teenagers allegedly assembled a crudely made cross by taping together broken chair legs. They then allegedly burned the cross inside the fenced yard of a black family that lived across the street from the house where petitioner was staying. Although this conduct could have been punished under any of a number of laws, one of the provisions under which respondent city of St. Paul chose to charge petitioner was the St. Paul Bias-Motivated Crime Ordinance, which provides:

> Whoever places on public or private property a symbol, object, appellation, characterization or graffiti, including, but not limited to, a burning cross or Nazi swastika, which one knows or has reasonable grounds to know arouses anger, alarm or resentment in others on the basis of race, color, creed, religion or gender commits disorderly conduct and shall be guilty of a misdemeanor.

Assuming that all of the expression reached by the ordinance is proscribable under the "fighting words" doctrine, we nonetheless conclude that the ordinance is facially unconstitutional in that it prohibits otherwise permitted speech solely on the basis of the subjects the speech addresses.

The First Amendment generally prevents government from proscribing speech, or even expressive conduct, because of disapproval of the ideas expressed. Content-based regulations are presumptively invalid.

[T]he exclusion of "fighting words" from the scope of the First Amendment simply means that the unprotected features of the words are, despite their verbal character, essentially a "nonspeech" element of communication. Fighting words are thus analogous to a noisy sound truck: Each is a "mode of speech," both can be used to convey an idea; but neither has, in and of itself, a claim upon the First Amendment. As with the sound truck, however, so also with fighting words: The government may not regulate use based on hostility -- or favoritism -- towards the underlying message expressed.

[W]e conclude that the ordinance is facially unconstitutional. Although the phrase, "arouses anger, alarm or resentment in others," has been limited to reach only those symbols or displays that amount to "fighting words," the remaining, unmodified terms make clear that the ordinance applies only to "fighting words" that insult, or provoke violence, "on the basis of race, color, creed, religion or gender." Displays containing abusive invective, no matter how vicious or severe, are permissible unless they are addressed to one of the specified disfavored topics. Those who wish to use "fighting words" in connection with other ideas -- to express hostility, for example, on the basis of political affiliation, union membership, or homosexuality -- are not covered. The First Amendment does not permit St. Paul to impose special prohibitions on speakers who express views on disfavored subjects.

In its practical operation, moreover, the ordinance goes even beyond mere content discrimination, to actual viewpoint discrimination. Displays containing some words -- odious racial epithets, for example -- would be prohibited to proponents of all views. But "fighting words" that do not themselves invoke race, color, creed, religion, or gender --  aspersions upon a person's mother, for example -- would seemingly be usable in the placards of those arguing in favor of racial, color, etc., tolerance and equality, but could not be used by those speakers' opponents.

What makes the anger, fear, sense of dishonor, etc., produced by violation of this ordinance distinct from the anger, fear, sense of dishonor, etc., produced by other fighting words is nothing other than the fact that it is caused by a distinctive idea, conveyed by a distinctive message. It is obvious that the symbols which will arouse "anger, alarm or resentment in others on the basis of race, color, creed, religion or gender" are those symbols that communicate a message of hostility based on one of these characteristics.

St. Paul has not singled out an especially offensive mode of expression -- it has not, for example, selected for prohibition only those fighting words that communicate ideas in a threatening (as opposed to a merely obnoxious) manner. Rather, it has proscribed fighting words of whatever manner that communicate messages of racial, gender, or religious intolerance. Selectivity of this sort creates the possibility that the city is seeking to handicap the expression of particular ideas.

St. Paul asserts that the ordinance helps to ensure the basic human rights of members of groups that have historically been subjected to discrimination, including the right of such group members to live in peace where they wish. We do not doubt that these interests are compelling, and that the ordinance can be said to promote them. The dispositive question is whether content discrimination is reasonably necessary to achieve St. Paul's compelling interests; it plainly is not. An ordinance not limited to the favored topics, for example, would have precisely the same beneficial effect. In fact the only interest distinctively served by the content limitation is that of displaying the city council's special hostility towards the particular biases thus singled out. That is precisely what the First Amendment forbids. The politicians of St. Paul are entitled to express that hostility -- but not through the means of imposing unique limitations upon speakers who (however benightedly) disagree.

Let there be no mistake about our belief that burning a cross in someone's yard is reprehensible. But St. Paul has sufficient means at its disposal to prevent such behavior without adding the First Amendment to the fire.

## DISCUSSION QUESTIONS

(1) What actions might St. Paul take, consistently with the First Amendment, to discourage "hate speech" against its citizens?

(2) Should burning a cross be considered "symbolic speech"?

(3) Several justices in the majority in this decision dissented in the *Texas v. Johnson* flag-burning case. Is it consistent to protect cross-burning, but not flag-burning, under the First Amendment?

## COLLIN v. SMITH
### 578 F.2d 1197 (7th Cir., 1978)

[T]he National Socialist Party of America (NSPA) is a political group described by its leader, Frank Collin, as a Nazi party. Among NSPA's more controversial and generally unacceptable beliefs are that black persons are biologically inferior to white persons, and should be expatriated to Africa as soon as possible; that American Jews have "inordinate . . . political and financial power" in the world and are "in the forefront of the international Communist revolution." NSPA members affect a uniform reminiscent of those worn by members of the German Nazi Party during the Third Reich and display a swastika thereon and on a red, white, and black flag they frequently carry.

The Village of Skokie, Illinois has a large Jewish population, including as many as several thousand survivors of the Nazi holocaust in Europe before and during World War II.

NSPA announced plans to march in front of the Village Hall in Skokie on May 1, 1977. [T]the Village enacted three ordinances to prohibit demonstrations such as the one NSPA had threatened. This lawsuit seeks declaratory and injunctive relief against enforcement of the ordinances.

Village Ordinance No. 77-5-N-994 (hereinafter 994) is a comprehensive permit system for all parades or public assemblies of more than 50 persons. One of the prerequisites for a permit is a finding by the appropriate (officials) that the assembly

will not portray criminality, depravity or lack of virtue in, or incite violence, hatred abuse or hostility toward a person or group of persons by reason of reference to religious, racial, ethnic, national or regional affiliation.

Village Ordinance No. 77-5-N-995 (995) prohibits

the dissemination of any materials within the Village of Skokie which promotes and incites hatred against persons by reason of their race, national origin, or religion, and is intended to do so

"Dissemination of materials" includes

publication or display or distribution of posters, signs, handbills, or writings and public display of markings and clothing of symbolic significance.

Ordinance No. 77-5-N-996 (996) prohibits public demonstrations by members of political parties while wearing "military-style" uniforms.

Collin and NSPA applied for a permit to march on July 4, 1977, which was denied on the ground the application disclosed an intention to violate 996. The permit application stated that the march would last about a half hour, and would involve 30 to 50 demonstrators wearing uniforms including swastikas and carrying a party banner with a swastika and placards with statements thereon such as "White Free Speech," "Free Speech for the White Man," and "Free Speech for White America." A single file sidewalk march that would not disrupt traffic was proposed, without speeches or the distribution of handbills or literature.

We would hopefully surprise no one by confessing personal views that NSPA's beliefs and goals are repugnant to the core values held generally by residents of this country, and, indeed, to much of what we cherish in civilization. As judges sworn to defend the Constitution, however, we cannot decide this or any case on that basis.

[A]ppellees know full well that, in light of their views and the historical associations they would bring with them to Skokie, many people would find their demonstration extremely mentally and emotionally disturbing, or the suspicion that such a result may be relished by appellees.

But our task here is to decide whether the First Amendment protects the activity in which appellees wish to engage, not to render moral judgment on their views or tactics. First Amendment rights are truly precious and fundamental to our national life. Nor is this truth without relevance to the saddening historical images this case inevitably arouses. It is, after all, in part the fact that our constitutional system protects minorities unpopular at a particular time or place from governmental harassment and intimidation, that distinguishes life in this country from life under the Third Reich.

[W]e are unable to deny that the activities in which the appellees wish to engage are within the ambit of the First Amendment. [A]lthough marching, parading, and picketing, because they involve conduct implicating significant interests in maintaining public order, are less protected than pure speech, they are nonetheless subject to First Amendment protection.

[T]he Nazi demonstration could be subjected to reasonable regulation of its time, place, and manner. No objection is raised by the Village to the suggested time, place, or manner of the demonstration, except the general assertion that in the place of Skokie, in these times, given the content of appellees' views and symbols, the demonstration and its symbols and speech should be prohibited. Because the ordinances turn on the content of the demonstration, they are necessarily not time, place, or manner regulations.

We first consider ordinance 995, prohibiting the dissemination of materials which would promote hatred towards persons on the basis of their heritage.

While some would no doubt label appellees' views and symbols obscene, the constitutional rule that obscenity is unprotected applies only to material with erotic content. Furthermore, the Village tells us that it does not rely on a fear of responsive violence to justify the ordinance and does not suggest that there will be any physical violence if the march is held.

[I]t is said that the content criminalized by 995 is "totally lacking in social content," and that it consists of "false statements of fact" in which there is "no constitutional value." No handbills are to be distributed; no speeches are planned. To the degree that the symbols in question can be said to assert anything specific, it must be the Nazi ideology, which cannot be treated as a mere false "fact." [T]here can be no legitimate start down such a road. The asserted falseness of Nazi dogma, and, indeed, its general repudiation, simply do not justify its suppression.

The Village's [next] argument is that the Nazi march, involving as it does the display of uniforms and swastikas, will create a substantive evil that it has a right to prohibit: the infliction of psychic trauma on resident holocaust survivors and other Jewish residents.

It would be grossly insensitive to deny, as we do not, that the proposed demonstration would seriously disturb, emotionally and mentally, at least some, and probably many of the Village's residents.

It is said that the proposed march is not speech, or even "speech plus," but rather an invasion, intensely menacing no matter how peacefully conducted. There is room under the First Amendment for the government to protect targeted listeners from offensive speech, but only when the speaker intrudes on the privacy of the home, or a captive audience cannot practically avoid exposure.

This case does not involve intrusion into people's homes. There need be no captive audience, as Village residents may simply avoid the Village Hall for thirty minutes on a Sunday afternoon. Absent such intrusion or captivity, there is no justifiable substantial privacy interest to save 995 from constitutional infirmity, when it attempts, by fiat, to declare the entire Village, at all times, a privacy zone that may be sanitized from the offensiveness of Nazi ideology and symbols.

Because 994 gives to Village "officials the power to deny use of a forum in advance of actual expression," it is a prior restraint, which thus "comes to this Court with a 'heavy presumption' against its constitutional validity."

[W]e feel compelled to express our repugnance at the doctrines which the appellees desire to profess publicly. The result we have reached is dictated by the fundamental proposition that if these civil rights are to remain vital for all, they must protect not only those society deems acceptable, but also those whose ideas it quite justifiably rejects and despises.

DISSENT: Under these circumstances, the appearance of plaintiffs' group in Skokie may be so extremely offensive and of such little social utility as to be beyond the protection of the First Amendment.

There is no dispute that speech may not be suppressed merely because it offends its listeners. At some point, however, considerations of a neutral desire to maintain the public peace and general welfare come into play in determining whether activities should be allowed. Where the activity is, as here, by its nature and by the circumstances, a threat to a reasonable attempt to maintain the public order, it cannot claim to go unregulated under the auspices that content may not properly be considered.

## DISCUSSION QUESTIONS

(1) What changes in the facts here might justify restriction on the free speech of the Nazis who wish to parade in Skokie?

(2) Should "absence of social utility" in the content of a message be the basis for a denial of the First Amendment protection of speech?

### Obscenity, Pornography, and Indecency

### ROTH v. UNITED STATES
354 U.S. 476 (U.S. Supreme Court, 1957)

In *Roth*, the primary constitutional question is whether the federal obscenity statute violates the First Amendment that "Congress shall make no law . . . abridging the freedom of speech, or of the press . . . ."

Roth conducted a business in New York in the publication and sale of books, photographs and magazines. He used circulars and advertising matter to solicit sales. He was convicted [of] mailing obscene circulars and advertising, and an obscene book, in violation of the federal obscenity statute.

The dispositive question is whether obscenity is utterance within the area of protected speech and press. Although this is the first time the question has been squarely presented to this Court, expressions found in numerous opinions indicate that this Court has always assumed that obscenity is not protected by the freedoms of speech and press.

The guaranties of freedom of expression in effect in 10 of the 14 States which by 1792 had ratified the Constitution, gave no absolute protection for every utterance. [A]ll of those States made either blasphemy or profanity, or both, statutory crimes.

In light of this history, it is apparent that the unconditional phrasing of the First Amendment was not intended to protect every utterance. [T]here is sufficiently contemporaneous evidence to show that obscenity was outside the protection intended for speech and press.

The protection given speech and press was fashioned to assure unfettered interchange of ideas for the bringing about of political and social changes desired by the people. All ideas having even the slightest redeeming social importance -- unorthodox ideas, controversial ideas, even ideas hateful to the prevailing climate of opinion -- have the full protection of the guaranties, unless excludable because they encroach upon the limited area of more important interests. But implicit in the history of the First Amendment is the rejection of obscenity as utterly without redeeming social importance. We hold that obscenity is not within the area of constitutionally protected speech or press.

[S]ex and obscenity are not synonymous. Obscene material is material which deals with sex in a manner appealing to prurient interest. The portrayal of sex, e.g., in art, literature and scientific works, is not itself sufficient reason to deny material the constitutional protection of freedom of speech and press.

The fundamental freedoms of speech and press have contributed greatly to the development and well-being of our free society and are indispensable to its continued growth. It is therefore vital that the standards for judging obscenity safeguard the protection of freedom of speech and press for material which does not treat sex in a manner appealing to prurient interest.

The early leading standard of obscenity allowed material to be judged merely by the effect of an isolated excerpt upon particularly susceptible persons. Some American courts substituted this test: whether to the average person, applying contemporary community standards, the dominant theme of the material taken as a whole appeals to prurient interest. The [early] test, judging obscenity by the effect of isolated passages upon the most susceptible persons, might well encompass material legitimately treating with sex, and so it must be rejected as unconstitutionally restrictive of the freedoms of speech and press. On the other hand, the substituted standard provides safeguards adequate to withstand the charge of constitutional infirmity.

The federal obscenity statute makes punishable the mailing of material that is "obscene, lewd, lascivious, or filthy . . . or other publication of an indecent character."

Many decisions have recognized that these obscenity statutes are not precise. This Court, however, has consistently held that lack of precision is not itself offensive to the requirements of due process. "The Constitution does not require impossible standards"; all that is required is that the language "conveys sufficiently definite warning as to the proscribed conduct when measured by common understanding and practices." These words give adequate warning of the conduct proscribed.

In summary, then, we hold that these statutes, applied according to the proper standard for judging obscenity, do not offend constitutional safeguards against convictions based upon protected material, or fail to give men in acting adequate notice of what is prohibited.

CONCUR: [B]ecause we are operating in a field of expression and because broad language here may eventually be applied to the arts and sciences and freedom of communication, I would limit our decision to the facts before us and to the validity of the statutes in question as applied.

That there is a social problem presented by obscenity is attested by the expression of the legislatures of the forty-eight States as well as the Congress. To recognize the existence of a problem, however, does not require that we sustain any and all measures adopted to meet that problem. The history of the application of laws designed to suppress the obscene demonstrates convincingly that the power of government can be invoked under them against great art or literature, scientific treatises, or works exciting social controversy. The line dividing the salacious or pornographic from literature or science is not straight and unwavering. Present laws depend largely upon the effect that the materials may have upon those who receive them. It is manifest that the same object may have a different impact, varying according to the part of the community it reached.

DISSENT: When we sustain these convictions, we make the legality of a publication turn on the purity of thought which a book or tract instills in the mind of the reader. I do not think we can approve that standard and be faithful to the command of the First Amendment.

The test of obscenity the Court endorses today gives the censor free range over a vast domain. To allow the State to step in and punish mere speech or publication that the judge or the jury thinks has an undesirable impact on thoughts but that is not shown to be a part of unlawful action is drastically to curtail the First Amendment.

If we were certain that impurity of sexual thoughts impelled to action, we would be on less dangerous ground in punishing the distributors of this sex literature. But it is by no means clear that obscene literature is a significant factor in influencing substantial deviations from community standards.

The absence of dependable information on the effect of obscene literature on human conduct should make us wary. It should put us on the side of protecting society's interest in literature, unless it can be said that the particular publication has an impact on action that the government can control.

The standard of what offends "the common conscience of the community" conflicts, in my judgment, with the command of the First Amendment. Certainly that standard would not be an acceptable one if religion, economics, politics or philosophy were involved. How does it become a constitutional standard when literature treating with sex is concerned?

Any test that turns on what is offensive to the community's standards is too loose, too capricious, too destructive of freedom of expression to be squared with the First Amendment. This is community censorship in one of its worst forms. It creates a regime where in the battle between the literati and the Philistines, the Philistines are certain to win.

I can understand (and at times even sympathize) with programs of civic groups and church groups to protect and defend the existing moral standards of the community. When speech alone is involved, I do not think that government, consistently with the First Amendment, can become the sponsor of any of these movements. Government should be concerned with antisocial conduct, not with utterances. [L]iterature should not be suppressed merely because it offends the moral code of the censor.

[T]he test that suppresses a cheap tract today can suppress a literary gem tomorrow. All it need do is to incite a lascivious thought or arouse a lustful desire. The list of books that judges or juries can place in that category is endless.

I would give the broad sweep of the First Amendment full support. I have the same confidence in the ability of our people to reject noxious literature as I have in their capacity to sort out the true from the false in theology, economics, politics, or any other field.

## DISCUSSION QUESTIONS

(1) Is the test of "obscenity" here sufficiently clear to enable enforcement by the courts that does not repress constitutionally protected speech?

(2) Should the Court follow the actual language of the first Amendment and disregard the practices of the American colonies over two centuries ago in interpreting the meaning of "free speech"?

(3) What would constitute proof that obscene material causes antisocial behavior?

## STANLEY v. GEORGIA
### 394 U.S. 557 (U.S. Supreme Court, 1969)

An investigation of appellant's alleged bookmaking activities led to the issuance of a search warrant for appellant's home. [W]hile looking through a desk drawer in an upstairs bedroom, one of the federal agents found three reels of eight-millimeter film. Using a projector and screen found in an upstairs living room, they viewed the films. The state officer concluded that they were obscene and seized them. Since a further examination of the bedroom indicated that appellant occupied it, he was charged with possession of obscene matter and placed under arrest. He was later indicted for "knowingly hav[ing] possession of . . . obscene matter" in violation of Georgia law. Appellant was tried before a jury and convicted.

Appellant argues that the Georgia obscenity statute, insofar as it punishes mere private possession of obscene matter, violates the First Amendment, as made applicable to the States by the Fourteenth Amendment. [W]e agree that the mere private possession of obscene matter cannot constitutionally be made a crime.

The question before us is whether "a statute imposing criminal sanctions upon the mere [knowing] possession of obscene matter" is constitutional.

It is now well established that the Constitution protects the right to receive information and ideas. This right to receive information and ideas, regardless of their social worth, is fundamental to our free society. [A]lso fundamental is the right to be free, except in very limited circumstances, from unwanted governmental intrusions into one's privacy.

Whatever may be the justifications for other statutes regulating obscenity, we do not think they reach into the privacy of one's own home. If the First Amendment means anything, it means that a State has no business telling a man, sitting alone in his own house, what books he may read or what films he may watch. Our whole constitutional heritage rebels at the thought of giving government the power to control men's minds.

Georgia asserts the right to protect the individual's mind from the effects of obscenity. We are not certain that this argument amounts to anything more than the assertion that the State has the right to control the moral content of a person's thoughts. To some, this may be a noble purpose, but it is wholly inconsistent with the philosophy of the First Amendment. Nor is it relevant that obscene materials are arguably devoid of any ideological content. The line between the transmission of ideas and mere entertainment is much too elusive for this Court to draw, if indeed such a line can be drawn at all. Whatever the power of the state to control public dissemination of ideas inimical to the public morality, it cannot constitutionally premise legislation on the desirability of controlling a person's private thoughts.

Georgia asserts that exposure to obscene materials may lead to deviant sexual behavior or crimes of sexual violence. There appears to be little empirical basis for that assertion. Given the present state of knowledge, the State may no more prohibit mere possession of obscene matter on the ground that it may lead to antisocial conduct than it may prohibit possession of chemistry books on the ground that they may lead to the manufacture of homemade spirits.

We hold that the First and Fourteenth Amendments prohibit making mere private possession of obscene material a crime. As we have said, the States retain broad power to regulate obscenity; that power simply does not extend to mere possession by the individual in the privacy of his own home.

## DISCUSSION QUESTIONS

(1) Is it consistent for the court to approve prosecutions for the sale of "obscene" material (in *Roth*), but not for possession of such material?

(2) The Court says there is no empirical evidence that reading obscene material causes violence. Three decades later, if new empirical data could be produced, should the conclusions here be reversed?

## MILLER v. CALIFORNIA
### 413 U.S. 15 (U.S. Supreme Court, 1973)

This is one of a group of "obscenity-pornography" cases being reviewed by the Court in a re-examination of standards enunciated in earlier cases.

Appellant conducted a mass mailing campaign to advertise the sale of illustrated books, euphemistically called "adult" material. After a jury trial, he was convicted of distributing obscene matter.

This case involves the application of a State's criminal obscenity statute to a situation in which sexually explicit materials have been thrust by aggressive sales action upon unwilling recipients who had in no way indicated any desire to receive such materials. This Court has recognized that the States have a legitimate interest in prohibiting dissemination or exhibition of obscene material when the mode of dissemination carries with it a significant danger of offending the sensibilities of unwilling recipients or of exposure to juveniles.

Apart from the initial formulation in the *Roth* case, no majority of the Court has been able to agree on a standard to determine what constitutes obscene, pornographic material subject to regulation under the States' police power. This is an area in which there are few eternal verities.

This much has been categorically settled by the Court, that obscene material is unprotected by the First Amendment. We acknowledge, however, the inherent dangers of undertaking to regulate any form of expression. As a result, we now confine the permissible scope of such regulation to works which depict or describe sexual conduct. That conduct must be specifically defined by the applicable state law.

The basic guidelines for the trier of fact must be: (a) whether "the average person, applying contemporary community standards" would find that the work, taken as a whole, appeals to the prurient interest, (b) whether the work depicts or describes, in a patently offensive way, sexual conduct specifically defined by the applicable state law; and (c) whether the work, taken as a whole, lacks serious literary, artistic, political, or scientific value.

We emphasize that it is not our function to propose regulatory schemes for the States. It is possible, however, to give a few plain examples of what a state statute could define for regulation under part (b) of the standard announced in this opinion:

(a) Patently offensive representations or descriptions of ultimate sexual acts, normal or perverted, actual or simulated.

(b) Patently offensive representations or descriptions of masturbation, excretory functions, and lewd exhibition of the genitals.

Under the holdings announced today, no one will be subject to prosecution for the sale or exposure of obscene materials unless these materials depict or describe patently offensive "hard core" sexual conduct specifically defined by the regulating state law, as written or construed. We are satisfied that these specific prerequisites will provide fair notice to a dealer in such materials that his activities may bring prosecution.

[T]oday, for the first time since *Roth* was decided, a majority of this Court has agreed on concrete guidelines to isolate "hard core" pornography from expression protected by the First Amendment.

This may not be an easy road, free from difficulty. But no amount of "fatigue" should lead us to adopt a convenient "institutional" rationale -- an absolutist, "anything goes" view of the First Amendment -- because it will lighten our burdens.

Under a National Constitution, fundamental First Amendment limitations on the powers of the States do not vary from community to community, but this does not mean that there are, or should or can be, fixed, uniform national standards of precisely what appeals to the "prurient interest" or is "patently offensive." These are essentially questions of fact, and our Nation is simply too big and too diverse for this Court to reasonably expect that such standards could be articulated for all 50 States in a single formulation, even assuming the prerequisite consensus exists. To require a State to structure obscenity proceedings around evidence of a national "community standard" would be an exercise in futility.

One can concede that the "sexual revolution" of recent years may have had useful byproducts in striking layers of prudery from a subject long irrationally kept from needed ventilation. But it does not follow that no regulation of patently offensive "hard core" materials is needed or permissible; civilized people do not allow unregulated access to heroin because it is a derivative of medicinal morphine.

In sum, we (a) reaffirm the *Roth* holding that obscene material is not protected by the First Amendment; (b) hold that such material can be regulated by the States, subject to the specific safeguards enunciated above, without a showing that the material is "utterly without redeeming social value"; and (c) hold that obscenity is to be determined by applying "contemporary community standards," not "national standards."

DISSENT: Today the Court retreats from the earlier formulations of the constitutional test and undertakes to make new definitions. This effort, like the earlier ones, is earnest and well intentioned. The difficulty is that we do not deal with constitutional terms, since "obscenity" is not mentioned in the Constitution or Bill of Rights.

Obscenity -- which even we cannot define with precision -- is a hodge-podge. To send men to jail for violating standards they cannot understand, construe, and apply is a monstrous thing to do in a Nation dedicated to fair trials and due process.

The idea that the First Amendment permits punishment for ideas that are "offensive" to the particular judge or jury sitting in judgment is astounding. No greater leveler of speech or literature has ever been designed. To give the power to the censor, as we do today, is to make a sharp and radical break with the traditions of a free society. The First Amendment was not fashioned as a vehicle for dispensing tranquilizers to the people. Its prime function was to keep debate open to "offensive" as well as to "staid" people. The use of the standard "offensive" gives authority to government that cuts the very vitals out of the First Amendment. As is intimated by the Court's opinion, the materials before us may be garbage. But so is much of what is said in political campaigns, in the daily press, on TV, or over the radio. By reason of the First Amendment -- and solely because of it -- speakers and publishers have not been threatened or subdued because their thoughts and ideas may be "offensive" to some.

If there are to be restraints on what is obscene, then a constitutional amendment should be the way of achieving the end. There are societies where religion and mathematics are the only free segments. It would be a dark day for America if that were our destiny. But the people can make it such if they choose to write obscenity into the Constitution and define it.

# DISCUSSION QUESTIONS

(1) Does the three-pronged test for "obscenity" announced here resolve the problems identified in the earlier cases?

(2) Would a Constitutional amendment banning "obscenity" be advisable? Would it resolve the problems the Court has encountered in defining "obscenity"? How should "obscenity" be defined in such an amendment?

## SOUTHEASTERN PROMOTIONS v. CONRAD
### 420 U.S. 546 (U.S. Supreme Court, 1975)

The issue in this case is whether First Amendment rights were abridged when respondents denied petitioner the use of a municipal facility in Chattanooga, Tenn., for the showing of the controversial rock musical "Hair."

Petitioner, Southeastern Promotions, Ltd., is a New York corporation engaged in the business of promoting and presenting theatrical productions for profit. On October 29, 1971, it applied for the use of the Tivoli, a privately owned Chattanooga theater under long-term lease to the city, to present "Hair" there for six days beginning November 23.

Respondents are the directors of the Chattanooga Memorial Auditorium, a municipal theater. Shortly after receiving Southeastern's application, the directors met, and voted to reject it. None of them had seen the play or read the script, but they understood from outside reports that the musical, as produced elsewhere, involved nudity and obscenity on stage. [R]espondents determined that the production would not be "in the best interest of the community." Southeastern was so notified but no written statement of reasons was provided.

[P]etitioner, alleging that respondents' action abridged its First Amendment rights, sought a preliminary injunction [and later] a permanent injunction permitting it to use [a municipal] auditorium.

We hold that respondents' rejection of petitioner's application to use this public forum accomplished a prior restraint under a system lacking in constitutionally required minimal procedural safeguards. Respondents' action is indistinguishable in its censoring effect from the official actions consistently identified as prior restraints in a long line of this Court's decisions.

The board's judgment effectively kept the musical off stage. Respondents did not permit the show to go on and rely on law enforcement authorities to prosecute for anything illegal that occurred. Rather, they denied the application in anticipation that the production would violate the law. Respondents' action was no less a prior restraint because the public facilities happened to be municipal theaters. None of the circumstances qualifying as an established exception to the doctrine of prior restraint was present. Nor was rejection of the application based on any regulation of time, place, or manner related to the nature of the facility or applications from other users. No rights of individuals in surrounding areas were violated by noise or any other aspect of the production. There was no captive audience.

Only if we were to conclude that live drama is unprotected by the First Amendment -- or subject to a totally different standard from that applied to other forms of expression -- could we possibly find no prior restraint here. Each medium of expression must be assessed for First Amendment purposes by standards suited to it, for each may present its own problems. By its nature, theater usually is the acting out -- or singing out -- of the written word, and frequently mixes speech with live action or conduct. But that is no reason to hold theater subject to a drastically different standard.

In order to be held lawful, respondents' action must have been accomplished with procedural safeguards that reduce the danger of suppressing constitutionally protected speech. We conclude that the standard, whatever it may have been, was not implemented by the board under a system with appropriate and necessary procedural safeguards.

Procedural safeguards were lacking here in several respects. The board's system did not provide a procedure for prompt judicial review. Effective review on the merits was not obtained until more than five months later. Throughout, it was petitioner, not the board, that bore the burden of obtaining judicial review. It was petitioner that had the burden of persuasion at the preliminary hearing if not at the later stages of the litigation. Respondents did not file a formal answer to the complaint for five months after petitioner sought review. During the time prior to judicial determination, the restraint altered the status quo. Petitioner was forced to forgo the initial dates planned for the engagement and to seek to schedule the performance at a later date. The delay and uncertainty inevitably discouraged use of the forum.

Whatever the reasons may have been for the board's exclusion of the musical, it could not escape the obligation to afford appropriate procedural safeguards. We need not decide whether the standard of obscenity applied was sufficiently precise or substantively correct, or whether the production is in fact obscene. The standard, whatever it may be, must be implemented under a system that assures prompt judicial review with a minimal restriction of First Amendment rights necessary under the circumstances.

[The denial of the injunction sought is] Reversed.

DISSENT [DOUGLAS]: While I agree with the Court's conclusion that the actions of the respondents constituted an impermissible prior restraint upon the performance of petitioner's rock musical, the injuries inflicted upon petitioner's First Amendment rights cannot be treated adequately or averted in the future by the simple application of a few procedural band-aids. The critical flaw in this case lies in the very nature of the content screening in which respondents have engaged.

A municipal theater is no less a forum for the expression of ideas than is a public park, or a sidewalk; the forms of expression adopted in such a forum may be more expensive and more structured than those typically seen in our parks and streets, but they are surely no less entitled to the shelter of the First Amendment. As soon as municipal officials are permitted to pick and choose, as they are in all existing socialist regimes, between those productions which are "clean and healthful and culturally uplifting" in content and those which are not, the path is cleared for a regime of censorship under which full voice can be given only to those views which meet with the approval of the power that be.

There was much testimony concerning the pungent social and political commentary which the musical "Hair" levels against various sacred cows of our society: the Vietnam war, the draft, and the puritanical conventions of the Establishment. This commentary is undoubtedly offensive to some, but its contribution to social consciousness and intellectual ferment is a positive one. In this respect, the musical's often ribald humor and trenchant social satire may someday merit comparison to the most highly regarded works of Aristophanes, a fellow debunker of established tastes and received wisdom, yet one whose offerings would doubtless meet with a similarly cold reception at the hands of Establishment censors. No matter how many procedural safeguards may be imposed, any system which permits governmental officials to inhibit or control the flow of disturbing and unwelcome ideas to the public threatens serious diminution of the breadth and richness of our cultural offerings.

DISSENT [REHNQUIST]: The Court treat[s] a community-owned theater as if it were the same as a city park or city street, which it is not. Here we deal with municipal action by the city of Chattanooga, not prohibiting or penalizing the expression of views in dramatic form by citizens at large, but rather managing its municipal auditorium.

But the apparent effect of the Court's decision is to tell the managers of municipal auditoriums that they may exercise no selective role whatsoever in deciding what performances may be booked. The auditoriums in question here have historically been devoted to "clean, healthful entertainment"; they have accepted only productions not inappropriate for viewing by children so that the facilities might serve as a place for entertaining the whole family. Viewed apart from any constitutional limitations, such a policy would undoubtedly rule out much worthwhile adult entertainment. But if it is the desire of the citizens of Chattanooga, who presumably have paid for and own the facilities, that the attractions to be shown there should not be of the kind which would offend any substantial number of potential theatergoers, I do not think the policy can be described as arbitrary or unreasonable. Whether or not the production of "Hair" is obscene, the findings of fact do indicate that it is not entertainment designed for the whole family.

## DISCUSSION QUESTIONS

(1) Should a city be required to accord the same First Amendment rights to productions in city-owned theaters as it does to speech in city parks and streets?

(2) Would "Hair" count as "obscenity" under the *Miller* test?

## NATIONAL ENDOWMENT FOR THE ARTS v. FINLEY
### 524 U.S. 569 (U.S. Supreme Court, 1998)

The National Foundation on the Arts and Humanities Act, as amended in 1990, requires the Chairperson of the National Endowment for the Arts (NEA) to ensure that "artistic excellence and artistic merit are the criteria by which [grant] applications are judged, taking into consideration general standards of decency and respect for the diverse beliefs and values of the

American public." 20 U.S.C. 954(d)(1). We conclude that 954(d)(1) is facially valid, as it neither inherently interferes with First Amendment rights nor violates constitutional vagueness principles.

With the establishment of the NEA in 1965, Congress embarked on a "broadly conceived national policy of support for the . . . arts in the United States," pledging federal funds to "help create and sustain not only a climate encouraging freedom of thought, imagination, and inquiry but also the material conditions facilitating the release of . . . creative talent."

Throughout the NEA's history, only a handful of the agency's roughly 100,000 awards have generated formal complaints about misapplied funds or abuse of the public's trust. Two provocative works, however, prompted public controversy in 1989 and led to congressional revaluation of the NEA's funding priorities and efforts to increase oversight of its grant-making procedures. Congress debated several proposals to reform the NEA's grant-making process when it considered the agency's reauthorization in 1990. Ultimately, Congress adopted a bipartisan compromise between Members opposing any funding restrictions and those favoring some guidance to the agency. [T]he Amendment became 954(d)(1), which directs the Chairperson, in establishing procedures to judge the artistic merit of grant applications, to "take into consideration general standards of decency and respect for the diverse beliefs and values of the American public."

The four individual respondents in this case, Karen Finley, John Fleck, Holly Hughes, and Tim Miller, are performance artists who applied for NEA grants before 954(d)(1) was enacted. [I]n June 1990, the NEA informed respondents that they had been denied funding. Respondents filed suit, alleging that the NEA had violated their First Amendment rights by rejecting the applications on political grounds.

The District Court then granted summary judgment in favor of respondents on their facial constitutional challenge to 954(d)(1) and enjoined enforcement of the provision. A divided panel of the Court of Appeals affirmed the District Court's ruling. We granted *certiorari*, and now reverse the judgment of the Court of Appeals.

Respondents raise a facial constitutional challenge to 954(d)(1), and consequently they confront "a heavy burden" in advancing their claim. To prevail, respondents must demonstrate a substantial risk that application of the provision will lead to the suppression of speech.

Respondents argue that the provision is a paradigmatic example of viewpoint discrimination because it rejects any artistic speech that either fails to respect mainstream values or offends standards of decency. It is clear, however, that the text of 954(d)(1) imposes no categorical requirement. The advisory language stands in sharp contrast to congressional efforts to prohibit the funding of certain classes of speech. When Congress has in fact intended to affirmatively constrain the NEA's grant-making authority, it has done so in no uncertain terms..

That 954(d)(1) admonishes the NEA merely to take "decency and respect" into consideration, and that the legislation was aimed at reforming procedures rather than precluding speech, undercut respondents' argument that the provision inevitably will be utilized as a tool for invidious viewpoint discrimination. In cases where we have struck down legislation as facially unconstitutional, the dangers were both more evident and more substantial. Thus, we do not perceive a realistic danger that 954(d)(1) will compromise First Amendment values. Given the varied interpretations of the criteria and the vague exhortation to "take them into consideration," it seems unlikely that this provision will introduce any greater element of selectivity than the determination of "artistic excellence" itself.

The NEA has limited resources and it must deny the majority of the grant applications that it receives, including many that propose "artistically excellent" projects. [W]e have no occasion here to address an as-applied challenge in a situation where the denial of a grant may be shown to be the product of invidious viewpoint discrimination. If the NEA were to leverage its power to award subsidies on the basis of subjective criteria into a penalty on disfavored viewpoints, then we would confront a different case. We have stated that, even in the provision of subsidies, the Government may not "aim at the suppression of dangerous ideas," and if a subsidy were "manipulated" to have a "coercive effect," then relief could be appropriate.

Finally, although the First Amendment certainly has application in the subsidy context, we note that the Government may allocate competitive funding according to criteria that would be impermissible were direct regulation of speech or a criminal penalty at stake.

In the context of selective subsidies, it is not always feasible for Congress to legislate with clarity. Indeed, if this statute is unconstitutionally vague, then so too are all government programs awarding scholarships and grants on the basis of subjective criteria such as "excellence." To accept respondents' vagueness argument would be to call into question the constitutionality of these government programs and countless others like them.

Section 954(d)(1) merely adds some imprecise considerations to an already subjective selection process. It does not, on its face, impermissibly infringe on First or Fifth Amendment rights.

CONCUR: I think that 954(d)(1) must be evaluated as written, rather than as distorted by the agency it was meant to control. By its terms, it establishes content- and viewpoint-based criteria upon which grant applications are to be evaluated. And that is perfectly constitutional. That conclusion is not altered by the fact that the statute does not "compel" the denial of funding. [T]he conclusion of viewpoint discrimination is not affected by the fact that what constitutes "decency" or "the diverse beliefs and values of the American people" is difficult to pin down. Those who wish to create indecent and disrespectful art are as unconstrained now as they were before the enactment of this statute. Avant-garde artistes such as respondents remain entirely free to *epater les bourgeois*; they are merely deprived of the additional satisfaction of having the bourgeoisie taxed to pay for it.

DISSENT: The decency and respect proviso mandates viewpoint-based decisions in the disbursement of government subsidies, and the Government has wholly failed to explain why the statute should be afforded an exemption from the fundamental rule of the First Amendment that viewpoint discrimination in the exercise of public authority over expressive activity is unconstitutional. The Court's conclusions that the proviso is not viewpoint based, that it is not a regulation, and that the NEA may permissibly engage in viewpoint-based discrimination, are all patently mistaken.

What if the statute required a panel to apply criteria "taking into consideration the centrality of Christianity to the American cultural experience," or
"taking into consideration whether the artist is a communist," or "taking into
consideration the political message conveyed by the art," or even "taking
into consideration the superiority of the white race"? Would the Court hold
these considerations facially constitutional, merely because the statute had
no requirement to give them any particular, much less controlling, weight? I
assume not. In such instances, the Court would hold that the First Amendment bars the government from considering viewpoint when it decides whether to subsidize private speech, and a statute that mandates the consideration of viewpoint is quite obviously unconstitutional.

The NEA is a subsidy scheme created to encourage expression of a
diversity of views from private speakers. So long as Congress chooses to
subsidize expressive endeavors at large, it has no business requiring the
NEA to turn down funding applications of artists and exhibitors who devote
their "freedom of thought, imagination, and inquiry" to defying our tastes,
our beliefs, or our values.

Since the decency and respect proviso of 954(d)(1) is substantially
overbroad and carries with it a significant power to chill artistic production
and display, it should be struck down. The Court does not strike down the
proviso. Instead, it preserves the irony of a statutory mandate to deny recognition to virtually any expression capable of causing offense in any quarter
as the most recent manifestation of a scheme enacted to "create and sustain .
. . a climate encouraging freedom of thought, imagination, and inquiry."

## DISCUSSION QUESTIONS

(1) Does the so-called "decency clause" chill future artistic expression?
(2) What limits should be placed on government funding of the arts?
(3) Is a government grant for the arts analogous to a public forum? A
city park? A public theater?

## AMERICAN BOOKSELLERS ASSOCIATION, INC. v. HUDNUT
### 771 F.2d 323 (7th Cir., 1985)

Indianapolis enacted an ordinance defining "pornography" as a practice that
discriminates against women. "Pornography" is to be redressed through the
administrative and judicial methods used for other discrimination. The
City's definition of "pornography" is considerably different from "obscenity," which the Supreme Court has held is not protected by the First Amendment.

"Pornography" under the ordinance is "the graphic sexually explicit
subordination of women, whether in pictures or in words, that also includes
one or more of the following:

(1) Women are presented as sexual objects who enjoy pain or humiliation; or (2) Women are presented as sexual objects who experience
sexual pleasure in being raped; or (3) Women are presented as sexual
objects tied up or cut up or mutilated or bruised or physically hurt, or as

dismembered or truncated or fragmented or severed into body parts; or (4) Women are presented as being penetrated by objects or animals; or (5) Women are presented in scenarios of degradation, injury abasement, torture, shown as filthy or inferior, bleeding, bruised, or hurt in a context that makes these conditions sexual; or (6) Women are presented as sexual objects for domination, conquest, violation, exploitation, possession, or use, or through postures or positions of servility or submission or display."

The statute provides that the "use of men, children, or transsexuals in the place of women in paragraphs (1) through (6) above shall also constitute pornography under this section."

The Indianapolis ordinance does not refer to prurient interest, to offensiveness, or to the standards of the community. It demands attention to particular depictions, not to the work judged as a whole. It is irrelevant under the ordinance whether the work has literary, artistic, political, or scientific value. The City point[s] to these omissions as virtues. They maintain that pornography influences attitudes, and the statute is a way to alter the socialization of men and women rather than to vindicate community standards of offensiveness. And as one of the principal drafters of the ordinance has asserted, "if a woman is subjected, why should it matter that the work has other value?" (Catharine A. MacKinnon)

Those supporting the ordinance say that it will play an important role in reducing the tendency of men to view women as sexual objects, a tendency that leads to both unacceptable attitudes and discrimination in the workplace and violence away from it. Those opposing the ordinance point out that much radical feminist literature is explicit and depicts women in ways forbidden by the ordinance. It is unclear how Indianapolis would treat works from James Joyce's *Ulysses* to Homer's *Iliad*; both depict women as submissive objects for conquest and domination.

The ordinance discriminates on the ground of the content of the speech. Speech treating women in the approved way -- in sexual encounters "premised on equality" -- is lawful no matter how sexually explicit. Speech treating women in the disapproved way -- as submissive in matters sexual or as enjoying humiliation -- is unlawful no matter how significant the literary, artistic, or political qualities of the work taken as a whole. The state may not ordain preferred viewpoints in this way. The Constitution forbids the state to declare one perspective right and silence opponents.

Under the First Amendment the government must leave to the people the evaluation of ideas. Totalitarian governments today rule much of the planet, practicing suppression of billions and spreading dogma that may enslave others. One of the things that separates our society is our absolute right to propagate opinions that the government finds wrong or even hateful.

W]e accept the premises of this legislation. Depictions of subordination tend to perpetuate subordination. The subordinate status of women in turn leads to affront and lower pay at work, insult and injury at home, battery and rape on the streets.

Yet this simply demonstrates the power of pornography as speech. All of these unhappy effects depend on mental intermediation. Pornography affects how people see the world, their fellows, and social relations. If pornography is what pornography does, so is other speech.

Racial bigotry, anti-semitism, violence on television, reporters' biases -- these and many more influence the culture and shape our socialization. None is directly answerable by more speech, unless that speech too finds its place in the popular culture. Yet all is protected as speech, however insidious. Any other answer leaves the government in control of all of the institutions of culture, the great censor and director of which thoughts are good for us. If the fact that speech plays a role in a process of conditioning were enough to permit governmental regulation, that would be the end of freedom of speech.

Much of Indianapolis's argument rests on the belief that when speech is "unanswerable," and the metaphor that there is a "marketplace of ideas" does not apply, the First Amendment does not apply either. The metaphor is honored; Milton's *Aeropagitica* and John Stewart Mill's *On Liberty* defend freedom of speech on the ground that the truth will prevail, and many of the most important cases under the First Amendment recite this position. The Framers undoubtedly believed it. As a general matter it is true. But the Constitution does not make the dominance of truth a necessary condition of freedom of speech. To say that it does would be to confuse an outcome of free speech with a necessary condition for the application of the amendment.

The definition of "pornography" is unconstitutional. Much speech is dangerous. Chemists whose work might help someone build a bomb, political theorists whose papers might start political movements that lead to riots, speakers whose ideas attract violent protesters, all these and more leave loss in their wake.

No amount of struggle with particular words and phrases in this ordinance can leave anything in effect. The district court came to the same conclusion. Its judgment is therefore AFFIRMED

## DISCUSSION QUESTIONS

(1) If evidence could be produced that pornography directly caused violence against women, would that be sufficient to meet the objections of the Court here to this ordinance?

(2) Should the stirring defense of free speech here also support protecting "obscenity" under the First Amendment?

# CHAPTER 6. RELIGIOUS FREEDOM

## EMPLOYMENT DIV., DEPT. OF HUMAN RESOURCES OF OREGON v. SMITH
494 U.S. 872 (U.S. Supreme Court, 1990)

This case requires us to decide whether the Free Exercise Clause of the First Amendment permits the State of Oregon to include religiously inspired peyote use within the reach of its general criminal prohibition on use of that drug, and thus permits the State to deny unemployment benefits to persons dismissed from their jobs because of such religiously inspired use.

Alfred Smith and Galen Black were fired from their jobs with a private drug rehabilitation organization because they ingested peyote for sacramental purposes at a ceremony of the Native American Church, of which both are members. When respondents applied to Employment Division for unemployment compensation, they were determined to be ineligible for benefits because they had been discharged for work-related "misconduct."

[T]he Oregon Supreme Court has confirmed that Oregon does prohibit the religious use of peyote, [and] we proceed to consider whether that prohibition is permissible under the Free Exercise Clause.

The Free Exercise Clause of the First Amendment, which has been made applicable to the States by incorporation into the Fourteenth Amendment, provides that "Congress shall make no law respecting an establishment of religion, or prohibiting the free exercise thereof . . . ." The free exercise of religion means, first and foremost, the right to believe and profess whatever religious doctrine one desires.

But the "exercise of religion" often involves not only belief and profession but the performance of (or abstention from) physical acts: assembling with others for a worship service, participating in sacramental use of bread and wine, proselytizing, abstaining from certain foods or certain modes of transportation. It would be true, we think, that a State would be "prohibiting the free exercise [of religion]" if it sought to ban such acts or abstentions only when they are engaged in for religious reasons, or only because of the religious belief that they display.

Respondents in the present case, however, seek to carry the meaning of "prohibiting the free exercise [of religion]" one large step further. They contend that their religious motivation for using peyote places them beyond the reach of a criminal law that is not specifically directed at their religious practice, and that is concededly constitutional as applied to those who use the drug for other reasons.

We have never held that an individual's religious beliefs excuse him from compliance with an otherwise valid law prohibiting conduct that the State is free to regulate.

It is not surprising that a number of States have made an exception to their drug laws for sacramental peyote use. But to say that a nondiscriminatory religious-practice exemption is permitted, or even that it is desirable, is not to say that it is constitutionally required.

Because respondents' ingestion of peyote was prohibited under Oregon law, and because that prohibition is constitutional, Oregon may, consistent with the Free Exercise Clause, deny respondents unemployment compensation when their dismissal results from use of the drug.

DISSENT: In weighing the clear interest of respondents in the free exercise of their religion against Oregon's asserted interest in enforcing its drug laws, it is important to articulate in precise terms the state interest involved. It is not the State's broad interest in fighting the critical "war on drugs" that must be weighed against respondents' claim, but the State's narrow interest in refusing to make an exception for the religious, ceremonial use of peyote.

The State's interest in enforcing its prohibition, in order to be sufficiently compelling to outweigh a free exercise claim, cannot be merely abstract or symbolic. In this case, the State actually has not evinced any concrete interest in enforcing its drug laws against religious users of peyote. Oregon has never sought to prosecute respondents, and does not claim that it has made significant enforcement efforts against other religious users of peyote. The State's asserted interest thus amounts only to the symbolic preservation of an unenforced prohibition.

The State proclaims an interest in protecting the health and safety of its citizens from the dangers of unlawful drugs. It offers, however, no evidence that the religious use of peyote has ever harmed anyone.

The carefully circumscribed ritual context in which respondents used peyote is far removed from the irresponsible and unrestricted recreational use of unlawful drugs. The Native American Church's internal restrictions on, and supervision of, its members' use of peyote substantially obviate the State's health and safety concerns. There is considerable evidence that the spiritual and social support provided by the church has been effective in combating the tragic effects of alcoholism on the Native American population.

The State also seeks to support its refusal to make an exception for religious use of peyote by invoking its interest in abolishing drug trafficking. There is, however, practically no illegal traffic in peyote. Peyote simply is not a popular drug; its distribution for use in religious rituals has nothing to do with the vast and violent traffic in illegal narcotics that plagues this country.

Finally, the State argues that granting an exception for religious peyote use would erode its interest in the uniform, fair, and certain enforcement of its drug laws. The State fears that, if it grants an exemption for religious peyote use, a flood of other claims to religious exemptions will follow. It would then be placed in a dilemma, it says, between allowing a patchwork of exemptions that would hinder its law enforcement efforts, and risking a violation of the Establishment Clause by arbitrarily limiting its religious exemptions. This argument, however, could be made in almost any free exercise case.

The State's apprehension of a flood of other religious claims is purely speculative. Almost half the States, and the Federal Government, have maintained an exemption for religious peyote use for many years, and apparently have not found themselves overwhelmed by claims to other religious exemptions.

Respondents believe, and their sincerity has never been at issue, that the peyote plant embodies their deity, and eating it is an act of worship and communion. Without peyote, they could not enact the essential ritual of their religion. If Oregon can constitutionally prosecute them for this act of worship, they, may be "forced to migrate to some other and more tolerant region." This potentially devastating impact must be viewed in light of the federal policy -- reached in reaction to many years of religious persecution and intolerance -- of protecting the religious freedom of Native Americans.

The American Indian Religious Freedom Act, in itself, may not create rights enforceable against government action restricting religious freedom, but this Court must scrupulously apply its free exercise analysis to the religious claims of Native Americans, however unorthodox they may be. Otherwise, both the First Amendment and the stated policy of Congress will offer to Native Americans merely an unfulfilled and hollow promise.

For these reasons, I conclude that Oregon's interest in enforcing its drug laws against religious use of peyote is not sufficiently compelling to outweigh respondents' right to the free exercise of their religion. Since the State could not constitutionally enforce its criminal prohibition against respondents, the interests underlying the State's drug laws cannot justify its denial of unemployment benefits. The State of Oregon cannot, consistently with the Free Exercise Clause, deny respondents unemployment benefits.

## DISCUSSION QUESTIONS

(1) How is this case different from the support for free exercise of the Santaria religion in *Church of the Lukumi Babalu Aye v. City of Hialeah*?

(2) Is this decision consistent with the deference shown to the Amish religion in *Wisconsin v. Yoder*?

(3) Should government defer to the practices of various religious groups only when those practices are otherwise legal?

## WALLACE v. JAFFREE
### 472 U.S. 38 (U.S. Supreme Court, 1985)

[T]he question for decision is whether [Alabama statute] 16-1-20.1, which authorizes a period of silence for "meditation or voluntary prayer," is a law respecting the establishment of religion within the meaning of the First Amendment.

Before analyzing the precise issue that is presented to us, it is appropriate to recall how firmly embedded in our constitutional jurisprudence is the proposition that the several States have no greater power to restrain the individual freedoms protected by the First Amendment than does the Congress of the United States.

Just as the right to speak and the right to refrain from speaking are complementary components of a broader concept of individual freedom of mind, so also the individual's freedom to choose his own creed is the counterpart of his right to refrain from accepting the creed established by the majority. At one time it was thought that this right merely proscribed the preference of one Christian sect over another, but would not require equal respect for the conscience of the infidel, the atheist, or the adherent of a non-Christian faith such as Islam or Judaism. [T]he Court has unambiguously concluded that the individual freedom of conscience protected by the First Amendment embraces the right to select any religious faith or none at all. This conclusion derives support not only from the interest in respecting the individual's freedom of conscience, but also from the conviction that religious beliefs worthy of respect are the product of free and voluntary choice by the faithful, and from recognition of the fact that the political interest in forestalling intolerance extends beyond intolerance among Christian sects -- or even intolerance among "religions" -- to encompass intolerance of the disbeliever and the uncertain. The State of Alabama, no less than the Congress of the United States, must respect that basic truth.

The sponsor of 16-1-20.1, Senator Donald Holmes, inserted into the legislative record -- apparently without dissent -- a statement indicating that the legislation was an "effort to return voluntary prayer" to the public schools. In response to the question whether he had any purpose for the legislation other than returning voluntary prayer to public schools, he stated: "No, I did not have no other purpose in mind." The State did not present evidence of any secular purpose.

[W]henever the State itself speaks on a religious subject, one of the questions that we must ask is "whether the government intends to convey a message of endorsement or disapproval of religion." The well-supported findings -- that 16-1-20.1 was intended to convey a message of state approval of prayer activities in the public schools -- make it unnecessary to evaluate the practical significance of the addition of the words "or voluntary prayer" to the statute. Keeping in mind "both the fundamental place held by the Establishment Clause in our constitutional scheme and the myriad, subtle ways in which Establishment Clause values can be eroded," we conclude that 16-1-20.1 violates the First Amendment.

DISSENT [BURGER]: To suggest that a moment-of-silence statute that includes the word "prayer" unconstitutionally endorses religion, while one that simply provides for a moment of silence does not, manifests not neutrality but hostility toward religion. For decades our opinions have stated that hostility toward any religion or toward all religions is as much forbidden by the Constitution as is an official establishment of religion. The Alabama Legislature has no more "endorsed" religion than a state or the Congress does when it provides for legislative chaplains, or than this Court does when it opens each session with an invocation to God.

The notion that the Alabama statute is a step toward creating an established church borders on, if it does not trespass into, the ridiculous. The statute does not remotely threaten religious liberty; it affirmatively furthers the values of religious freedom and tolerance that the Establishment Clause was designed to protect. Without pressuring those who do not wish to pray, the statute simply creates an opportunity to think, to plan, or to pray if one wishes -- as Congress does by providing chaplains and chapels. It accommodates the purely private, voluntary religious choices of the individual pupils who wish to pray while at the same time creating a time for nonreligious reflection for those who do not choose to pray. The statute also provides a meaningful opportunity for schoolchildren to appreciate the absolute constitutional right of each individual to worship and believe as the individual wishes. The statute "endorses" only the view that the religious observances of others should be tolerated and, where possible, accommodated. If the government may not accommodate religious needs when it does so in a wholly neutral and noncoercive manner, the "benevolent neutrality" that we have long considered the correct constitutional standard will quickly translate into the "callous indifference" that the Court has consistently held the Establishment Clause does not require.

DISSENT [REHNQUIST]: The Establishment Clause did not require government neutrality between religion and irreligion nor did it prohibit the Federal Government from providing nondiscriminatory aid to religion. There is simply no historical foundation for the proposition that the Framers intended to build the "wall of separation."

The Framers intended the Establishment Clause to prohibit the designation of any church as a "national" one. The Clause was also designed to stop the Federal Government from asserting a preference for one religious denomination or sect over others. [N]othing in the Establishment Clause requires government to be strictly neutral between religion and irreligion, nor does that Clause prohibit Congress or the States from pursuing legitimate secular ends through nondiscriminatory sectarian means.

It would come as much of a shock to those who drafted the Bill of Rights as it will to a large number of thoughtful Americans today to learn that the Constitution, as construed by the majority, prohibits the Alabama Legislature from "endorsing" prayer.

## DISCUSSION QUESTIONS

(1) Should the constitutionality of a statute depend mainly on the statements of state legislators concerning their intent?

(2) Is school prayer more appropriately seen as the "free exercise of religion" or as "establishment of a state religion"?

## EDWARDS v. AGUILLARD
### 482 U.S. 578 (U.S. Supreme Court, 1987)

The question for decision is whether Louisiana's "Balanced Treatment for Creation-Science and Evolution-Science in Public School Instruction" Act (Creationism Act) is facially invalid as violative of the Establishment Clause of the First Amendment.

The Creationism Act forbids the teaching of the theory of evolution in public schools unless accompanied by instruction in "creation science." No school is required to teach evolution or creation science. If either is taught, however, the other must also be taught. The theories of evolution and creation science are statutorily defined as "the scientific evidences for [creation or evolution] and inferences from those scientific evidences."

The Establishment Clause forbids the enactment of any law "respecting an establishment of religion." The Court has applied a three-pronged test to determine whether legislation comports with the Establishment Clause.

First, the legislature must have adopted the law with a secular purpose. Second, the statute's principal or primary effect must be one that neither advances nor inhibits religion. Third, the statute must not result in an excessive entanglement of government with religion. State action violates the Establishment Clause if it fails to satisfy any of these prongs.

The Court has been particularly vigilant in monitoring compliance with the Establishment Clause in elementary and secondary schools. Families entrust public schools with the education of their children, but condition their trust on the understanding that the classroom will not purposely be used to advance religious views that may conflict with the private beliefs of the student and his or her family. Students in such institutions are impressionable and their attendance is involuntary.

In this case, appellants have identified no clear secular purpose for the Louisiana Act. True, the Act's stated purpose is to protect academic freedom. [H]owever, the Act was not designed to further that goal. The Act does not grant teachers a flexibility that they did not already possess to supplant the present science curriculum with the presentation of theories, besides evolution, about the origin of life.

If the Louisiana Legislature's purpose was solely to maximize the comprehensiveness and effectiveness of science instruction, it would have encouraged the teaching of all scientific theories about the origins of humankind. But under the Act's requirements, teachers who were once free to teach any and all facets of this subject are now unable to do so. Moreover, the Act fails even to ensure that creation science will be taught, but instead requires the teaching of this theory only when the theory of evolution is taught. Thus the Act does not serve to protect academic freedom, but has the distinctly different purpose of discrediting "evolution by counterbalancing its teaching at every turn with the teaching of creationism."

[W]e need not be blind in this case to the legislature's preeminent religious purpose in enacting this statute. There is a historic and contemporaneous link between the teachings of certain religious denominations and the teaching of evolution. The preeminent purpose of the Louisiana Legislature was clearly to advance the religious viewpoint that a supernatural being created humankind. The term "creation science" was defined as embracing this particular religious doctrine by those responsible for the passage of the Creationism Act. The legislative history reveals that the term "creation science" embodies the religious belief that a supernatural creator was responsible for the creation of humankind.

Furthermore, it is not happenstance that the legislature required the teaching of a theory that coincided with this religious view. The legislative history documents that the Act's primary purpose was to change the science curriculum of public schools in order to provide persuasive advantage to a particular religious doctrine that rejects the factual basis of evolution in its entirety. The sponsor of the Creationism Act explained during the legislative hearings that his disdain for the theory of evolution resulted from the support that evolution supplied to views contrary to his own religious beliefs. The legislation therefore sought to alter the science curriculum to reflect endorsement of a religious view that is antagonistic to the theory of evolution. Because the primary purpose of the Creationism Act is to advance a particular religious belief, the Act endorses religion in violation of the First Amendment.

The Louisiana Creationism Act advances a religious doctrine by requiring either the banishment of the theory of evolution from public school classrooms or the presentation of a religious viewpoint that rejects evolution in its entirety. The Act violates the Establishment Clause of the First Amendment because it seeks to employ the symbolic and financial support of government to achieve a religious purpose.

DISSENT: [T]he fact that creation science coincides with the beliefs of certain religions, a fact upon which the majority relies heavily, does not itself justify invalidation of the Act.

The censorship of creation science has at least two harmful effects. First, it deprives students of knowledge of one of the two scientific explanations for the origin of life and leads them to believe that evolution is proven fact; thus, their education suffers and they are wrongly taught that science has proved their religious beliefs false. Second, it violates the Establishment Clause. The United States Supreme Court has held that secular humanism is a religion. Belief in evolution is a central tenet of that religion. Thus, by censoring creation science and instructing students that evolution is fact, public school teachers are now advancing religion in violation of the Establishment Clause.

The people of Louisiana, including those who are Christian fundamentalists, are quite entitled, as a secular matter, to have whatever scientific evidence there may be against evolution presented in their schools. Perhaps what the Louisiana Legislature has done is unconstitutional because there is no such evidence, and the scheme they have established will amount to no more than a presentation of the Book of Genesis. But we cannot say that on the evidence before us, which includes ample uncontradicted testimony that "creation science" is a body of scientific knowledge rather than revealed belief. Infinitely less can we say that the scientific evidence for evolution is so conclusive that no one could be gullible enough to believe that there is any real scientific evidence to the contrary, so that the legislation's stated purpose must be a lie. Yet that illiberal judgment is ultimately the basis on which the Court's facile rejection of the Louisiana Legislature's purpose must rest.

## DISCUSSION QUESTIONS

(1) Are there any circumstances under which creationism should be taught in the public schools? Could this be done, consistently with the First Amendment ?

(2) Is this decision consistent with the decision in *Wallace v. Jaffree* on school prayer?

# ELK GROVE v. NEWDOW
## No. 02-1624 (U.S. Supreme Court, 2004)

Each day elementary school teachers in the Elk Grove Unified School District lead their classes in recitation of the Pledge of Allegiance. Michael A. Newdow is an atheist whose daughter participates in that daily exercise. Because the Pledge contains the words "under God," he views the School District's policy as a religious indoctrination of his child that violates the First Amendment. [W]e granted *certiorari* to review the First Amendment issue and, preliminarily, whether Newdow has standing to invoke the jurisdiction of the federal courts. We conclude that Newdow lacks standing.

[T]he Pledge of Allegiance evolved as a common public acknowledgement of the ideals that our flag symbolizes. Its recitation is a patriotic exercise designed to foster national unity and pride in those principles.

Under California law, "every public elementary school" must begin each day with "appropriate patriotic exercises." The Elk Grove Unified School District has implemented the state law by requiring that "[e]ach elementary school class recite the pledge of allegiance to the flag once each day." [T]he School District permits students who object on religious grounds to abstain from the recitation.

Newdow is an atheist who was ordained more than 20 years ago in a ministry that "espouses the religious philosophy that the true and eternal bonds of righteousness and virtue stem from reason rather than mythology." The complaint seeks a declaration that the words "under God" violated the Establishment and Free Exercise Clauses of the United States Constitution.

Sandra Banning, the mother of Newdow's daughter, declared that although she and Newdow shared "physical custody" of their daughter, a state-court order granted her "exclusive legal custody" of the child, "including the sole right to represent [the daughter's] legal interests and make all decision[s] about her education" and welfare.

In our view, it is improper for the federal courts to entertain a claim by a plaintiff whose standing to sue is founded on family law rights that are in dispute when prosecution of the lawsuit may have an adverse effect on the person who is the source of the plaintiff's claimed standing.

CONCUR [REHNQUIST]: The Court erects a novel principle in order to avoid reaching the merits of the constitutional claim. I dissent from that ruling. On the merits, I conclude that the policy that requires teachers to lead willing students in reciting the Pledge of Allegiance, which includes the words "under God," does not violate the Establishment Clause.

Congress amended the Pledge to include the phrase "under God" in 1954. The amendment's purpose was to contrast this country's belief in God with the Soviet Union's embrace of atheism. To the millions of people who regularly recite the Pledge, "under God" might mean several different things: that God has guided the destiny of the United States or that the United States exists under God's authority.

I do not believe that "under God" in the Pledge converts its recital into a "religious exercise." [I]t is a declaration of belief in allegiance and loyalty to the United States flag and the Republic that it represents. The phrase "under God" is in no sense a prayer, nor an endorsement of any religion.

The Constitution only requires that schoolchildren be entitled to abstain from the ceremony if they chose to do so. To give the parent of such a child a sort of "heckler's veto" over a patriotic ceremony willingly participated in by other students, simply because the Pledge of Allegiance contains the descriptive phrase "under God," is an unwarranted extension of the Establishment Clause, an extension which would have the unfortunate effect of prohibiting a commendable patriotic observance.

CONCUR [O'CONNOR]: I conclude that the respondent does have standing to bring his claim before a federal court. I believe that school district's policy of having its teachers lead students in voluntary recitations of the Pledge of Allegiance does not offend the Establishment Clause.

The Court has permitted government, in some instances, to refer to or commemorate religion in public life. I believe that although these references speak in the language of religious belief, they are more properly understood as employing the idiom for essentially secular purposes. One such purpose is to commemorate the role of religion in our history. In my view, some references to religion in public life and government are the inevitable consequence of our Nation's origins. It is unsurprising that a Nation founded by religious refugees and dedicated to religious freedom should find references to divinity in its symbols, songs, mottoes, and oaths. Eradicating such references would sever ties to a history that sustains this Nation even today.

For centuries, we have marked important occasions or pronouncements with references to God and invocations of divine assistance. Such references can serve to solemnize an occasion instead of to invoke divine provenance. The reasonable observer, fully aware of our national history and the origins of such practices, would not perceive these acknowledgments as signifying a government endorsement of any specific religion, or even of religion over non-religion.

Given the values that the Establishment Clause was meant to serve, I believe that government can acknowledge or refer to the divine without offending the Constitution. This category of "ceremonial deism" most clearly encompasses such things as the national motto ("In God We Trust"), religious references in traditional patriotic songs such as the Star-Spangled Banner, and the words with which the Marshal of this Court opens each of its sessions ("God save the United States and this honorable Court"). These references are not minor trespasses upon the Establishment Clause to which I turn a blind eye. Instead, their history, character, and context prevent them from being constitutional violations at all.

This case requires us to determine whether the appearance of the phrase "under God" in the Pledge of Allegiance constitutes an instance of such ceremonial deism. I conclude that it does.

The constitutional value of ceremonial deism turns on a shared understanding of its legitimate nonreligious purposes. That sort of understanding can exist only when a given practice has been in place for a significant portion of the Nation's history, and when it is observed by enough persons that it can fairly be called ubiquitous. By contrast, novel or uncommon references to religion can more easily be perceived as government endorsements because the reasonable observer cannot be presumed to be fully familiar with their origins. As a result, in examining whether a given practice constitutes an instance of ceremonial deism, its "history and ubiquity" will be of great importance.

Fifty years have passed since the words "under God" were added, a span of time that is not inconsiderable given the relative youth of our Nation. In that time, the Pledge has become, alongside the singing of the Star-Spangled Banner, our most routine ceremonial act of patriotism; countless schoolchildren recite it daily, and their religious heterogeneity reflects that of the Nation as a whole. As a result, the Pledge and the context in which it is employed are familiar and nearly inseparable in the public mind.

It is true that some of the legislators who voted to add the phrase "under God" to the Pledge may have done so in an attempt to attach to it an overtly religious message. But their intentions cannot decide our inquiry. First, those legislators also had permissible secular objectives--they meant, for example, to acknowledge the religious origins of our Nation's belief in the "individuality and the dignity of the human being." Second--and more critically--the subsequent social and cultural history of the Pledge shows that its original secular character was not transformed by its amendment.

[N]o religious acknowledgment could claim to be an instance of ceremonial deism if it explicitly favored one particular religious belief system over another. The Pledge does not refer to a nation "under Jesus" or "under Vishnu," but instead acknowledges religion in a general way: a simple reference to a generic "God." Of course, some religions--Buddhism, for instance--are not based upon a belief in a separate Supreme Being. But one would be hard pressed to imagine a brief solemnizing reference to religion that would adequately encompass every religious belief expressed by any citizen of this Nation. The phrase "under God," conceived and added at a time when our national religious diversity was neither as robust nor as well recognized as it is now, represents a tolerable attempt to acknowledge religion and to invoke its solemnizing power without favoring any individual religious sect or belief system.

A final factor that makes the Pledge an instance of ceremonial deism is its highly circumscribed reference to God. Any coercion that persuades an onlooker to participate in an act of ceremonial deism is inconsequential, as an Establishment Clause matter, because such acts are simply not religious in character. As a result, symbolic references to religion that qualify as instances of ceremonial deism will pass the coercion test as well as the endorsement test.

## DISCUSSION QUESTIONS

(1) A new lawsuit has been filed by several parents in California, who clearly have standing, raising the same substantive challenge to the Pledge of Allegiance that was raised by Newdow. Based on the concurring opinions here, what is the likely outcome of that suit on the merits?

(2) Does the pledge offend the religious views of Buddhists? Of atheists? Of other religions represented in this country?

(3) Is the long history of ceremonial references to "God" in this nation's history sufficient to justify continuation of this language in the Pledge?

110

# CHAPTER 7. RACIAL DISCRIMINATION
## AND AFFIRMATIVE ACTION

## KOREMATSU v. UNITED STATES
323 U.S. 214 (U.S. Supreme Court, 1944)

The petitioner, an American citizen of Japanese descent, was convicted in a federal district court for remaining in San Leandro, California, a "Military Area," contrary to Civilian Exclusion Order No. 34 of the U.S. Army, which directed that after May 9, 1942, all persons of Japanese ancestry should be excluded from that area. No question was raised as to petitioner's loyalty to the United States. Exclusion Order No. 34, issued after we were at war with Japan, declared that "the successful prosecution of the war requires every possible protection against espionage and against sabotage to national-defense material, national-defense premises, and national-defense utilities."

[E]xclusion of those of Japanese origin was deemed necessary because of the presence of an unascertained number of disloyal members of the group, most of whom we have no doubt were loyal to this country. The judgment that exclusion of the whole group was a military imperative answers the contention that the exclusion was in the nature of group punishment based on antagonism to those of Japanese origin. That there were members of the group who retained loyalties to Japan has been confirmed by investigations made subsequent to the exclusion. Approximately five thousand American citizens of Japanese ancestry refused to swear unqualified allegiance to the United States and to renounce allegiance to the Japanese Emperor, and several thousand evacuees requested repatriation to Japan.

We uphold the exclusion order as of the time it was made and when the petitioner violated it. In doing so, we are not unmindful of the hardships imposed upon a large group of American citizens. But hardships are part of war, and war is an aggregation of hardships. All citizens alike, both in and out of uniform, feel the impact of war in greater or lesser measure. Citizenship has its responsibilities as well as its privileges, and in time of war the burden is always heavier. Compulsory exclusion of large groups of citizens from their homes, except under circumstances of direst emergency and peril, is inconsistent with our basic governmental institutions. But when under conditions of modern warfare our shores are threatened by hostile forces, the power to protect must be commensurate with the threatened danger.

It is said that we are dealing here with the case of imprisonment of a citizen in a concentration camp solely because of his ancestry, without evidence or inquiry concerning his loyalty and good disposition towards the United States. Regardless of the true nature of the assembly and relocation centers -- and we deem it unjustifiable to call them concentration camps with all the ugly connotations that term implies -- we are dealing specifically with nothing but an exclusion order. To cast this case into outlines of racial prejudice, without reference to the real military dangers which were presented, merely confuses the issue. Korematsu was not excluded from the Military Area because of hostility to him or his race. He was excluded because we are at war with the Japanese Empire, because the properly constituted military authorities feared an invasion of our West Coast and felt constrained to take proper security measures, because they decided that the military urgency of the situation demanded that all citizens of Japanese ancestry be segregated from the West Coast temporarily, and finally, because Congress, reposing its confidence in this time of war in our military leaders -- as inevitably it must -- determined that they should have the power to do just this. We cannot -- by availing ourselves of the calm perspective of hindsight -- now say that at that time these actions were unjustified.

DISSENT [MURPHY]: This exclusion goes over "the very brink of constitutional power" and falls into the ugly abyss of racism. Justification for the exclusion is sought mainly upon questionable racial and sociological grounds not ordinarily within the realm of expert military judgment, supplemented by certain semi-military conclusions drawn from an unwarranted use of circumstantial evidence. Individuals of Japanese ancestry are condemned because they are said to be "a large, unassimilated, tightly knit racial group, bound to an enemy nation by strong ties of race, culture, custom and religion." They are claimed to be given to "emperor worshipping ceremonies" and to "dual citizenship." Japanese language schools and allegedly pro-Japanese organizations are cited as evidence of possible group disloyalty.

No one denies that there were some disloyal persons of Japanese descent on the Pacific Coast who did all in their power to aid their ancestral land. Similar disloyal activities have been engaged in by many persons of German, Italian and even more pioneer stock in our country. But to infer that examples of individual disloyalty prove group disloyalty and justify discriminatory action against the entire group is to deny that under our system of law individual guilt is the sole basis for deprivation of rights.

DISSENT [JACKSON]: [I]f any fundamental assumption underlies our system, it is that guilt is personal and not inheritable. Even if all of one's antecedents had been convicted of treason, the Constitution forbids its penalties to be visited upon him. [H]ere is an attempt to make an otherwise innocent act a crime merely because this prisoner is the son of parents as to whom he had no choice, and belongs to a race from which there is no way to resign.

## DISCUSSION QUESTIONS

(1) In 1988, the U.S. Congress authorized an apology and reparations of $20,000 each to Japanese-Americans who had been interned during World War II. Was this adequate compensation? Why did it take over four decades for Congress to admit this serious violation of Civil Rights?

(2) Do any racial groups today suffer from the kind of stereotyping assumed by the Supreme Court in this decision?

## PLESSY v. FERGUSON
163 U.S. 537 (U.S. Supreme Court, 1896)

This case turns upon the constitutionality of an act of the General Assembly of the State of Louisiana, passed in 1890, providing for separate railway carriages for the white and colored races.

Plessy, being a passenger between two stations within the State of Louisiana, was assigned by officers of the company to the coach used for the race to which he belonged, but he insisted upon going into a coach used by the race to which he did not belong.

The object of the [Fourteenth] amendment was undoubtedly to enforce the absolute equality of the two races before the law, but in the nature of things it could not have been intended to abolish distinctions based upon color, or to enforce social, as distinguished from political equality, or a commingling of the two races upon terms unsatisfactory to either. Laws permitting, and even requiring, their separation in places where they are liable to be brought into contact do not necessarily imply the inferiority of either race to the other, and have been generally, if not universally, recognized as within the competency of the state legislatures in the exercise of their police power. The most common instance of this is connected with the establishment of separate schools for white and colored children, which has been held to be a valid exercise of the legislative power even by courts of States where the political rights of the colored race have been longest and most earnestly enforced. Gauged by this standard, we cannot say that a law which authorizes or even requires the separation of the two races in public conveyances is unreasonable, or obnoxious to the Fourteenth Amendment.

The argument assumes that social prejudices may be overcome by legislation, and that equal rights cannot be secured to the negro except by an enforced commingling of the two races. We cannot accept this proposition. If the two races are to meet upon terms of social equality, it must be the result of natural affinities, a mutual appreciation of each other's merits and a voluntary consent of individuals. Legislation is powerless to eradicate racial instincts or to abolish distinctions based upon physical differences, and the attempt to do so can only result in accentuating the difficulties of the present situation. If the civil and political rights of both races be equal one cannot be inferior to the other civilly or politically. If one race be inferior to the other socially, the Constitution cannot put them upon the same plane.

DISSENT: [I]n view of the Constitution, in the eye of the law, there is in this country no superior, dominant, ruling class of citizens. There is no caste here. Our Constitution is color-blind, and neither knows nor tolerates classes among citizens. In respect of civil rights, all citizens are equal before the law. The humblest is the peer of the most powerful. The law regards man as man, and takes no account of his surroundings or of his color when his civil rights as guaranteed by the supreme law of the land are involved. It is, therefore, to be regretted that this high tribunal, the final expositor of the fundamental law of the land, has reached the conclusion that it is competent for a State to regulate the enjoyment by citizens of their civil rights solely upon the basis of race.

In my opinion, the judgment this day rendered will, in time, prove to be pernicious. The recent amendments of the Constitution, it was supposed, had eradicated these principles from our institutions. But it seems that we have yet, in some of the States, a dominant race -- a superior class of citizens, which assumes to regulate the enjoyment of civil rights, common to all citizens, upon the basis of race. The present decision, it may well be apprehended, will not only stimulate aggressions, more or less brutal and irritating, upon the admitted rights of colored citizens, but will encourage the belief that it is possible, by means of state enactments, to defeat the beneficent purposes which the people of the United States had in view when they adopted the recent amendments of the Constitution, by one of which the blacks of this country were made citizens of the United States and of the States in which they respectively reside, and whose privileges and immunities, as citizens, the States are forbidden to abridge. Sixty millions of whites are in no danger from the presence here of eight millions of blacks. The destinies of the two races, in this country, are indissolubly linked together, and the interests of both require that the common government of all shall not permit the seeds of race hate to be planted under the sanction of law. What can more certainly arouse race hate, what more certainly create and perpetuate a feeling of distrust between these races, than state enactments, which, in fact, proceed on the ground that colored citizens are so inferior and degraded that they cannot be allowed to sit in public coaches occupied by white citizens? That is the real meaning of such legislation.

The arbitrary separation of citizens, on the basis of race, while they are on a public highway, is a badge of servitude wholly inconsistent with the civil freedom and the equality before the law established by the Constitution. It cannot be justified upon any legal grounds.

If evils will result from the commingling of the two races upon public highways established for the benefit of all, they will be infinitely less than those that will surely come from state legislation regulating the enjoyment of civil rights upon the basis of race. We boast of the freedom enjoyed by our people above all other peoples. But it is difficult to reconcile that boast with a state of the law which, practically, puts the brand of servitude and degradation upon a large class of our fellow-citizens, our equals before the law. The thin disguise of "equal" accommodations for passengers in railroad coaches will not mislead any one, nor atone for the wrong this day done.

## DISCUSSION QUESTIONS

(1) The doctrine of "separate but equal" upheld in this decision was overturned 58 years later in *Brown vs. Board of Education*. Compare the reasoning in that case with the reasoning in the dissent here in *Plessy*.

(2) What does "equal" mean in a legal context? How do the justices here understand its meaning? How do we understand its meaning today?

## BROWN v. BOARD OF EDUCATION OF TOPEKA
### 347 U.S. 483 (U.S. Supreme Court, 1954)

These cases come to us from the States of Kansas, South Carolina, Virginia, and Delaware. They are premised on different facts and different local conditions, but a common legal question justifies their consideration together.

In each of the cases, minors of the Negro race, through their legal representatives, seek the aid of the courts in obtaining admission to the public schools of their community on a nonsegregated basis. In each instance, they had been denied admission to schools attended by white children under laws requiring or permitting segregation according to race. This segregation was alleged to deprive the plaintiffs of the equal protection of the laws under the Fourteenth Amendment.

The plaintiffs contend that segregated public schools are not "equal" and cannot be made "equal," and that hence they are deprived of the equal protection of the laws. Because of the obvious importance of the question presented, the Court took jurisdiction.

Reargument was largely devoted to the circumstances surrounding the adoption of the Fourteenth Amendment in 1868. It covered exhaustively consideration of the Amendment in Congress, ratification by the states, then existing practices in racial segregation, and the views of proponents and opponents of the Amendment. This discussion and our own investigation convince us that, although these sources cast some light, it is not enough to resolve the problem with which we are faced. At best, they are inconclusive.

In the first cases in this Court construing the Fourteenth Amendment, decided shortly after its adoption, the Court interpreted it as proscribing all state-imposed discriminations against the Negro race. The doctrine of "separate but equal" did not make its appearance in this Court until 1896 in *Plessy v. Ferguson*, involving not education but transportation. American courts have since labored with the doctrine for over half a century.

[T]here are findings that the Negro and white schools involved have been equalized, or are being equalized, with respect to buildings, curricula, qualifications and salaries of teachers, and other "tangible" factors. Our decision, therefore, cannot turn on merely a comparison of these tangible factors in the Negro and white schools involved in each of the cases. We must look instead to the effect of segregation itself on public education.

[W]e cannot turn the clock back to 1868 when the Amendment was adopted, or even to 1896 when *Plessy v. Ferguson* was written. We must consider public education in the light of its full development and its present place in American life throughout the Nation. Only in this way can it be determined if segregation in public schools deprives these plaintiffs of the equal protection of the laws.

Today, education is perhaps the most important function of state and local governments. Compulsory school attendance laws and the great expenditures for education both demonstrate our recognition of the importance of education to our democratic society. It is required in the performance of our most basic public responsibilities, even service in the armed forces. It is the very foundation of good citizenship. Today it is a principal instrument in awakening the child to cultural values, in preparing him for later professional training, and in helping him to adjust normally to his environment. In these days, it is doubtful that any child may reasonably be expected to succeed in life if he is denied the opportunity of an education. Such an opportunity, where the state has undertaken to provide it, is a right which must be made available to all on equal terms.

We come then to the question presented: Does segregation of children in public schools solely on the basis of race, even though the physical facilities and other "tangible" factors may be equal, deprive the children of the minority group of equal educational opportunities? We believe that it does.

To separate [children in grade and high schools] from others of similar age and qualifications solely because of their race generates a feeling of inferiority as to their status in the community that may affect their hearts and minds in a way unlikely ever to be undone. Whatever may have been the extent of psychological knowledge at the time of *Plessy v. Ferguson*, this finding is amply supported by modern authority. Any language in *Plessy v. Ferguson* contrary to this finding is rejected.

We conclude that in the field of public education the doctrine of "separate but equal" has no place. Separate educational facilities are inherently unequal. Therefore, we hold that the plaintiffs and others similarly situated for whom the actions have been brought are, by reason of the segregation complained of, deprived of the equal protection of the laws guaranteed by the Fourteenth Amendment.

## DISCUSSION QUESTIONS

(1) What factors are the source of the inherent inequality in separate facilities of concern to the court? Is it solely economic disparity?

(2) Some of the psychological data relied on by the Court have been challenged by social scientists. Does this effect the reasoning in this decision? How significant is empirical data in supporting the conclusions?

## REGENTS OF THE UNIVERSITY OF CALIFORNIA v. BAKKE
### 438 U.S. 265 (U.S. Supreme Court, 1978)

JUSTICE POWELL: This case presents a challenge to the special admissions program of the Medical School of the University of California at Davis, which is designed to assure the admission of a specified number of students from certain minority groups.

The Medical School of the University of California at Davis opened in 1968. Over the next two years, the faculty devised a special admissions program to increase the representation of "disadvantaged" students in each Medical School class. The special program consisted of a separate admissions system operating in coordination with the regular admissions process.

Allan Bakke is a white male who applied to the Davis Medical School in both 1973 and 1974. In both years Bakke's application was considered under the general admissions program. After the second rejection, Bakke filed [this] suit in the Superior Court of California.

[T]he parties fight over the proper characterization of the special admissions program. Petitioner prefers to view it as establishing a "goal" of minority representation. Respondent labels it a racial quota. This semantic distinction is beside the point: The special admissions program is undeniably a classification based on race and ethnic background. To the extent that there existed a pool of at least minimally qualified minority applicants to fill the 16 special admissions seats, white applicants could compete only for 84 seats in the entering class, rather than the 100 open to minority applicants. Whether this limitation is described as a quota or a goal, it is a line drawn on the basis of race and ethnic status.

The guarantees of the Fourteenth Amendment extend to all persons.

The guarantee of equal protection cannot mean one thing when applied to one individual and something else when applied to a person of another color. If both are not accorded the same protection, then it is not equal. Racial and ethnic distinctions of any sort are inherently suspect and thus call for the most exacting judicial examination.

This perception of racial and ethnic distinctions is rooted in our Nation's constitutional and demographic history. The Court's initial view of the Fourteenth Amendment was that its "one pervading purpose" was "the freedom of the slave race, the security and firm establishment of that freedom, and the protection of the newly-made freeman and citizen from the oppressions of those who had formerly exercised dominion over him."

By [the twentieth century] it was no longer possible to peg the guarantees of the Fourteenth Amendment to the struggle for equality of one racial minority. [T]he United States had become a Nation of minorities. As the Nation filled with the stock of many lands, the reach of the Clause was gradually extended to all ethnic groups seeking protection from official discrimination.

Although many of the Framers of the Fourteenth Amendment conceived of its primary function as bridging the vast distance between members of the Negro race and the white "majority," the Amendment itself was framed in universal terms, without reference to color, ethnic origin, or condition of prior servitude.

Petitioner urges us to adopt for the first time a more restrictive view of the Equal Protection Clause and hold that discrimination against members of the white "majority" cannot be suspect if its purpose can be characterized as "benign." The clock of our liberties, however, cannot be turned back to 1868. It is far too late to argue that the guarantee of equal protection to all persons permits the recognition of special wards entitled to a degree of protection greater than that accorded others.

[T]he white "majority" itself is composed of various minority groups, most of which can lay claim to a history of prior discrimination at the hands of the State and private individuals. Not all of these groups can receive preferential treatment and corresponding judicial tolerance of distinctions drawn in terms of race and nationality, for then the only "majority" left would be a new minority of white Anglo-Saxon Protestants.

[T]here has been no determination by the legislature or [an] administrative agency that the University engaged in a discriminatory practice requiring remedial efforts. Moreover, the operation of petitioner's special admissions program prefers the designated minority groups at the expense of other individuals who are totally foreclosed from competition for the 16 special admissions seats in every Medical School class. Because of that foreclosure, some individuals are excluded from enjoyment of a state- provided benefit — admission to the Medical School — they otherwise would receive.

The special admissions program purports to serve the purposes of: (i) "reducing the historic deficit of traditionally disfavored minorities in medical schools and in the medical profession," (ii) countering the effects of societal discrimination; (iii) increasing the number of physicians who will practice in communities currently underserved; and (iv) obtaining the educational benefits that flow from an ethnically diverse student body.

Petitioner identifies, as [a] purpose of its program, improving the delivery of health-care services to communities currently underserved. It may be assumed that in some situations a State's interest in facilitating the health care of its citizens is sufficiently compelling to support the use of a suspect classification. But there is virtually no evidence in the record indicating that petitioner's special admissions program is either needed or geared to promote that goal. Petitioner simply has not carried its burden of demonstrating that it must prefer members of particular ethnic groups over all other individuals in order to promote better health-care delivery to deprived citizens.

The fourth goal asserted by petitioner is the attainment of a diverse student body. This clearly is a constitutionally permissible goal for an institution of higher education. Academic freedom, though not a specifically enumerated constitutional right, long has been viewed as a special concern of the First Amendment.

The diversity that furthers a compelling state interest encompasses a far broader array of qualifications and characteristics of which racial or ethnic origin is but a single though important element. Petitioner's special admissions program, focused solely on ethnic diversity, would hinder rather than further attainment of genuine diversity.

The experience of other university admissions programs, which take race into account in achieving the educational diversity, demonstrates that the assignment of a fixed number of places to a minority group is not a necessary means toward that end. [R]ace or ethnic background may be deemed a "plus" in a particular applicant's file, yet it does not insulate the individual from comparison with all other candidates for the available seats. The file of a particular black applicant may be examined for his potential contribution to diversity without the factor of race being decisive when compared, for example, with that of an applicant identified as an Italian-American if the latter is thought to exhibit qualities more likely to promote beneficial educational pluralism. Such qualities could include exceptional personal talents, unique work or service experience, leadership potential, maturity, demonstrated compassion, a history of overcoming disadvantage, ability to communicate with the poor, or other qualifications deemed important. [A]n admissions program operated in this way is flexible enough to consider all pertinent elements of diversity in light of the particular qualifications of each applicant, and to place them on the same footing for consideration, although not necessarily according them the same weight.

The fatal flaw in petitioner's preferential program is its disregard of individual rights as guaranteed by the Fourteenth Amendment. Such rights are not absolute. But when a State's distribution of benefits or imposition of burdens hinges on ancestry or the color of a person's skin, that individual is entitled to a demonstration that the challenged classification is necessary to promote a substantial state interest. For this reason, that portion of the California court's judgment holding petitioner's special admissions program invalid under the Fourteenth Amendment must be affirmed.

[T]he State has a substantial interest that legitimately may be served by a properly devised admissions program involving the competitive consideration of race and ethnic origin. For this reason, so much of the California court's judgment as enjoins petitioner from any consideration of the race of any applicant must be reversed.

With respect to respondent's entitlement to an injunction directing his admission to the Medical School, petitioner has conceded that it could not carry its burden of proving that, but for the existence of its unlawful special admissions program, respondent still would not have been admitted. Hence, respondent is entitled to the injunction.

JUSTICE MARSHALL: I agree with the judgment of the Court only insofar as it permits a university to consider the race of an applicant in making admissions decisions. I do not agree that petitioner's admissions program violates the Constitution. [D]uring most of the past 200 years, the Constitution as interpreted by this Court did not prohibit the most ingenious and pervasive forms of discrimination against the Negro. Now, when a State acts to remedy the effects of that legacy of discrimination, I cannot believe that this same Constitution stands as a barrier.

Three hundred and fifty years ago, the Negro was dragged to this country in chains to be sold into slavery. Uprooted from his homeland and thrust into bondage for forced labor, the slave was deprived of all legal rights. It was unlawful to teach him to read; he could be sold away from his family and friends at the whim of his master; and killing or maiming him was not a crime.

The denial of human rights was etched into the American Colonies' first attempts at establishing self-government. When the colonists determined to seek their independence from England, they drafted a unique document proclaiming as "self-evident" that "all men are created equal" and are endowed "with certain unalienable Rights," including those to "Life, Liberty and the pursuit of Happiness." The self-evident truths and the unalienable rights were intended, however, to apply only to white men.

The implicit protection of slavery embodied in the Declaration of Independence was made explicit in the Constitution. In their declaration of the principles that were to provide the cornerstone of the new Nation, the Framers made it plain that "we the people" did not include those whose skins were the wrong color.

The status of the Negro as property was officially erased by his emancipation at the end of the Civil War. But the long-awaited emancipation, while freeing the Negro from slavery, did not bring him citizenship or equality in any meaningful way. Despite the passage of the Thirteenth, Fourteenth, and Fifteenth Amendments, the Negro was systematically denied the rights those Amendments were supposed to secure. The combined actions and inactions of the State and Federal Governments maintained Negroes in a position of legal inferiority for another century after the Civil War.

The enforced segregation of the races continued into the middle of the 20th century. [I]t was not until 1948 that an end to segregation in the military was ordered by President Truman. And the history of the exclusion of Negro children from white public schools is too well known and recent to require repeating here. That Negroes were deliberately excluded from public graduate and professional schools is also well established.

The position of the Negro today in America is the tragic but inevitable consequence of centuries of unequal treatment. In light of the sorry history of discrimination and its devastating impact on the lives of Negroes, bringing the Negro into the mainstream of American life should be a state interest of the highest order. To fail to do so is to ensure that America will forever remain a divided society.

I do not believe that the Fourteenth Amendment requires us to accept that fate. Neither its history nor our past cases lend any support to the conclusion that a university may not remedy the cumulative effects of society's discrimination by giving consideration to race in an effort to increase the number and percentage of Negro doctors.

While I applaud the judgment of the Court that a university may consider race in its admissions process, it is more than a little ironic that, after several hundred years of class-based discrimination against Negroes, the Court is unwilling to hold that a class-based remedy for that discrimination is permissible. [T]oday's judgment ignores the fact that for several hundred years Negroes have been discriminated against, not as individuals, but rather solely because of the color of their skins. It is unnecessary in 20th-century America to have individual Negroes demonstrate that they have been victims of racial discrimination; the racism of our society has been so pervasive that none, regardless of wealth or position, has managed to escape its impact. The experience of Negroes in America has been different in kind, not just in degree, from that of other ethnic groups. It is not merely the history of slavery alone but also that a whole people were marked as inferior by the law. The dream of America as the great melting pot has not been realized for the Negro; because of his skin color he never made it into the pot.

It is because of a legacy of unequal treatment that we now must permit the institutions of this society to give consideration to race in making decisions about who will hold the positions of influence, affluence, and prestige in America. For far too long, the doors to those positions have been shut to Negroes. If we are ever to become a fully integrated society, one in which the color of a person's skin will not determine the opportunities available to him or her, we must be willing to take steps to open those doors. I do not believe that anyone can truly look into America's past and still find that a remedy for the effects of that past is impermissible.

## DISCUSSION QUESTIONS

(1) Does the history of race-based discrimination against Negroes support race-based remedies, as argued by Justice Marshall (the first African-American justice on the Supreme Court and the NAACP attorney who represented the school children in *Brown vs. Board of Education)*?

(2) African-Americans, American Indians, Asians, and Mexican-Americans were all eligible for the special program. Does the argument from the history of slavery and the discredited policy of "separate but equal" justify the inclusion of all these racial minorities in the Davis program? What additional arguments support their inclusion?"

(3) Should affirmative action programs be assessed solely in terms of "equal rights"? Are consequences also relevant?

# GRUTTER v. BOLLINGER
## 539 U.S. 306 (U.S. Supreme Court, 2003)

This case requires us to decide whether the use of race as a factor in student admissions by the University of Michigan Law School is unlawful.

The Law School ranks among the Nation's top law schools. Seeking to "admit a group of students who individually and collectively are among the most capable," the Law School looks for individuals with "substantial promise for success in law school" and "a strong likelihood of succeeding in the practice of law and contributing in diverse ways to the well-being of others." More broadly, the Law School seeks "a mix of students with varying backgrounds and experiences who will respect and learn from each other." In 1992, the dean of the Law School charged a faculty committee with crafting a written admissions policy to implement these goals. The hallmark of that policy is its focus on academic ability coupled with a flexible assessment of applicants' talents, experiences, and potential "to contribute to the learning of those around them." The policy requires admissions officials to evaluate each applicant based on all the information available in the file, including a personal statement, letters of recommendation, and an essay describing the ways in which the applicant will contribute to the life and diversity of the Law School. In reviewing an applicant's file, admissions officials must consider the applicant's undergraduate grade point average (GPA) and Law School Admissions Test (LSAT) score because they are important (if imperfect) predictors of academic success in law school.

The policy aspires to "achieve that diversity which has the potential to enrich everyone's education and thus make a law school class stronger than the sum of its parts." The policy recognizes "many possible bases for diversity admissions." The policy does, however, reaffirm the Law School's long-standing commitment to "one particular type of diversity," that is, "racial and ethnic diversity with special reference to the inclusion of students from groups which have been historically discriminated against, like African-Americans, Hispanics and Native Americans, who without this commitment might not be represented in our student body in meaningful numbers." By enrolling a "'critical mass' of [underrepresented] minority students," the Law School seeks to "ensure their ability to make unique contributions to the character of the Law School."

Barbara Grutter is a white Michigan resident who applied to the Law School with a 3.8 grade point average and 161 LSAT score. The Law School initially placed petitioner on a waiting list, but subsequently rejected her application. [P]etitioner filed suit in the United States District Court for the Eastern District of Michigan. Petitioner alleged that respondents discriminated against her on the basis of race in violation of the Fourteenth Amendment; Title VI of the Civil Rights Act of 1964.

Petitioner further alleged that her application was rejected because the Law School uses race as a "predominant" factor, giving applicants who belong to certain minority groups "a significantly greater chance of admission than students with similar credentials from disfavored racial groups." Petitioner also alleged that respondents "had no compelling interest to justify their use of race in the admissions process."

We granted *certiorari* to resolve a question of national importance: Whether diversity is a compelling interest that can justify the narrowly tailored use of race in selecting applicants for admission to public universities.

In the *Bakke* case, we reviewed a racial set-aside program that reserved 16 out of 100 seats in a medical school class for members of certain minority groups. The decision produced six separate opinions, none of which commanded a majority of the Court. The only holding for the Court in *Bakke* was that a "State has a substantial interest that legitimately may be served by a properly devised admissions program involving the competitive consideration of race and ethnic origin." Since this Court's splintered decision in *Bakke*, Justice Powell's opinion announcing the judgment of the Court has served as the touchstone for constitutional analysis of race-conscious admissions policies.

[T]oday we endorse Justice Powell's view that student body diversity is a compelling state interest that can justify the use of race in university admissions.

The Equal Protection Clause provides that no State shall "deny to any person within its jurisdiction the equal protection of the laws. " Because the Fourteenth Amendment "protects persons, not groups," all "governmental action based on race--a group classification long recognized as in most circumstances irrelevant and therefore prohibited--should be subjected to detailed judicial inquiry to ensure that the personal right to equal protection of the laws has not been infringed."

Today, we hold that the Law School has a compelling interest in attaining a diverse student body. The Law School's educational judgment that such diversity is essential to its educational mission is one to which we defer. Our scrutiny of the interest asserted by the Law School is no less strict for taking into account complex educational judgments in an area that lies primarily within the expertise of the university.

Our conclusion that the Law School has a compelling interest in a diverse student body is informed by our view that attaining a diverse student body is at the heart of the Law School's proper institutional mission, and that "good faith" on the part of a university is "presumed" absent "a showing to the contrary."

We have repeatedly acknowledged the overriding importance of preparing students for work and citizenship, describing education as pivotal to "sustaining our political and cultural heritage" with a fundamental role in maintaining the fabric of society. [T]he diffusion of knowledge and opportunity through public institutions of higher education must be accessible to all individuals regardless of race or ethnicity. Effective participation by members of all racial and ethnic groups in the civic life of our Nation is essential if the dream of one Nation, indivisible, is to be realized.

We find that the Law School's admissions program bears the hallmarks of a narrowly tailored plan. As Justice Powell made clear in *Bakke*, truly individualized consideration demands that race be used in a flexible, nonmechanical way. It follows from this mandate that universities cannot establish quotas for members of certain racial groups or put members of those groups on separate admissions tracks. Nor can universities insulate applicants who belong to certain racial or ethnic groups from the competition for admission. Universities can, however, consider race or ethnicity more flexibly as a "plus" factor in the context of individualized consideration of each and every applicant.

The Law School's goal of attaining a critical mass of underrepresented minority students does not transform its program into a quota. "Some attention to numbers," without more, does not transform a flexible admissions system into a rigid quota. [B]etween 1993 and 2000, the number of African-American, Latino, and Native-American students in each class at the Law School varied from 13.5 to 20.1 percent, a range inconsistent with a quota.

The United States advocates "percentage plans," recently adopted by public undergraduate institutions in Texas, Florida, and California to guarantee admission to all students above a certain class-rank threshold in every high school in the State. The United States does not, however, explain how such plans could work for graduate and professional schools. Moreover, even assuming such plans are race-neutral, they may preclude the university from conducting the individualized assessments necessary to assemble a student body that is not just racially diverse, but diverse along all the qualities valued by the university. We are satisfied that the Law School adequately considered race-neutral alternatives currently capable of producing a critical mass without forcing the Law School to abandon the academic selectivity that is the cornerstone of its educational mission.

[R]ace-conscious admissions policies must be limited in time. This requirement reflects that racial classifications, however compelling their goals, are potentially so dangerous that they may be employed no more broadly than the interest demands. Enshrining a permanent justification for racial preferences would offend this fundamental equal protection principle. We see no reason to exempt race-conscious admissions programs from the requirement that all governmental use of race must have a logical end point.

It has been 25 years since Justice Powell first approved the use of race to further an interest in student body diversity in the context of public higher education. Since that time, the number of minority applicants with high grades and test scores has indeed increased. We expect that 25 years from now, the use of racial preferences will no longer be necessary to further the interest approved today.

In summary, the Equal Protection Clause does not prohibit the Law School's narrowly tailored use of race in admissions decisions to further a compelling interest in obtaining the educational benefits that flow from a diverse student body.

CONCUR [GINSBURG]: [M]any minority students encounter markedly inadequate and unequal educational opportunities. As lower school education in minority communities improves, an increase in the number of such students may be anticipated. From today's vantage point, one may hope, but not firmly forecast, that progress toward nondiscrimination and genuinely equal opportunity will make it safe to sunset affirmative action.

DISSENT [SCALIA]: [T]he Law School's mystical "critical mass" justification for its discrimination by race challenges even the most gullible mind. The admissions statistics show it to be a sham to cover a scheme of racially proportionate admissions.

If it is appropriate for the University of Michigan Law School to use racial discrimination for the purpose of putting together a "critical mass" that will convey generic lessons in socialization and good citizenship, surely it is no less appropriate--indeed, particularly appropriate--for the civil service system of the State of Michigan to do so. There, also, those exposed to "critical masses" of certain races will presumably become better Americans, better Michiganders, better civil servants. And surely private employers cannot be criticized--indeed, should be praised--if they also "teach" good citizenship to their adult employees through a patriotic, all-American system of racial discrimination in hiring. The nonminority individuals who are deprived of a legal education, a civil service job, or any job at all by reason of their skin color will surely understand.

DISSENT AND CONCUR [THOMAS]: Frederick Douglass, speaking to a group of abolitionists almost 140 years ago, delivered a message lost on today's majority: "In regard to the colored people, there is always more that is benevolent, I perceive, than just, manifested towards us. What I ask for the negro is not benevolence, not pity, not sympathy, but simply justice. . . . I have had but one answer from the beginning. Do nothing with us! Your doing with us has already played the mischief with us. All I ask is, give him a chance to stand on his own legs! Let him alone! . . . Your interference is doing him positive injury."

Like Douglass, I believe blacks can achieve in every avenue of American life without the meddling of university administrators. The Constitution does not, however, tolerate institutional devotion to the status quo in admissions policies when such devotion ripens into racial discrimination. The Law School, of its own choosing, and for its own purposes, maintains an exclusionary admissions system that it knows produces racially disproportionate results. Racial discrimination is not a permissible solution to the self-inflicted wounds of this elitist admissions policy.

I agree with the Court's holding that racial discrimination in higher education admissions will be illegal in 25 years. I respectfully dissent from the remainder of the Court's opinion and the judgment, however, because I believe that the Law School's current use of race violates the Equal Protection Clause and that the Constitution means the same thing today as it will in 300 months.

## DISCUSSION QUESTIONS

(1) Is the goal of a "critical mass" of minority students any different from an illegal quota system in admissions?

(2) Are the benefits of a diverse student body for all sufficient to justify a race-conscious admissions policy?

(3) Does the Michigan admissions program actually harm minorities by stigmatizing them?

# THE COALITION v. PETE WILSON
## 122 F.3d 692 (9<sup>th</sup> Cir., 1997)

We must decide whether a provision of the California Constitution prohibiting public race and gender preferences violates the Equal Protection Clause of the United States Constitution.

On November 5, 1996, the people of the State of California adopted the California Civil Rights Initiative as an amendment to their Constitution. The initiative, which appeared on the ballot as Proposition 209, provides in relevant part that

> [t]he state shall not discriminate against, or grant preferential treatment to, any individual or group on the basis of race, sex, color, ethnicity, or national origin in the operation of public employment, public education, or public contracting.

Proposition 209 passed by a margin of 54 to 46 percent. On the day after the election, several individuals and groups claiming to represent the interests of racial minorities and women filed a complaint in the [Federal court] against several officials and political subdivisions of the State of California. The complaint alleges that Proposition 209, first, denies racial minorities and women the equal protection of the laws guaranteed by the Fourteenth Amendment, and, second, is void under the Supremacy Clause because it conflicts with the Civil Rights Act of 1964, and Title IX of the Educational Amendments of 1972. As relief, plaintiffs seek a declaration that Proposition 209 is unconstitutional and a permanent injunction enjoining the State from implementing and enforcing it.

As a matter of "conventional" equal protection analysis, there is simply no doubt that Proposition 209 is constitutional. The Equal Protection Clause guarantees that the government will not classify individuals on the basis of impermissible criteria. Most laws, of course -- perhaps all -- classify individuals one way or another. Individuals receive, or correspondingly are denied, governmental benefits on the basis of income, disability, veteran status, age, occupation and countless other grounds.

The general rule does not apply, however, when a law classifies individuals by race or gender. To be constitutional, a racial classification, regardless of its purported motivation, must be narrowly tailored to serve a compelling governmental interest, an extraordinary justification. The first step in determining whether a law violates the Equal Protection Clause is to identify the classification that it draws. Proposition 209 provides that the State of California shall not discriminate against, or grant preferential treatment to, any individual or group on the basis of race or gender. Rather than classifying individuals by race or gender, Proposition 209 prohibits the State from classifying individuals by race or gender. A law that prohibits the State from classifying individuals by race or gender *a fortiori* does not classify individuals by race or gender. Proposition 209's ban on race and gender preferences, as a matter of law and logic, does not violate the Equal Protection Clause in any conventional sense.

As a matter of "political structure" analysis, however, plaintiffs challenge the level of government at which the State of California has prohibited race and gender preferences. Plaintiffs contend that Proposition 209 imposes an unequal "political structure" that denies women and minorities a right to seek preferential treatment from the lowest level of government.

Can a statewide ballot initiative deny equal protection to members of a group that constitutes a majority of the electorate that enacted it? Is it possible for a majority of voters impermissibly to stack the political deck against itself? It would seem to make little sense to apply "political structure" equal protection principles where the group alleged to face special political burdens itself constitutes a majority of the electorate.

The difficulty, however, lies in reconciling what seems to be that eminently sensible conclusion with the principle that the Fourteenth Amendment guarantees equal protection to individuals and not to groups. That the Fourteenth Amendment affords individuals, not groups, the right to demand equal protection is a fundamental first principle of "conventional" equal protection jurisprudence.

Where a state denies someone a job, an education, or a seat on the bus because of her race or gender, the injury to that individual is clear. The person who wants to work, study, or ride but cannot because she is black or a woman is denied equal protection. Where, as here, a state prohibits race or gender preferences at any level of government, the injury to any specific individual is utterly inscrutable. No one contends that individuals have a constitutional right to preferential treatment solely on the basis of their race or gender. Quite the contrary. What, then, is the personal injury that members of a group suffer when they cannot seek preferential treatment on the basis of their race or gender from local government?

While the Constitution protects against obstructions to equal treatment, it erects obstructions to preferential treatment by its own terms. The alleged "equal protection" burden that Proposition 209 imposes on those who would seek race and gender preferences is a burden that the Constitution itself imposes. That the Constitution permits the rare race-based or gender-based preference hardly implies that the state cannot ban them altogether.

[W]e must conclude that, as a matter of law, Proposition 209 does not violate the United States Constitution. With no constitutional injury on the merits as a matter of law, there is no threat of irreparable injury or hardship to tip the balance in plaintiffs' favor.

## DISCUSSION QUESTIONS

(1) Is the nation at a point in its history where the approach of Proposition 209 is the best way to ensure true "equal protection"?

(2) Should California, to be fair, now also ban preferences based on political connections, wealth, disability, veterans-status, age, alumni parents, and athletic ability? Which preferences should be allowed and which banned in public employment and education?

(3) Should 209 be extended to private employment and education?

# CHAPTER 8. SEX DISCRIMINATION AND HARASSMENT

## Sex Discrimination

## CALIFORNIA FEDERAL SAVINGS & LOAN ASSN. v. GUERRA
### 479 U.S. 272 (U.S. Supreme Court, 1987)

The question presented is whether the Civil Rights Act of 1964, as amended by the Pregnancy Discrimination Act of 1978 [PDA], pre-empts a state statute that requires employers to provide leave and reinstatement to employees disabled by pregnancy.

California's Fair Employment and Housing Act (FEHA), prohibits discrimination in employment and housing. In September 1978, California amended the FEHA to proscribe certain forms of employment discrimination on the basis of pregnancy. Subdivision (b)(2) is the only portion of the statute that applies to employers subject to [the PDA]. It requires these employers to provide female employees an unpaid pregnancy disability leave of up to four months. Respondent Fair Employment and Housing Commission, the state agency authorized to interpret the FEHA, has construed (b)(2) to require California employers to reinstate an employee returning from pregnancy leave to the job she previously held, unless it is no longer available due to business necessity. In the latter case, the employer must make a reasonable, good-faith effort to place the employee in a substantially similar job. The statute does not compel employers to provide paid leave to pregnant employees. [T]he only benefit pregnant workers actually derive from (b)(2) is a qualified right to reinstatement.

Congress passed the Pregnancy Discrimination Act of 1978. The PDA specifies that sex discrimination includes discrimination on the basis of pregnancy.

California Federal Savings & Loan Association (Cal Fed) has a facially neutral leave policy that permits employees who have completed three months of service to take unpaid leaves of absence for a variety of reasons, including disability and pregnancy. Although it is Cal Fed's policy to try to provide an employee taking unpaid leave with a similar position upon returning, Cal Fed expressly reserves the right to terminate an employee who has taken a leave of absence if a similar position is not available.

Lillian Garland was employed by Cal Fed as a receptionist for several years. In January 1982, she took a pregnancy disability leave. When she was able to return to work in April of that year, Garland was informed that her job had been filled and that there were no receptionist or similar positions available. Garland filed a complaint with [the] Department of Fair Employment and Housing, which issued an administrative accusation against Cal Fed on her behalf.

In determining whether a state statute is pre-empted by federal law and therefore invalid under the Supremacy Clause of the Constitution, our sole task is to ascertain the intent of Congress. [I]n those areas where Congress has not completely displaced state regulation, federal law may nonetheless pre-empt state law to the extent it actually conflicts with federal law.

In order to decide whether the California statute requires or permits employers to violate the PDA, or is inconsistent with the purposes of the statute, we must determine whether the PDA prohibits the States from requiring employers to provide reinstatement to pregnant workers, regardless of their policy for disabled workers generally.

Congress had before it extensive evidence of discrimination against pregnancy, particularly in disability and health insurance programs. We find it significant that Congress was aware of state laws similar to California's but apparently did not consider them inconsistent with the PDA.

We emphasize the limited nature of the benefits (b)(2) provides. The statute is narrowly drawn to cover only the period of actual physical disability on account of pregnancy, childbirth, or related medical conditions. [U]nlike the protective labor legislation prevalent earlier in this century, (b)(2) does not reflect archaic or stereotypical notions about pregnancy and the abilities of pregnant workers.

Section (b)(2) does not compel California employers to treat pregnant workers better than other disabled employees; it merely establishes benefits that employers must, at a minimum, provide to pregnant workers. Employers are free to give comparable benefits to other disabled employees, thereby treating "women affected by pregnancy" no better than "other persons not so affected but similar in their ability or inability to work."

[P]etitioners' challenge to (b)(2) fails. The statute is not pre-empted by the PDA, because it is not inconsistent with the purposes of the federal statute, nor does it require the doing of an act which is unlawful under [the PDA].

## DISCUSSION QUESTIONS

(1) Is the provision of employment rights to pregnant women unfair discrimination against men and nonpregnant women?

(2) How can the government require nondiscrimination against pregnant women without reinforcing old stereotypes about them?

### INTERNATIONAL UNION, UAW v. JOHNSON CONTROLS
499 U.S. 187 (U.S. Supreme Court, 1991)

In this case we are concerned with an employer's gender-based fetal-protection policy. May an employer exclude a fertile female employee from certain jobs because of its concern for the health of the fetus the woman might conceive?

Johnson Controls, Inc., manufactures batteries. In the manufacturing process, the element lead is a primary ingredient. Occupational exposure to lead entails health risks, including the risk of harm to any fetus carried by a female employee.

Before the Civil Rights Act of 1964 became law, Johnson Controls did not employ any woman in a battery-manufacturing job. In June 1977, however, it announced its first official policy concerning its employment of women in lead-exposure work. Johnson Controls "stopped short of excluding women capable of bearing children from lead exposure," but emphasized that a woman who expected to have a child should not choose a job in

128

which she would have such exposure. Between 1979 and 1983, eight employees became pregnant while maintaining blood lead levels in excess of the critical level noted by the Occupational Safety and Health Administration (OSHA) for a worker who was planning to have a family. The company responded by announcing a broad exclusion of women from jobs that exposed them to lead:

"It is [Johnson Controls'] policy that women who are pregnant or who are capable of bearing children will not be placed into jobs involving lead exposure or which could expose them to lead through the exercise of job bidding, bumping, transfer or promotion rights."

In April 1984, petitioners filed in [Federal] Court a class action challenging Johnson Controls' fetal-protection policy as sex discrimination that violated Title VII of the Civil Rights Act of 1964.

The bias in Johnson Controls' policy is obvious. Fertile men, but not fertile women, are given a choice as to whether they wish to risk their reproductive health for a particular job. Respondent's fetal-protection policy explicitly discriminates against women on the basis of their sex.

Johnson Controls' policy classifies on the basis of gender and childbearing capacity, rather than fertility alone. Despite evidence in the record about the debilitating effect of lead exposure on the male reproductive system, Johnson Controls is concerned only with the harms that may befall the unborn offspring of its female employees. Johnson Controls' policy is facially discriminatory because it requires only a female employee to produce proof that she is not capable of reproducing.

Our conclusion is bolstered by the Pregnancy Discrimination Act (PDA), [which] has now made clear that discrimination based on a woman's pregnancy is, on its face, discrimination because of her sex." Johnson Controls explicitly classifies on the basis of potential for pregnancy. Under the PDA, such a classification must be regarded in the same light as explicit sex discrimination. Respondent has chosen to treat all its female employees as potentially pregnant; that choice evinces discrimination on the basis of sex.

[T]he absence of a malevolent motive does not convert a facially discriminatory policy into a neutral policy with a discriminatory effect. Whether an employment practice involves disparate treatment through explicit facial discrimination does not depend on why the employer discriminates but rather on the explicit terms of the discrimination. The beneficence of an employer's purpose does not undermine the conclusion that an explicit gender-based policy is sex discrimination.

We hold that Johnson Controls' fetal-protection policy is sex discrimination forbidden under Title VII unless respondent can establish that sex is a "bona fide occupational qualification." [BFOQ]

Johnson Controls argues that its fetal-protection policy falls within the so-called safety exception to the BFOQ. Our case law makes clear that the safety exception is limited to instances in which sex or pregnancy actually interferes with the employee's ability to perform the job. Johnson Controls suggests, however, that we expand the exception to allow fetal-protection policies that mandate particular standards for pregnant or fertile women. We decline to do so. Such an expansion contradicts not only the language of the BFOQ and the narrowness of its exception, but also the plain language and history of the PDA.

We conclude that the language of both the BFOQ provision and the PDA, as well as the legislative history and the case law, prohibit an employer from discriminating against a woman because of her capacity to become pregnant unless her reproductive potential prevents her from performing the duties of her job. [A]n employer must direct its concerns about a woman's ability to perform her job safely and efficiently to those aspects of the woman's job-related activities that fall within the "essence" of the particular business.

Fertile women participate in the manufacture of batteries as efficiently as anyone else. Johnson Controls' professed moral and ethical concerns about the welfare of the next generation do not suffice to establish a BFOQ of female sterility. Decisions about the welfare of future children must be left to the parents who conceive, bear, support, and raise them rather than to the employers who hire those parents.

More than 40 States currently recognize a right to recover for a prenatal injury based either on negligence or on wrongful death. According to Johnson Controls, the company complies with the lead standard developed by OSHA and warns its female employees about the damaging effects of lead. It is worth noting that OSHA gave the problem of lead lengthy consideration and concluded that "there is no basis whatsoever for the claim that women of childbearing age should be excluded from the workplace in order to protect the fetus or the course of pregnancy." Instead, OSHA established a series of mandatory protections which, taken together, "should effectively minimize any risk to the fetus and newborn child." Without negligence, it would be difficult for a court to find liability on the part of the employer.

Concern for a woman's existing or potential offspring historically has been the excuse for denying women equal employment opportunities. Congress in the PDA prohibited discrimination on the basis of a woman's ability to become pregnant. We do no more than hold that the PDA means what it says.

It is no more appropriate for the courts than it is for individual employers to decide whether a woman's reproductive role is more important to herself and her family than her economic role. Congress has left this choice to the woman as hers to make.

## DISCUSSION QUESTIONS

(1) In this decision, does the Court appropriately address the rights of women? Of men? Of the future children of employees?

(2) What course of action should Johnson Controls now follow to respond to the court's decision and the concern about the health of fetuses?

## MICHAEL M. v. SUPERIOR COURT OF SONOMA COUNTY
450 U.S. 464 (U.S. Supreme Court, 1981)

The question presented in this case is whether California's "statutory rape" law violates the Equal Protection Clause of the Fourteenth Amendment.

[The statute] defines unlawful sexual intercourse as "an act of sexual intercourse accomplished with a female not the wife of the perpetrator, where the female is under the age of 18 years." The statute thus makes men alone criminally liable for the act of sexual intercourse.

In 1978, a complaint was filed in the Municipal Court of Sonoma County, alleging that petitioner, then a 17 1/2-year-old male, had had unlawful sexual intercourse with Sharon, a 16 1/2-year-old female.

We are satisfied not only that the prevention of illegitimate pregnancy is at least one of the "purposes" of the statute, but also that the State has a strong interest in preventing such pregnancy. At the risk of stating the obvious, teenage pregnancies, which have increased dramatically over the last two decades, have significant social, medical, and economic consequences for both the mother and her child, and the State.

We need not be medical doctors to discern that young men and young women are not similarly situated with respect to the problems and the risks of sexual intercourse. Only women may become pregnant, and they suffer disproportionately the profound physical, emotional, and psychological consequences of sexual activity. The statute here protects women from sexual intercourse at an age when those consequences are particularly severe.

The question thus boils down to whether a State may attack the problem of sexual intercourse and teenage pregnancy directly by prohibiting a male from having sexual intercourse with a minor female. We hold that such a statute is sufficiently related to the State's objectives to pass constitutional muster.

Because virtually all of the significant harmful and inescapably identifiable consequences of teenage pregnancy fall on the young female, a legislature acts well within its authority when it elects to punish only the participant who, by nature, suffers few of the consequences of his conduct. It is hardly unreasonable for a legislature acting to protect minor females to exclude them from punishment. Moreover, the risk of pregnancy itself constitutes a substantial deterrence to young females. No similar natural sanctions deter males. A criminal sanction imposed solely on males thus serves to roughly "equalize" the deterrents on the sexes.

[W]e cannot say that a gender-neutral statute would be as effective as the statute California has chosen to enact. The State persuasively contends that a gender-neutral statute would frustrate its interest in effective enforcement. Its view is that a female is surely less likely to report violations of the statute if she herself would be subject to criminal prosecution. In an area already fraught with prosecutorial difficulties, we decline to hold that the Equal Protection Clause requires a legislature to enact a statute so broad that it may well be incapable of enforcement.

[T]he statute does not rest on the assumption that males are generally the aggressors. It is instead an attempt by a legislature to prevent illegitimate teenage pregnancy by providing an additional deterrent for men. The age of the man is irrelevant since young men are as capable as older men of inflicting the harm sought to be prevented.

In upholding the California statute we also recognize that this is not a case where a statute is being challenged on the grounds that it "invidiously discriminates" against females. To the contrary, the statute places a burden on males which is not shared by females. But we find nothing to suggest that men, because of past discrimination or peculiar disadvantages, are in need of the special solicitude of the courts. Nor is this a case where the gender classification rests on "the baggage of sexual stereotypes." [T]he statute reasonably reflects the fact that the consequences of sexual intercourse and pregnancy fall more heavily on the female than on the male.

DISSENT: I am convinced that there is only one proper resolution of this issue: the classification must be declared unconstitutional.

Common sense suggests that a gender-neutral statutory rape law is potentially a greater deterrent of sexual activity than a gender-based law, for the simple reason that a gender-neutral law subjects both men and women to criminal sanctions and thus arguably has a deterrent effect on twice as many potential violators. The State's failure to prove that a gender-neutral law would be a less effective deterrent than a gender-based law, like the State's failure to prove that a gender-neutral law would be difficult to enforce, should have led this Court to invalidate [this statute].

Until very recently, no California court had suggested that the purpose of California's statutory rape law was to protect young women from the risk of pregnancy. Indeed, the historical development demonstrates that the law was initially enacted on the premise that young women, in contrast to young men, were to be deemed legally incapable of consenting to an act of sexual intercourse. Because their chastity was considered particularly precious, those young women were felt to be uniquely in need of the State's protection. In contrast, young men were assumed to be capable of making such decisions for themselves; the law therefore did not offer them any special protection.

It is perhaps because the gender classification in California's statutory rape law was initially designed to further these outmoded sexual stereotypes, rather than to reduce the incidence of teenage pregnancies, that the State has been unable to demonstrate a substantial relationship between the classification and its newly asserted goal. But whatever the reason, the State has not shown that [it] is any more effective than a gender-neutral law would be in deterring minor females from engaging in sexual intercourse.

## DISCUSSION QUESTIONS

(1) Does this statutory rape law reflect outmoded stereotypes about women and men?

(2) Is the threat of criminal prosecution an effective deterrent against teenage pregnancies and sexually transmitted diseases?

## UNITED STATES v. VIRGINIA
### 518 U.S. 515 (U.S. Supreme Court, 1996)

Virginia's public institutions of higher learning include an incomparable military college, Virginia Military Institute (VMI). The United States maintains that the Constitution's equal protection guarantee precludes Virginia from reserving exclusively to men the unique educational opportunities VMI affords. We agree.

VMI's distinctive mission is to produce "citizen-soldiers," men prepared for leadership in civilian life and in military service. VMI has notably succeeded in its mission to produce leaders; among its alumni are military generals, Members of Congress, and business executives.

Neither the goal of producing citizen-soldiers nor VMI's implementing methodology is inherently unsuitable to women. And the school's impressive record in producing leaders has made admission desirable to some women. VMI's program "is directed at preparation for both military and civilian life"; "only about 15% of VMI cadets enter career military service."

In 1990, prompted by a complaint filed with the Attorney General by a female high-school student, the United States sued the Commonwealth of Virginia and VMI, alleging that VMI's exclusively male admission policy violated the Equal Protection Clause of the Fourteenth Amendment.

Virginia proposed a parallel program for women: Virginia Women's Institute for Leadership (VWIL). The 4-year, state-sponsored undergraduate program would be located at Mary Baldwin College, a private liberal arts school for women. Although VWIL would share VMI's mission the VWIL program would differ from VMI in academic offerings, methods of education, and financial resources.

[T]his case present[s] two ultimate issues. First, does Virginia's exclusion of women from the educational opportunities provided by VMI deny to women the equal protection of the laws guaranteed by the Fourteenth Amendment? Second, if VMI's "unique" situation -- as Virginia's sole single-sex public institution of higher education -- offends the Constitution's equal protection principle, what is the remedial requirement?

Today's skeptical scrutiny of official action denying rights or opportunities based on sex responds to volumes of history. [N]ot until 1920 did women gain a constitutional right to the franchise. And for a half century thereafter, it remained the prevailing doctrine that government could withhold from women opportunities accorded men so long as any "basis in reason" could be conceived for the discrimination.

In 1971, for the first time in our Nation's history, this Court ruled in favor of a woman who complained that her State had denied her the equal protection of its laws. Since [then], the Court has repeatedly recognized that neither federal nor state government acts compatibly with the equal protection principle when a law or official policy denies to women, simply because they are women, full citizenship stature -- equal opportunity to aspire, achieve, participate in and contribute to society based on their individual talents and capacities.

Without equating gender classifications to classifications based on race or national origin, the Court has carefully inspected official action that closes a door or denies opportunity to women (or to men). "Inherent differences" between men and women, we have come to appreciate, remain cause for celebration, but not for denigration of the members of either sex or for artificial constraints on an individual's opportunity. Sex classifications may not be used, as they once were, to create or perpetuate the legal, social, and economic inferiority of women.

[W]e conclude that Virginia has shown no "exceedingly persuasive justification" for excluding all women from the citizen-soldier training afforded by VMI. We therefore [hold] that Virginia [has] violated the Fourteenth Amendment's Equal Protection Clause.

VWIL affords women no opportunity to experience the rigorous military training for which VMI is famed. Instead, the VWIL program uses a "cooperative method" of education "which reinforces self-esteem." Virginia maintains that these methodological differences are "justified pedagogically," based on "important differences between men and women in learning and developmental needs," "psychological and sociological differences" Virginia describes as "real" and "not stereotypes."

[G]eneralizations about "the way women are," estimates of what is appropriate for most women, no longer justify denying opportunity to women whose talent and capacity place them outside the average description. In myriad respects other than military training, VWIL does not qualify as VMI's equal. VWIL's student body, faculty, course offerings, and facilities hardly match VMI's. Nor can the VWIL graduate anticipate the benefits associated with VMI's 157-year history, the school's prestige, and its influential alumni network.

Virginia, while maintaining VMI for men only, has failed to provide any "comparable single-gender women's institution." Instead, the Commonwealth has created a VWIL program fairly appraised as a "pale shadow" of VMI. Virginia has not shown substantial equality in the separate educational opportunities the Commonwealth supports at VWIL and VMI.

DISSENT: The potential of today's decision for widespread disruption of existing institutions lies in its application to private single-sex education. Government support is immensely important to private educational institutions. The issue will be whether the government itself would be violating the Constitution by providing state support to single-sex colleges.

## DISCUSSION QUESTIONS

(1) How does the rejection of the proposed "separate but equal" program at Mary Baldwin compare with the *Brown* court's rejection of separate but equal" programs for different races?

(2) Should gender discrimination be reviewed with the same standard of "strict scrutiny" accorded racial discrimination?

(3) Should private single-sex colleges be found unconstitutional?

### Sexual Harassment

### MERITOR SAVINGS BANK v. VINSON
477 U.S. 57 (U.S. Supreme Court, 1986)

This case presents important questions concerning workplace "sexual harassment" brought under Title VII of the Civil Rights Act of 1964.

In 1974, respondent Mechelle Vinson met Sidney Taylor, a vice president of what is now Meritor Savings Bank and manager of one of its branch offices. With Taylor as her supervisor, respondent started as a teller-trainee, and was promoted to teller, head teller, and assistant branch manager. [I]t is undisputed that her advancement there was based on merit alone. In September 1978, respondent notified Taylor that she was taking sick leave for an indefinite period. On November 1, 1978, the bank discharged her for excessive use of that leave.

Respondent brought this action against Taylor and the bank, claiming that during her four years at the bank she had "constantly been subjected to sexual harassment" by Taylor in violation of Title VII. She sought injunctive relief, compensatory and punitive damages against Taylor and the bank, and attorney's fees.

Respondent testified that during her probationary period as a teller-trainee, Taylor treated her in a fatherly way and made no sexual advances. Shortly thereafter, however, he invited her out to dinner and, during the course of the meal, suggested that they go to a motel to have sexual relations. At first she refused, but out of what she described as fear of losing her job she eventually agreed. According to respondent, Taylor thereafter made repeated demands upon her for sexual favors, usually at the branch, both during and after business hours; she estimated that over the next several years she had intercourse with him some 40 or 50 times. In addition, respondent testified that Taylor fondled her in front of other employees, followed her into the women's restroom when she went there alone, exposed himself to her, and even forcibly raped her on several occasions. These activities ceased after 1977, when she started going with a steady boyfriend.

Respondent also testified that because she was afraid of Taylor she never reported his harassment to any of his supervisors and never attempted to use the bank's complaint procedure.

Taylor denied respondent's allegations of sexual activity, testifying that he never fondled her, never made suggestive remarks to her, never engaged in sexual intercourse with her, and never asked her to do so.

The District Court denied relief. The Court of Appeals for the District of Columbia Circuit reversed. We granted *certiorari*, and now affirm.

Title VII of the Civil Rights Act of 1964 makes it "an unlawful employment practice for an employer . . . to discriminate against any individual with respect to his compensation, terms, conditions, or privileges of employment, because of such individual's race, color, religion, sex, or national origin."

Without question, when a supervisor sexually harasses a subordinate because of the subordinate's sex, that supervisor "discriminate[s]" on the basis of sex. [T]he language of Title VII is not limited to "economic" or "tangible" discrimination. The phrase "terms, conditions, or privileges of employment" evinces a congressional intent "'to strike at the entire spectrum of disparate treatment of men and women'" in employment. The EEOC Guidelines fully support the view that harassment leading to noneconomic injury can violate Title VII.

In defining "sexual harassment," the Guidelines first describe the kinds of workplace conduct that may be actionable under Title VII. These include "[unwelcome] sexual advances, requests for sexual favors, and other verbal or physical conduct of a sexual nature." Relevant to the charges at issue in this case, the Guidelines provide that such sexual misconduct constitutes prohibited "sexual harassment," whether or not it is directly linked to the grant or denial of an economic *quid pro quo*, where "such conduct has the purpose or effect of unreasonably interfering with an individual's work performance or creating an intimidating, hostile, or offensive working environment."

In concluding that so-called "hostile environment" (i.e., non *quid pro quo*) harassment violates Title VII, the EEOC drew upon a substantial body of judicial decisions and EEOC precedent holding that Title VII affords employees the right to work in an environment free from discriminatory intimidation, ridicule, and insult. Courts have uniformly held, and we agree that a plaintiff may establish a violation of Title VII by proving that discrimination based on sex has created a hostile or abusive work environment.

Of course, not all workplace conduct that may be described as "harassment" affects a "term, condition, or privilege" of employment within the meaning of Title VII. For sexual harassment to be actionable, it must be sufficiently severe or pervasive "to alter the conditions of [the victim's] employment and create an abusive working environment." Respondent's allegations in this case -- which include not only pervasive harassment but also criminal conduct of the most serious nature -- are plainly sufficient to state a claim for "hostile environment" sexual harassment. [W]e hold that a claim of "hostile environment" sex discrimination is actionable under Title VII.

## DISCUSSION QUESTIONS

(1) This was the first recognition by the U.S. Supreme Court of a Civil Right not to be sexually harassed in the workplace. From the facts here, does this seem like an appropriate area for government intervention?

(2) What additional examples of workplace "harassment" would be protected by the Civil Rights Act under the court's reasoning here? What examples of workplace "harassment" would *not* be protected?

## HARRIS v. FORKLIFT SYSTEMS
### 510 U.S. 17 (U.S. Supreme Court, 1993)

In this case we consider the definition of a discriminatorily "abusive work environment" (also known as a "hostile work environment") under Title VII of the Civil Rights Act of 1964.

Teresa Harris worked as a manager at Forklift Systems, an equipment rental company, from April 1985 until October 1987. Charles Hardy was Forklift's president. [T]hroughout Harris' time at Forklift, Hardy often insulted her because of her gender and often made her the target of unwanted sexual innuendos. Hardy told Harris on several occasions, in the presence of other employees, "You're a woman, what do you know" and "We need a man as the rental manager"; at least once, he told her she was "a dumb ass woman." Again in front of others, he suggested that the two of them "go to the Holiday Inn to negotiate [Harris'] raise." Hardy occasionally asked Harris and other female employees to get coins from his front pants pocket. He threw objects on the ground in front of Harris and other women, and asked them to pick the objects up. He made sexual innuendos about Harris' and other women's clothing.

In mid-August 1987, Harris complained to Hardy about his conduct. Hardy said he was surprised that Harris was offended, claimed he was only joking, and apologized. He also promised he would stop, and based on this assurance Harris stayed on the job. But in early September, Hardy began anew: While Harris was arranging a deal with one of Forklift's customers, he asked her, again in front of other employees, "What did you do, promise the guy . . . some [sex] Saturday night?" On October 1, Harris collected her paycheck and quit.

Harris then sued Forklift, claiming that Hardy's conduct had created an abusive work environment for her because of her gender. We granted *certiorari*, to [determine] whether conduct, to be actionable as "abusive work environment" harassment (no *quid pro quo* harassment issue is present here), must "seriously affect [an employee's] psychological well-being" or lead the plaintiff to "suffer injury."

Title VII of the Civil Rights Act of 1964 makes it "an unlawful employment practice for an employer . . . to discriminate against any individual with respect to his compensation, terms, conditions, or privileges of employment, because of such individual's race, color, religion, sex, or national origin." [T]his language "is not limited to 'economic' or 'tangible' discrimination. The phrase 'terms, conditions, or privileges of employment' evinces a congressional intent 'to strike at the entire spectrum of disparate treatment of men and women' in employment," which includes requiring people to work in a discriminatorily hostile or abusive environment. When the workplace is permeated with "discriminatory intimidation, ridicule, and insult," that is "sufficiently severe or pervasive to alter the conditions of the victim's employment and create an abusive working environment," Title VII is violated.

This standard, which we reaffirm today, takes a middle path between making actionable any conduct that is merely offensive and requiring the conduct to cause a tangible psychological injury. Conduct that is not severe or pervasive enough to create an objectively hostile or abusive work environment -- an environment that a reasonable person would find hostile or abusive -- is beyond Title VII's purview.

Title VII comes into play before the harassing conduct leads to a nervous breakdown. A discriminatorily abusive work environment, even one that does not seriously affect employees' psychological well-being, can and often will detract from employees' job performance, discourage employees from remaining on the job, or keep them from advancing in their careers. Moreover, even without regard to these tangible effects, the very fact that the discriminatory conduct was so severe or pervasive that it created a work environment abusive to employees because of their race, gender, religion, or national origin offends Title VII.

[W]hether an environment is "hostile" or "abusive" can be determined only by looking at all the circumstances. These may include the frequency of the discriminatory conduct; its severity; whether it is physically threatening or humiliating, or a mere offensive utterance; and whether it unreasonably interferes with an employee's work performance. The effect on the employee's psychological well-being is, of course, relevant to determining whether the plaintiff actually found the environment abusive. But while psychological harm, like any other relevant factor, may be taken into account, no single factor is required.

CONCUR: The critical issue is whether members of one sex are exposed to disadvantageous conditions of employment to which members of the other sex are not exposed. [T]the inquiry should center, dominantly, on whether the discriminatory conduct has unreasonably interfered with the plaintiff's work performance. It suffices to prove that a reasonable person subjected to the discriminatory conduct would find that the harassment so altered working conditions as to "make it more difficult to do the job."

## DISCUSSION QUESTIONS

(1) Does the decision here restrict speech which should be protected under the First Amendment?

(2) Is the central concern here the economic harm from being unable to carry out one's job responsibilities appropriately?

## GEBSER v. LAGO VISTA INDEPENDENT SCHOOL DISTRICT
### 524 U.S. 274 (U.S. Supreme Court, 1998)

The question in this case is when a school district may be held liable in damages for the sexual harassment of a student by one of the district's teachers. We conclude that damages may not be recovered unless an official of the school district who has authority to institute corrective measures has actual notice of, and is deliberately indifferent to, the teacher's misconduct.

In the spring of 1991, when petitioner Alida Star Gebser was an eighth-grade student in Lago Vista Independent School District, she joined a high school book discussion group led by Frank Waldrop, a teacher at Lago Vista's high school. Lago Vista received federal funds at all pertinent times. Gebser entered high school in the fall and was assigned to classes taught by Waldrop in both semesters. He initiated sexual contact with Gebser in the spring, when, while visiting her home ostensibly to give her a book, he kissed and fondled her. The two had sexual intercourse on a number of occasions during the remainder of the school year. Their relationship continued the following school year, and they often had intercourse during class time, although never on school property.

Gebser did not report the relationship to school officials, testifying that while she realized Waldrop's conduct was improper, she was uncertain how to react and she wanted to continue having him as a teacher. [I]n 1993, a police officer discovered Waldrop and Gebser engaging in sexual intercourse and arrested Waldrop. Lago Vista terminated his employment, and the Texas Education Agency revoked his teaching license.

Gebser and her mother filed suit against Lago Vista and Waldrop, raising claims against the school district under Title IX. They sought compensatory and punitive damages from both defendants.

Title IX provides that, "no person . . . shall, on the basis of sex, be excluded from participation in, be denied the benefits of, or be subjected to discrimination under any education program or activity receiving Federal financial assistance." Title IX is also enforceable through an implied private right of action [and] monetary damages.

[W]e conclude that it would "frustrate the purposes" of Title IX to permit a damages recovery against a school district for a teacher's sexual harassment of a student without actual notice to a school district official. [I]t does not appear that Congress contemplated unlimited recovery in damages against a funding recipient where the recipient is unaware of discrimination in its programs.

The number of reported cases involving sexual harassment of students in schools confirms that harassment unfortunately is an all too common aspect of the educational experience. No one questions that a student suffers extraordinary harm when subjected to sexual harassment and abuse by a teacher, and that the teacher's conduct is reprehensible and undermines the basic purposes of the educational system. The issue in this case, however, is whether the independent misconduct of a teacher is attributable to the school district that employs him.

## DISCUSSION QUESTIONS

(1) Should school districts be held accountable, through payment of damages, for sexual harassment of students by any of their employees?

(2) If school districts were liable for paying damages in cases like this, would they be more likely to aggressively educate and supervise their teachers and students to prevent sexual harassment?

## ONCALE v. SUNDOWNER OFFSHORE SERVICES
### 523 U.S. 75 (U.S. Supreme Court, 1998)

This case presents the question whether workplace harassment can violate Title VII's prohibition against "discrimination . . . because of . . . sex," when the harasser and the harassed employee are of the same sex.

Oncale was working for Sundowner Offshore Services on [an] oil platform in the Gulf of Mexico. On several occasions, Oncale was forcibly subjected to sex-related, humiliating actions in the presence of the crew. [He was] also physically assaulted in a sexual manner, and threatened with rape.

Oncale's complaints produced no remedial action. Oncale eventually quit -- asking that his pink slip reflect that he "voluntarily left due to sexual harassment and verbal abuse." Oncale filed a complaint against Sundowner, alleging that he was discriminated against in his employment because of his sex.

Title VII of the Civil Rights Act of 1964 provides that "it shall be an unlawful employment practice for an employer . . . to discriminate against any individual with respect to his compensation, terms, conditions, or privileges of employment, because of such individual's race, color, religion, sex, or national origin." Title VII's prohibition of discrimination "because of

. . . sex" protects men as well as women, and in the related context of racial discrimination in the workplace we have rejected any conclusive presumption that an employer will not discriminate against members of his own race. [W]e hold today that nothing in Title VII necessarily bars a claim of discrimination "because of . . . sex" merely because the plaintiff and the defendant are of the same sex.

We see no justification for a categorical rule excluding same-sex harassment claims from the coverage of Title VII. [M]ale-on-male sexual harassment in the workplace was assuredly not the principal evil Congress was concerned with when it enacted Title VII. But statutory prohibitions often go beyond the principal evil to cover reasonably comparable evils, and it is ultimately the provisions of our laws rather than the principal concerns of our legislators by which we are governed. Title VII prohibits "discrimination . . . because of . . . sex" in the "terms" or "conditions" of employment. Our holding that this includes sexual harassment must extend to sexual harassment of any kind that meets the statutory requirements.

[T]he statute does not reach genuine but innocuous differences in the ways men and women routinely interact with members of the same sex and of the opposite sex. The prohibition of harassment on the basis of sex requires neither asexuality nor androgyny in the workplace; it forbids only behavior so objectively offensive as to alter the "conditions" of the victim's employment. We have always regarded that requirement as crucial, and as sufficient to ensure that courts and juries do not mistake ordinary socializing in the workplace -- such as male-on-male horseplay or intersexual flirtation -- for discriminatory "conditions of employment."

We have emphasized, moreover, that the objective severity of harassment should be judged from the perspective of a reasonable person in the plaintiff's position, considering "all the circumstances." In same-sex (as in all) harassment cases, that inquiry requires careful consideration of the social context in which particular behavior occurs and is experienced by its target. A professional football player's working environment is not severely or pervasively abusive, for example, if the coach smacks him on the buttocks as he heads onto the field-even if the same behavior would reasonably be experienced as abusive by the coach's secretary (male or female) back at the office. Common sense, and an appropriate sensitivity to social context, will enable courts and juries to distinguish between simple teasing or roughhousing among members of the same sex, and conduct which a reasonable person in the plaintiff's position would find severely hostile or abusive.

[W]e conclude that sex discrimination consisting of same-sex sexual harassment is actionable under Title VII.

## DISCUSSION QUESTIONS

(1) As Congress did not intend this protection when it passed the Civil Rights Act, is this holding appropriate?

(2) What is the "reasonable person" standard used here? Is it an effective guide for evaluating alleged "harassment" in the workplace?

# CHAPTER 9. CAPITAL PUNISHMENT

## FURMAN v. GEORGIA
### 408 U.S. 238 (U.S. Supreme Court, 1972)

The Court holds that the imposition and carrying out of the death penalty in these cases constitute cruel and unusual punishment in violation of the Eighth and Fourteenth Amendments.

It has been assumed that punishment by death is not cruel, unless the manner of execution can be said to be inhuman and barbarous. What may be said of the validity of a law on the books and what may be done with the law in its application do, or may, lead to quite different conclusions.

It would seem to be incontestable that the death penalty inflicted on one defendant is "unusual" if it discriminates against him by reason of his race, religion, wealth, social position, or class, or if it is imposed under a procedure that gives room for the play of such prejudices.

In a Nation committed to equal protection of the laws there is no permissible "caste" aspect of law enforcement. Yet we know that discretion in imposing the death penalty enables the penalty to be selectively applied, feeding prejudices against the accused if he is poor and despised, and lacking political clout, or if he is a member of a suspect or unpopular minority, and saving those who by social position may be in a more protected position.

A law that stated that anyone making more than $50,000 would be exempt from the death penalty would plainly fall, as would a law that said that blacks, those who never went beyond the fifth grade in school, those who made less than $3,000 a year, or those who were unpopular or unstable should be the only people executed. A law which reaches that result in practice has no more sanctity than a law which in terms provides the same.

[T]hese discretionary statutes are unconstitutional in their operation. They are pregnant with discrimination and discrimination is an ingredient not compatible with the idea of equal protection of the laws that is implicit in the ban on "cruel and unusual" punishments.

CONCUR [BRENNAN]: It is a denial of human dignity for the State arbitrarily to subject a person to an unusually severe punishment that society has indicated it does not regard as acceptable, and that cannot be shown to serve any penal purpose more effectively than a less drastic punishment.

[T]he State may not arbitrarily inflict an unusually severe punishment. The outstanding characteristic of our present practice of punishing criminals by death is the infrequency with which we resort to it. The evidence is conclusive that death is not the ordinary punishment for any crime.

The States' primary claim is that death is a necessary punishment because it prevents the commission of capital crimes more effectively than any less severe punishment. The first part of this claim is that the infliction of death is necessary to stop the individuals executed from committing further crimes. The answer to this is that if a criminal convicted of a capital crime poses a danger to society, effective administration of the State's pardon and parole laws can delay or deny his release from prison, and techniques of isolation can eliminate or minimize the danger while he remains confined.

The more significant argument is that the threat of death prevents the commission of capital crimes because it deters potential criminals who would not be deterred by the threat of imprisonment. The argument is not based upon evidence that the threat of death is a superior deterrent. Indeed, the available evidence uniformly indicates, although it does not conclusively prove, that the threat of death has no greater deterrent effect than the threat of imprisonment.

There is, however, another aspect to the argument that the punishment of death is necessary for the protection of society. The infliction of death, the States urge, serves to manifest the community's outrage at the commission of the crime. It is, they say, a concrete public expression of moral indignation that inculcates respect for the law and helps assure a more peaceful community. Moreover, we are told, not only does the punishment of death exert this widespread moralizing influence upon community values, it also satisfies the popular demand for grievous condemnation of abhorrent crimes and thus prevents disorder, lynching, and attempts by private citizens to take the law into their own hands.

The question is not whether death serves these supposed purposes of punishment, but whether death serves them more effectively than imprisonment. There is no evidence whatever that utilization of imprisonment rather than death encourages private blood feuds and other disorders. Furthermore, it is doubtful that the infliction of death by the State does in fact strengthen the community's moral code; if the deliberate extinguishment of human life has any effect at all, it more likely tends to lower our respect for life and brutalize our values. That is why we no longer carry out public executions.

The other purpose suggested is retribution. Although it is difficult to believe that any State wishes to proclaim adherence to "naked vengeance," the States claim that death is the only fit punishment for capital crimes and that this retributive purpose justifies its infliction. When the overwhelming number of criminals who commit capital crimes go to prison, it cannot be concluded that death serves the purpose of retribution more effectively than imprisonment. The asserted public belief that murderers and rapists deserve to die is flatly inconsistent with the execution of a random few.

CONCUR [STEWART]: The penalty of death differs from all other forms of criminal punishment, not in degree but in kind. It is unique in its total irrevocability. And it is unique, finally, in its absolute renunciation of all that is embodied in our concept of humanity.

DISSENT [BURGER]: Those favoring retention start from the intuitive notion that capital punishment should act as the most effective deterrent and note that there is no convincing evidence that it does not. Comparative deterrence is not a matter that lends itself to precise measurement; to shift the burden to the States is to provide an illusory solution to an enormously complex problem. If it were proper to put the States to the test of demonstrating the deterrent value of capital punishment, we could just as well ask them to prove the need for life imprisonment or any other punishment. If the States are unable to adduce convincing proof rebutting such assertions, does it then follow that all punishments are suspect as being "cruel and unusual" within the meaning of the Constitution?

DISSENT [POWELL]: The possibility of racial bias in the trial and sentencing process has diminished in recent years. [T]he day is past when juries do not represent the minority group elements of the community. The assurance of fair trials for all citizens is greater today than at any previous time in our history. Because standards of criminal justice have "evolved" in a manner favorable to the accused, discriminatory imposition of capital punishment is far less likely today than in the past.

## DISCUSSION QUESTIONS

(1) Does capital punishment serve the main purposes of any punishment, including deterrence, retribution, and protection of society?

(2) Does discriminatory impact, if proven, show that capital punishment is unconstitutional?

## GREGG v. GEORGIA
### 428 U.S. 153 (U.S. Supreme Court, 1976)

The issue in this case is whether the imposition of the sentence of death for the crime of murder under the law of Georgia violates the Eighth and Fourteenth Amendments. We now hold that the punishment of death does not invariably violate the Constitution.

It is clear that the Eighth Amendment has not been regarded as a static concept. [A]n assessment of contemporary values concerning the infliction of a challenged sanction is relevant to the application of the Eighth Amendment. [T]his assessment does not call for a subjective judgment. It requires, rather, that we look to objective indicia that reflect the public attitude toward a given sanction.

But our cases also make clear that public perceptions of standards of decency with respect to criminal sanctions are not conclusive. [I]n assessing a punishment selected by a democratically elected legislature against the constitutional measure, we presume its validity. And a heavy burden rests on those who would attack the judgment of the representatives of the people.

[D]evelopments since *Furman* have undercut substantially the assumptions upon which their argument rested. Despite the continuing debate over the morality and utility of capital punishment, it is now evident that a large proportion of American society continues to regard it as an appropriate and necessary criminal sanction.

The most marked indication of society's endorsement of the death penalty for murder is the legislative response to *Furman*. The legislatures of at least 35 States have enacted new statutes that provide for the death penalty for at least some crimes that result in the death of another person. These statutes have attempted to address the concerns expressed by the Court in *Furman* primarily (i) by specifying the factors to be weighed and the procedures to be followed in deciding when to impose a capital sentence, or (ii) by making the death penalty mandatory for specified crimes.

The Court also must ask whether it comports with the basic concept of human dignity at the core of the Amendment. In part, capital punishment is an expression of society's moral outrage at particularly offensive conduct. This function may be unappealing to many, but it is essential in an ordered society that asks its citizens to rely on legal processes rather than self-help to vindicate their wrongs.

Statistical attempts to evaluate the worth of the death penalty as a deterrent to crimes by potential offenders have occasioned a great deal of debate. The results simply have been inconclusive.

We may nevertheless assume safely that there are murderers, such as those who act in passion, for whom the threat of death has little or no deterrent effect. But for many others, the death penalty undoubtedly is a significant deterrent.

We hold that the death penalty is not a form of punishment that may never be imposed, regardless of the circumstances of the offense, regardless of the character of the offender, and regardless of the procedure followed in reaching the decision to impose it.

[T]he concerns expressed in *Furman* that the penalty of death not be imposed in an arbitrary or capricious manner can be met by a carefully drafted statute that ensures that the sentencing authority is given adequate information and guidance. As a general proposition these concerns are best met by a system that provides for a bifurcated proceeding at which the sentencing authority is apprised of the information relevant to the imposition of sentence and provided with standards to guide its use of the information.

As an important additional safeguard against arbitrariness and caprice, the Georgia statutory scheme provides for automatic appeal of all death sentences to the State's Supreme Court. That court is required by statute to review each sentence of death and determine whether it was imposed under the influence of passion or prejudice, whether the evidence supports the jury's finding of a statutory aggravating circumstance, and whether the sentence is disproportionate compared to sentences imposed in similar cases.

[W]e hold that the statutory system under which Gregg was sentenced to death does not violate the Constitution.

## DISCUSSION QUESTIONS

(1) Do the procedural protections added to the Georgia death penalty statute adequately address the objections raised in *Furman*?

(2) Should public sentiment favoring the death penalty dictate what the Court considers to be constitutional?

## COKER v. GEORGIA
### 433 U.S. 584 (U.S. Supreme Court, 1977)

Georgia Code provides that "[a] person convicted of rape shall be punished by death or by imprisonment for life, or by imprisonment for not less than one nor more than 20 years." Petitioner Coker was convicted of rape and sentenced to death. Coker was granted a writ of *certiorari*, limited to the single claim, that the punishment of death for rape violates the Eighth Amendment, which proscribes "cruel and unusual punishments."

Under Gregg, a punishment is "excessive" and unconstitutional if it (1) makes no measurable contribution to acceptable goals of punishment and hence is nothing more than the purposeless and needless imposition of pain and suffering; or (2) is grossly out of proportion to the severity of the crime. A punishment might fail the test on either ground.

We have concluded that a sentence of death is grossly disproportionate and excessive punishment for the crime of rape and is therefore forbidden by the Eighth Amendment as cruel and unusual punishment.

Georgia is the sole jurisdiction in the United States at the present time that authorizes a sentence of death when the rape victim is an adult woman, and only two other jurisdictions provide capital punishment when the victim is a child. The current judgment with respect to the death penalty for rape is not wholly unanimous among state legislatures, but it obviously weighs very heavily on the side of rejecting capital punishment as a suitable penalty for raping an adult woman.

These recent events evidencing the attitude of state legislatures and sentencing juries do not wholly determine this controversy, for the Constitution contemplates that in the end our own judgment will be brought to bear on the question of the acceptability of the death penalty under the Eighth Amendment. Nevertheless, the legislative rejection of capital punishment for rape strongly confirms our own judgment, which is that death is indeed a disproportionate penalty for the crime of raping an adult woman.

We do not discount the seriousness of rape as a crime. It is highly reprehensible, both in a moral sense and in its almost total contempt for the personal integrity and autonomy of the female victim and for the latter's privilege of choosing those with whom intimate relationships are to be established. Short of homicide, it is the "ultimate violation of self." It is also a violent crime because it normally involves force, or the threat of force or intimidation, to overcome the will and the capacity of the victim to resist. Rape is very often accompanied by physical injury to the female and can also inflict mental and psychological damage. Because it undermines the community's sense of security, there is public injury as well.

Rape is without doubt deserving of serious punishment; but in terms of moral depravity and of the injury to the person and to the public, it does not compare with murder, which does involve the unjustified taking of human life. Life is over for the victim of the murderer; for the rape victim, life may not be nearly so happy as it was, but it is not over and normally is not beyond repair. We have the abiding conviction that the death penalty is an excessive penalty for the rapist who, as such, does not take human life.

DISSENT [POWELL]: The plurality does not limit its holding to the case before us or to similar cases. Rather, in an opinion that ranges well beyond what is necessary, it holds that capital punishment always - regardless of the circumstances - is a disproportionate penalty for the crime of rape. [I]n a case that does not require such an expansive pronouncement, the plurality draws a bright line between murder and all rapes - regardless of the degree of brutality of the rape or the effect upon the victim. I dissent because I am not persuaded that such a bright line is appropriate.

DISSENT [BURGER]: Whatever our individual views as to the wisdom of capital punishment, I cannot agree that it is constitutionally impermissible for a state legislature to make the "solemn judgment" to impose such penalty for the crime of rape. Accordingly, I would leave to the States the task of legislating in this area of the law.

(1) What punishment would be appropriate for rape and why?
(2) In considering Constitutional rights, how deferential should the Court be to the actions taken by state legislatures?

## McCLESKEY v. KEMP
### 481 U.S. 279 (U.S. Supreme Court, 1987)

This case presents the question whether a complex statistical study that indicates a risk that racial considerations enter into capital sentencing determinations proves that petitioner McCleskey's capital sentence is unconstitutional under the Eighth or Fourteenth Amendment.

McCleskey, a black man, was convicted of two counts of armed robbery and one count of murder of a white police officer during the course of the robbery. McCleskey [claims] that the Georgia capital sentencing process is administered in a racially discriminatory manner in violation of the Eighth and Fourteenth Amendments. In support of his claim, McCleskey proffered a statistical study (the Baldus study) that purports to show a disparity in the imposition of the death sentence in Georgia based on the race of the murder victim and, to a lesser extent, the race of the defendant.

Baldus found that the death penalty was assessed in 22% of the cases involving black defendants and white victims; 8% of the cases involving white defendants and white victims; 1% of the cases involving black defendants and black victims; and 3% of the cases involving white defendants and black victims. Similarly, Baldus found that prosecutors sought the death penalty in 70% of the cases involving black defendants and white victims; 32% of the cases involving white defendants and white victims; 15% of the cases involving black defendants and black victims; and 19% of the cases involving white defendants and black victims.

McCleskey's first claim is that the Georgia capital punishment statute violates the Equal Protection Clause of the Fourteenth Amendment. He argues that race has infected the administration of Georgia's statute. As a black defendant who killed a white victim, McCleskey claims that the Baldus study demonstrates that he was discriminated against because of his race and because of the race of his victim. [T]his claim must fail.

The Court has accepted statistics as proof of intent to discriminate in certain limited contexts. But the nature of the capital sentencing decision, and the relationship of the statistics to that decision, are fundamentally different from [those] cases. Each jury is unique in its composition, and the Constitution requires that its decision rest on consideration of innumerable factors that vary according to the characteristics of the individual defendant and the facts of the particular offense. Accordingly, we hold that the Baldus study is clearly insufficient to support an inference that any of the decisionmakers in McCleskey's case acted with discriminatory purpose.

McCleskey's claim, taken to its logical conclusion, throws into serious question the principles that underlie our entire criminal justice system. [I]f we accepted McCleskey's claim that racial bias has impermissibly tainted the capital sentencing decision, we could soon be faced with similar claims as to other types of penalty. Moreover, the claim that his sentence rests on the irrelevant factor of race easily could be extended to apply to claims based on unexplained discrepancies that correlate to membership in other minority groups, and even to gender. Similarly, since McCleskey's claim relates to the race of his victim, other claims could apply with equally logical force to statistical disparities that correlate with the race or sex of other actors in the criminal justice system, such as defense attorneys or judges. Also, there is no logical reason that such a claim need be limited to racial or sexual bias. If arbitrary and capricious punishment is the touchstone under the Eighth Amendment, such a claim could -- at least in theory -- be based upon any arbitrary variable, such as the defendant's facial characteristics, or the physical attractiveness of the defendant or the victim, that some statistical study indicates may be influential in jury decisionmaking. As these examples illustrate, there is no limiting principle to the type of challenge brought by McCleskey.

DISSENT: Granting relief to McCleskey, it is said, could lead to further constitutional challenges. That, of course, is no reason to deny McCleskey his rights under the Equal Protection Clause. If a grant of relief to him were to lead to a closer examination of the effects of racial considerations throughout the criminal justice system, the system, and hence society, might benefit. Where no such factors come into play, the integrity of the system is enhanced. Where such considerations are shown to be significant, efforts can be made to eradicate their impermissible influence and to ensure an evenhanded application of criminal sanctions.

## DISCUSSION QUESTIONS

(1) Should statistical data concerning evidence of discrimination ever be relevant or decisive in judicial reviews of punishment?

(2) What evidence, other than statistics, might be sufficient to show racial discrimination in the imposition of punishment?

### HERRERA v. COLLINS
506 U.S. 390 (U.S. Supreme Court, 1993)

Petitioner Leonel Torres Herrera was convicted of capital murder and sentenced to death in January 1982. In February 1992 -- 10 years after his conviction -- he urged in a petition that he was "actually innocent" of the murder for which he was sentenced to death, and that the Eighth Amendment's prohibition against cruel and unusual punishment therefore forbid his execution. He supported this claim with affidavits tending to show that his now-dead brother had been the perpetrator of the crime. Petitioner urges us to hold that this showing of innocence entitles him to relief in this federal proceeding. We hold that it does not.

Petitioner asserts that the Eighth and Fourteenth Amendments to the United States Constitution prohibit the execution of a person who is innocent of the crime for which he was convicted. But the evidence upon which petitioner's claim of innocence rests was not produced at his trial, but rather eight years later. In any system of criminal justice, "innocence" or "guilt" must be determined in some sort of a judicial proceeding.

Once a defendant has been afforded a fair trial and convicted of the offense for which he was charged, the presumption of innocence disappears. Here, it is not disputed that the State met its burden of proving at trial that petitioner was guilty of capital murder beyond a reasonable doubt. Thus, petitioner does not come before the Court as one who is "innocent," but, on the contrary, as one who has been convicted by due process of law of two brutal murders.

Petitioner's newly discovered evidence consists of affidavits. Petitioner's affidavits are particularly suspect in this regard because, with the exception of [one] affidavit, they consist of hearsay. The affidavits filed in this proceeding were given over eight years after petitioner's trial. No satisfactory explanation has been given as to why the affiants waited until the 11th hour -- and, indeed, until after the alleged perpetrator of the murders himself was dead -- to make their statements. Equally troubling, no explanation has been offered as to why petitioner pleaded guilty to the murder of [one of the victims].

Finally, the affidavits must be considered in light of the proof of petitioner's guilt at trial -- proof which included two eyewitness identifications, numerous pieces of circumstantial evidence, and a handwritten letter in which petitioner apologized for killing the officers and offered to turn himself in under certain conditions. That proof, even when considered alongside petitioner's belated affidavits, points strongly to petitioner's guilt.

## DISCUSSION QUESTIONS

(1) Should the government ever provide opportunities to convicted felons to introduce new evidence showing they are innocent?

(2) Does the new evidence here suggest that Herrera is in fact innocent or only that he should have the opportunity to try to prove, once again, that he is innocent?

## ATKINS v. VIRGINIA
536 U.S. 304 (U.S. Supreme Court, 2002)

Those mentally retarded persons who meet the law's requirements for criminal responsibility should be tried and punished when they commit crimes. Because of their disabilities in reasoning, judgment, and control of their impulses, however, they do not act with the level of moral culpability that characterizes the most serious adult criminal conduct. Moreover, their impairments can jeopardize the reliability and fairness of capital proceedings against mentally retarded defendants. [I]n the 13 years since we decided *Penry v. Lynaugh*, the American public, legislators, scholars, and judges have deliberated over the question whether the death penalty should ever be imposed on a mentally retarded criminal. The consensus reflected in those deliberations informs our answer to the question presented by this case: whether such executions are "cruel and unusual punishments" prohibited by the Eighth Amendment.

Atkins was convicted of abduction, armed robbery, and capital murder, and sentenced to death. Atkins and William Jones, armed with a semiautomatic handgun, abducted Eric Nesbitt, robbed him of the money on his person, drove him to an automated teller machine in his pickup truck where cameras recorded their withdrawal of additional cash, then took him to an isolated location where he was shot eight times and killed.

In the penalty phase, a forensic psychologist concluded that [Atkins] was "mildly mentally retarded." His conclusion was based on a standard intelligence test which indicated that Atkins had a full scale IQ of 59.

The jury sentenced Atkins to death. The Supreme Court of Virginia affirmed the imposition of the death penalty. [W]e granted *certiorari* to revisit the issue that we first addressed in the *Penry* case.

The Eighth Amendment provides: "Excessive bail shall not be required, nor excessive fines imposed, nor cruel and unusual punishments inflicted." "The basic concept underlying the Eighth Amendment is nothing less than the dignity of man. . . . The Amendment must draw its meaning from the evolving standards of decency that mark the progress of a maturing society.'

Proportionality review under those evolving standards should be informed by "'objective factors to the maximum possible extent.'" We have pinpointed that the "clearest and most reliable objective evidence of contemporary values is the legislation enacted by the country's legislatures."

It is not so much the number of these States that is significant, but the consistency of the direction of change. [T]he large number of States prohibiting the execution of mentally retarded persons (and the complete absence of States passing legislation reinstating the power to conduct such executions) provides powerful evidence that today our society views mentally retarded offenders as categorically less culpable than the average criminal. The evidence carries even greater force when it is noted that the legislatures that have addressed the issue have voted overwhelmingly in favor of the prohibition. Moreover, even in those States that allow the execution of mentally retarded offenders, the practice is uncommon, and it is fair to say that a national consensus has developed against it.

To the extent there is disagreement about the execution of mentally retarded offenders, it is in determining which offenders are in fact retarded.

This consensus unquestionably reflects widespread judgment about the relative culpability of mentally retarded offenders, and the relationship between mental retardation and the penological purposes served by the death penalty. Additionally, it suggests that some characteristics of mental retardation undermine the strength of the procedural protections that our capital jurisprudence steadfastly guards.

Mentally retarded persons frequently know the difference between right and wrong and are competent to stand trial. Because of their impairments, however, they have diminished capacities to understand and process information, to communicate, to abstract from mistakes and learn from experience, to engage in logical reasoning, to control impulses, and to understand the reactions of others. There is no evidence that they are more likely to engage in criminal conduct than others, but there is abundant evidence that they often act on impulse rather than pursuant to a premeditated plan, and that in group settings they are followers rather than leaders. Their deficiencies do not warrant an exemption from criminal sanctions, but they do diminish their personal culpability.

In light of these deficiencies, our death penalty jurisprudence provides two reasons consistent with the legislative consensus that the mentally retarded should be categorically excluded from execution. First, there is a serious question as to whether either justification that we have recognized as a basis for the death penalty applies to mentally retarded offenders.

With respect to retribution -- the interest in seeing that the offender gets his "just deserts" -- the severity of the appropriate punishment necessarily depends on the culpability of the offender. If the culpability of the average murderer is insufficient to justify the most extreme sanction available to the State, the lesser culpability of the mentally retarded offender surely does not merit that form of retribution.

The theory of deterrence is predicated upon the notion that the increased severity of the punishment will inhibit criminal actors from carrying out murderous conduct. Yet it is the same cognitive and behavioral impairments that make these defendants less morally culpable that also make it less likely that they can process the information of the possibility of execution as a penalty and, as a result, control their conduct based upon that information.

The reduced capacity of mentally retarded offenders provides a second justification for a categorical rule making such offenders ineligible for the death penalty. Mentally retarded defendants may be less able to give meaningful assistance to their counsel and are typically poor witnesses, and their demeanor may create an unwarranted impression of lack of remorse.

[W]e conclude that such punishment is excessive and that the Constitution "places a substantive restriction on the State's power to take the life" of a mentally retarded offender.

DISSENT: [T]he Court's assessment of the current legislative judgment regarding the execution of defendants like petitioner more resembles a *post hoc* rationalization for the majority's subjectively preferred result than any objective effort to ascertain the content of an evolving standard of decency.

To further buttress its appraisal of contemporary societal values, the Court marshals public opinion poll results and evidence that several professional organizations and religious groups have adopted official positions opposing the imposition of the death penalty upon mentally retarded offenders. [N]one should be accorded any weight on the Eight Amendment scale when the elected representatives of a State's populace have not deemed them persuasive enough to prompt legislative action.

## DISCUSSION QUESTIONS

(1) How much weight should the Court, in interpreting the Constitution, place on the opinions of state legislatures and the public?

(2) Should the analysis here of the diminished culpability of the mentally retarded extend to the mentally ill who know the difference between right and wrong?

# CHAPTER 10. BUSINESS ETHICS

## GRIMSHAW v. FORD
119 Cal. App. 3d 757 (Ct. of Appeal of California, 1981)

A 1972 Ford Pinto hatchback automobile unexpectedly stalled on a freeway, erupting into flames when it was rear ended by a car proceeding in the same direction. Mrs. Lilly Gray, the driver of the Pinto, suffered fatal burns and 13-year-old Richard Grimshaw, a passenger in the Pinto, suffered severe and permanently disfiguring burns on his face and entire body. Grimshaw and the heirs of Mrs. Gray sued Ford Motor Company and others. Following a six-month jury trial, verdicts were returned in favor of plaintiffs against Ford Motor Company. Grimshaw was awarded $2,516,000 compensatory damages and $125 million punitive damages; the Grays were awarded $559,680 in compensatory damages. On Ford's motion for a new trial, Grimshaw was required to remit all but $3-1/2 million of the punitive award as a condition of denial of the motion.

Ford assails the judgment as a whole, but the primary thrust of its appeal is directed against the punitive damage award. Ford contends that the punitive award was statutorily unauthorized and constitutionally invalid.

In 1968, Ford began designing a new subcompact automobile which ultimately became the Pinto. Ford's objective was to build a car at or below 2,000 pounds to sell for no more than $2,000. Ordinarily marketing surveys and preliminary engineering studies precede the styling of a new automobile line. Pinto, however, was a rush project, so that styling dictated engineering design to a greater degree than usual. Among the engineering decisions dictated by styling was the placement of the fuel tank.

During the development of the Pinto, prototypes were built and tested. The crash tests revealed that the Pinto's fuel system as designed could not meet the 20-mile-per-hour proposed [Federal] standard.

When a prototype failed the fuel system integrity test, the standard of care for engineers in the industry was to redesign and retest it. The vulnerability of the production Pinto's fuel tank at speeds of 20 and 30-miles-per- - hour fixed barrier tests could have been remedied by inexpensive "fixes," but Ford produced and sold the Pinto to the public without doing anything to remedy the defects. Design changes would have enhanced the integrity of the fuel tank system at relatively little cost per car.

The Pinto crash tests results had been forwarded up the chain of command to the ultimate decision-makers. [T]he highest level of Ford's management made the decision to go forward with the production of the Pinto, knowing that the gas tank was vulnerable to puncture and rupture at low rear impact speeds creating a significant risk of death or injury from fire and knowing that "fixes" were feasible at nominal cost. [M]anagement's decision was based on the cost savings from omitting or delaying the "fixes."

In deciding whether an award is excessive as a matter of law or was so grossly disproportionate as to raise the presumption that it was the product of passion or prejudice, the following factors should be weighed: The degree of reprehensibility of defendant's conduct, the wealth of the defendant, the amount of compensatory damages, and an amount which would serve as

151

a deterrent effect on like conduct by defendant and others who may be so inclined. Applying the foregoing criteria to the instant case, the punitive damage award as reduced by the trial court was well within reason.

[T]he reduced award [was not] excessive taking into account defendant's wealth and the size of the compensatory award. Nor was the size of the award excessive in light of its deterrent purpose. An award which is so small that it can be simply written off as a part of the cost of doing business would have no deterrent effect. An award which affects the company's pricing of its product and thereby affects its competitive advantage would serve as a deterrent. The award in question was far from excessive as a deterrent against future wrongful conduct by Ford and others.

Ford has failed to demonstrate that any errors or irregularities that may have occurred during the trial resulted in a miscarriage of justice.

## DISCUSSION QUESTIONS

(1) Did Ford have an ethical obligation to correct the known defects in the gas tank, regardless of cost? Did it have a duty to disclose to purchasers of the car the known defects?

(2) Are punitive damages an effective system of deterrence to keep large corporations from knowingly selling defective products? Is it a fair system?

## DEAL v. SPEARS
### 980 F.2d 1153 (8th Cir., 1992)

This civil action is based on the Omnibus Crime Control and Safe Streets Act of 1968. Sibbie Deal and Calvin Lucas seek damages against Deal's former employers, Newell and Juanita Spears, for the intentional interception and disclosure of plaintiffs' telephone conversations. [T]he District Court awarded statutory damages to Deal and Lucas in the amount of $40,000. We affirm.

Newell and Juanita Spears have owned and operated the White Oak Package Store near Camden, Arkansas, for about twenty years. The Spearses live in a mobile home adjacent to the store. The telephone in the store has an extension in the home, and is the only phone line.

Deal was an employee at the store from December 1988 until she was fired in August 1990. The store was burglarized in April 1990 and approximately $16,000 was stolen. The Spearses believed that it was an inside job and suspected that Deal was involved. Hoping to catch the suspect in an unguarded admission, Newell Spears purchased and installed a recording device on the extension phone in the mobile home. [T]he machine would automatically record all conversations made or received on either phone.

Calls were taped from June 27, 1990, through August 13, 1990. During that period, Deal was having an extramarital affair with Calvin Lucas. Deal and Lucas spoke on the telephone at the store long periods of time while Deal was at work. Deal also made or received numerous other personal telephone calls during her workday. Even before Newell Spears purchased the recorder, Deal was asked by her employers to cut down on her use of the phone for personal calls.

Newell Spears listened to virtually all twenty-two hours of the tapes he recorded, and Juanita Spears listened to some of them. On August 13, 1990, when Deal came in to work the evening shift, Newell Spears played a few seconds of the incriminating tape for Deal and then fired her. Deal and Lucas filed this action on August 29, 1990.

The Spearses argue that they are immune from liability under an exemption for business use of a telephone extension. We do not quarrel with the contention that the Spearses had a legitimate business reason for listening in. The Spearses might legitimately have monitored Deal's calls to the extent necessary to determine that the calls were personal and made or received in violation of store policy.

But the Spearses recorded twenty-two hours of calls, and Newell Spears listened to all of them without regard to their relation to his business interests. We conclude that the scope of the interception in this case takes us well beyond the boundaries of the ordinary course of business.

## DISCUSSION QUESTIONS

(1) Under what circumstances should it be legal for an employer to secretly tape the telephone conversations of an employee? When would it be ethical?

(2) What alternative approaches by the Spears' would be ethical to address the problems in their business?

## KASKY V. NIKE
27 Cal. 4th 939 (Supreme Court of California, 2002)

Acting on behalf of the public, plaintiff brought this action seeking monetary and injunctive relief under California laws designed to curb false advertising and unfair competition. Plaintiff alleged that defendant corporation, in response to public criticism, and to induce consumers to continue to buy its products, made false statements of fact about its labor practices and about working conditions in factories that make its products.

The issue here is whether defendant corporation's false statements are commercial or noncommercial speech for purposes of constitutional free speech analysis under the state and federal Constitutions. Resolution of this issue is important because commercial speech receives a lesser degree of protection than other forms of expression, and because governments may entirely prohibit commercial speech that is false or misleading.

· Because the messages in question were directed by a commercial speaker to a commercial audience, and because they made representations of fact about the speaker's own business operations for the purpose of promoting sales of its products, we conclude that these messages are commercial speech for purposes of applying state laws barring false and misleading commercial messages.

Our holding in no way prohibits any business enterprise from speaking out on issues of public importance or from vigorously defending its own labor practices. It means only that when a business enterprise, to promote and defend its sales and profits, makes factual representations about its own products or its own operations, it must speak truthfully. We emphasize that this lawsuit is still at a preliminary stage, and that whether any false representations were made is a disputed issue that has yet to be resolved.

Nike manufactures and sells athletic shoes and apparel. In 1997, it reported annual revenues of $ 9.2 billion, with annual expenditures for advertising and marketing of almost $ 1 billion. Most of Nike's products are manufactured by subcontractors in China, Vietnam, and Indonesia.

Beginning with a report on the television news program 48 Hours, and continuing with the publication of articles in the *Financial Times, the New York Times, the San Francisco Chronicle, the Buffalo News, the Oregonian, the Kansas City Star*, and the *Sporting News*, various persons and organizations alleged that in the factories where Nike products are made workers were paid less than the applicable local minimum wage; required to work overtime; allowed and encouraged to work more overtime hours than applicable local law allowed; subjected to physical, verbal, and sexual abuse; and exposed to toxic chemicals, noise, heat, and dust without adequate safety equipment, in violation of local occupational health and safety regulations.

In response, Nike made statements to the California consuming public that plaintiff alleges were false and misleading. Nike said that workers are protected from physical and sexual abuse, that they are paid in accordance with applicable local laws and regulations governing wages and hours, that they are paid on average double the applicable local minimum wage, that they receive a "living wage," that they receive free meals and health care, and that their working conditions are in compliance with applicable local laws and regulations governing occupational health and safety. Nike made these statements in press releases, in letters to newspapers, in a letter to university presidents and athletic directors, and in other documents distributed for public relations purposes.

California's unfair competition law (UCL) defines "unfair competition" to include "any unlawful, unfair or fraudulent business act or practice and unfair, deceptive, untrue or misleading advertising." The UCL's purpose is to protect both consumers and competitors by promoting fair competition in commercial markets for goods and services.

California's false advertising law makes it "unlawful for any person, . . . corporation . . ., or any employee thereof with intent directly or indirectly to dispose of real or personal property or to perform services . . . or to induce the public to enter into any obligation relating thereto, to make or disseminate . . . before the public in this state, . . . in any newspaper or other publication . . . or in any other manner or means whatever . . . any statement, concerning that real or personal property or those services . . . which is untrue or misleading, and which is known, or which by the exercise of reasonable care should be known, to be untrue or misleading . . . ."

This court has recognized that these laws prohibit "not only advertising which is false, but also advertising which[,] although true, is either actually misleading or which has a capacity, likelihood or tendency to deceive or confuse the public."

[I]t was not until the 1970's that the United States Supreme Court extended First Amendment protection to commercial messages. The high court observed that "the free flow of commercial information is indispensable" not only "to the proper allocation of resources in a free enterprise system" but also "to the formation of intelligent opinions as to how that system ought to be regulated or altered."

But the United States Supreme Court has explained that commercial speech that is false or misleading is not entitled to First Amendment protection and "may be prohibited entirely."

Because in the statements at issue here Nike was acting as a commercial speaker, because its intended audience was primarily the buyers of its products, and because the statements consisted of factual representations about its own business operations, we conclude that the statements were commercial speech for purposes of applying state laws designed to prevent false advertising and other forms of commercial deception.

For purposes of categorizing Nike's speech as commercial or noncommercial, it does not matter that Nike was responding to charges publicly raised by others and was thereby participating in a public debate.

As the United States Supreme Court has explained, false and misleading speech has no constitutional value in itself and is protected only in circumstances and to the extent necessary to give breathing room for the free debate of public issues. Commercial speech, because it is both more readily verifiable by its speaker and more hardy than noncommercial speech, can be effectively regulated to suppress false and actually or inherently misleading messages without undue risk of chilling public debate. With these basic principles in mind, we conclude that when a corporation, to maintain and increase its sales and profits, makes public statements defending labor practices and working conditions at factories where its products are made, those public statements are commercial speech that may be regulated to prevent consumer deception.

In concluding, we do not decide whether that speech was, as plaintiff has alleged, false or misleading.

DISSENT: While Nike's critics have taken full advantage of their right to " 'uninhibited, robust, and wide-open' " debate, the same cannot be said of Nike, the object of their ire. Handicapping one side in this important worldwide debate is both ill considered and unconstitutional. Full free speech protection for one side and strict liability for the other will hardly promote vigorous and meaningful debate.

The public at large, in addition to Nike's actual and intended customers, has the right to receive information from both sides of this international debate. Thus, not only Nike, but all of us, are the poorer for the majority's assault on free speech.

## DISCUSSION QUESTIONS

(1) Is it fair to Nike to restrict its right of free speech in responding to these allegations by its critics?

(2) Do corporations have an ethical obligation not to mislead the public with their public statements, or should they be free to say whatever they want, whenever they want?

# CHAPTER 11.  COMPUTER ETHICS

## UNITED STATES v. MORRIS
928 F.2d 504 (2nd Cir., 1991)

This appeal presents two narrow issues concerning a provision Congress recently adopted to strengthen protection against computer crimes. Section 2(d) of the Computer Fraud and Abuse Act of 1986 punishes anyone who intentionally accesses without authorization a category of computers known as "federal interest computers" and damages or prevents authorized use of information in such computers, causing loss of $1,000 or more. The issues raised are (1) whether the Government must prove not only that the defendant intended to access a federal interest computer, but also that the defendant intended to prevent authorized use of the computer's information and thereby cause loss; and (2) what satisfies the statutory requirement of "access without authorization."

These questions are raised on an appeal by Robert Tappan Morris, [convicted] of violating [the Act]. Morris released into INTERNET a computer program known as a "worm" that spread and multiplied, eventually causing computers at various educational institutions and military sites to "crash" or cease functioning.

We conclude that [the Act] does not require the Government to demonstrate that the defendant intentionally prevented authorized use and thereby caused loss. We also find that Morris acted "without authorization" within the meaning of [the Act]. We therefore affirm.

In 1988, Morris was a first-year graduate student in Cornell University's computer science Ph.D. program. When Morris entered Cornell, he was given an account on the computer at the Computer Science Division. Morris engaged in discussions with fellow graduate students about the security of computer networks and his ability to penetrate it.

Morris began work on a computer program, later known as the INTERNET "worm" or "virus." The goal of this program was to demonstrate the inadequacies of current security measures by exploiting the security defects that Morris had discovered. Morris designed the program to spread across a national network of computers after being inserted at one computer location connected to the network.

On November 2, 1988, Morris released the worm from a computer at the Massachusetts Institute of Technology. MIT was selected to disguise the fact that the worm came from Morris at Cornell. Morris soon discovered that the worm was replicating and reinfecting machines at a much faster rate than he had anticipated. Ultimately, many machines at locations around the country either crashed or became "catatonic." When Morris realized what was happening, he contacted a friend at Harvard to discuss a solution. Eventually, they sent an anonymous message from Harvard over the network, instructing programmers how to kill the worm and prevent reinfection. However, because the network route was clogged, this message did not get through until it was too late. Computers were affected at numerous installations, including leading universities, military sites, and medical research facilities. The estimated cost of dealing with the worm at each installation ranged from $200 to more than $53,000.

Morris was found guilty, following a jury trial, of violating [the Act]. He was sentenced to three years of probation, 400 hours of community service, a fine of $10,050, and the costs of his supervision.

Morris argues that the Government had to prove not only that he intended the unauthorized access of a computer, but also that he intended to prevent others from using it, and thus cause a loss. [T]he wording, structure, and purpose of the [Act] persuade us that the "intentionally" standard applies only to the "accesses" phrase, and not to its "damages" phrase.

Morris was authorized to use computers at Cornell, Harvard, and Berkeley, all of which were on INTERNET. The question is whether Morris's transmission of his worm constituted exceeding authorized access or accessing without authorization.

Morris's use of the SEND MAIL and finger demon features constituted access without authorization. Morris did not use either of those features in any way related to their intended function. He did not send or read mail nor discover information about other users; instead he found holes in both programs that permitted him a special and unauthorized access route into other computers.

Congress was punishing those, like Morris, who, with access to some computers that enable them to communicate on a network linking other computers, gain access to other computers to which they lack authorization and either trespass or cause damage or loss of $1,000 or more. Congress did not intend an individual's authorized access to one computer to protect him from prosecution, no matter what other computers he accesses.

## DISCUSSION QUESTIONS

(1) What Internet practices sufficiently deviate from their intended function that they should count as "unauthorized access"? Who determines what the "intended functions" are?

(2) Should people experimenting with security problems on the Internet with the goal of solving those problems be subject to the same punishment as people with malicious intentions to crash other peoples' computers?

## UNITED STATES v. ALKHABAZ
104 F.3d 1492 (6th Cir., 1997)

From November 1994 until approximately January 1995, [Abraham Jacob Alkhabaz, a.k.a. Jake] Baker and [Arthur] Gonda exchanged e-mail messages over the Internet, the content of which expressed a sexual interest in violence against women and girls.

Prior to this time, Baker had posted a number of fictional stories to "alt.sex.stories," a popular interactive Usenet news group. On January 9, Baker posted a story describing the torture, rape, and murder of a young woman who shared the name of one of Baker's classmates at the University of Michigan.

On February 9, Baker was arrested on a criminal complaint alleging violations of 18 U.S.C. 875(c), which prohibits interstate communications containing threats to kidnap or injure another person. On March 15, 1995, a federal grand jury returned [an] indictment, charging Baker and Gonda with five counts of violations of 18 U.S.C. 875(c).

[W]e conclude that the indictment failed to allege violations of Section 875(c). [I]n determining the sufficiency of the indictment against Baker, we must consider the elements of the offense that Congress intended to prohibit. Title 18, United States Code, Section 875(c) states:

Whoever transmits in interstate or foreign commerce any communication containing any threat to kidnap any person or any threat to injure the person of another, shall be fined under this title or imprisoned not more than five years, or both.

Accordingly, Section 875(c) requires proof that a reasonable person would have taken the defendant's statement as "a serious expression of an intention to inflict bodily harm."

[T]hreats are tools that are employed when one wishes to have some effect, or achieve some goal, through intimidation. Although it may offend our sensibilities, a communication objectively indicating a serious expression of an intention to inflict bodily harm cannot constitute a threat unless the communication also is conveyed for the purpose of furthering some goal through the use of intimidation.

[W]e hold that, to constitute "a communication containing a threat," a communication must be such that a reasonable person (1) would take the statement as a serious expression of an intention to inflict bodily harm, and (2) would perceive such expression as being communicated to effect some change or achieve some goal through intimidation.

[W]e conclude that the communications between Baker and Gonda do not constitute "communications containing a threat." Even if a reasonable person would take the communications as serious expressions of an intention to inflict bodily harm, no reasonable person would perceive such communications as being conveyed to achieve some goal through intimidation. Quite the opposite, Baker and Gonda apparently sent e-mail messages in an attempt to foster a friendship based on shared sexual fantasies.

We agree with the district court, that "whatever Baker's faults, and he is to be faulted, he did not violate 18 U.S.C. 875(c)."

DISSENT: Whether the originator of the message intended to intimidate or coerce anyone thereby is irrelevant. Rather, the pertinent inquiry is whether a jury could find that a reasonable recipient of the communication would objectively tend to believe that the speaker was serious about his stated intention.

By publishing his sadistic Jane Doe story on the Internet, Baker could reasonably foresee that his threats to harm Jane Doe would ultimately be communicated to her (as they were), and would cause her fear and intimidation, which in fact ultimately occurred. The majority may casually conclude within the security of chambers that Baker's threats conveyed to Jane Doe in his articles published on the Internet were nonintimidating. However, Jane Doe's reaction to those threats when brought to her attention evinces a contrary conclusion of a shattering traumatic reaction that resulted in recommended psychological counselling.

[A] rational jury could infer that the reason Baker published his Jane Doe story featuring the actual name of a young woman was the probability that its threats would be communicated to her and cause her to suffer fear, anxiety, and intimidation.

## DISCUSSION QUESTIONS

(1) What examples of communication on the Internet would count as a "threat" that violates this Federal statute?

(2) Is there a difference between a "virtual threat" on the Internet and a "real threat" in another context?

(3) Should Jake Baker escape moral criticism on the same basis as he escaped legal punishment?

## INTEL v. HAMIDI
30 Cal. 4th 1342 (Supreme Court of California, 2003)

Intel Corporation maintains an electronic mail system, connected to the Internet, through which messages between employees and those outside the company can be sent and received, and permits its employees to make reasonable nonbusiness use of this system. On six occasions over almost two years, Kourosh Kenneth Hamidi, a former Intel employee, sent e-mails criticizing Intel's employment practices to numerous current employees on Intel's electronic mail system. Hamidi breached no computer security barriers in order to communicate with Intel employees. He offered to, and did, remove from his mailing list any recipient who so wished. Hamidi's communications to individual Intel employees caused neither physical damage nor functional disruption to the company's computers, nor did they at any time deprive Intel of the use of its computers. The contents of the messages, however, caused discussion among employees and managers.

Intel brought suit, claiming that by communicating with its employees over the company's e-mail system Hamidi committed the tort of trespass to chattels.

[W]e conclude that under California law the tort does not encompass, and should not be extended to encompass, an electronic communication that neither damages the recipient computer system nor impairs its functioning. Such an electronic communication does not constitute an actionable trespass to personal property, i.e., the computer system, because it does not interfere with the possessor's use or possession of, or any other legally protected interest in, the personal property itself. The economic damage Intel claims to have suffered, i.e., loss of productivity caused by employees reading and reacting to Hamidi's messages and company efforts to block the messages, is not an injury to the company's interest in its computers--which worked as intended and were unharmed by the communications--any more than the personal distress caused by reading an unpleasant letter would be an injury to the recipient's mailbox, or the loss of privacy caused by an intrusive telephone call would be an injury to the recipient's telephone equipment.

Intel's claim fails not because e-mail transmitted through the Internet enjoys unique immunity, but because the trespass to chattels tort may not, in California, be proved without evidence of an injury to the plaintiff's personal property or legal interest.

Nor does our holding affect the legal remedies of Internet service providers (ISP's) against senders of unsolicited commercial bulk e-mail, also known as "spam." A series of federal district court decisions, has approved the use of trespass to chattels as a theory of spammers' liability to ISP's, based upon evidence that the vast quantities of mail sent by spammers both overburdened the ISP's own computers and made the entire computer system harder to use for recipients, the ISP's customers. In the present case, the claimed injury is located in the disruption or distraction caused to recipients by the contents of the e-mail messages, an injury entirely separate from, and not directly affecting, the possession or value of personal property.

Under California law, trespass to chattels "lies where an intentional interference with the possession of personal property has proximately caused injury."

Intel suggests that the requirement of actual harm does not apply here because it sought only injunctive relief, as protection from future injuries. But, in order to obtain injunctive relief the plaintiff must ordinarily show that the defendant's wrongful acts threaten to cause irreparable injuries, ones that cannot be adequately compensated in damages.

Though Hamidi sent thousands of copies of the same message on six occasions over 21 months, that number is minuscule compared to the amounts of mail sent by commercial operations. Hamidi's occasional advocacy messages cannot be compared to the burdens and costs caused ISP's and their customers by the ever-rising deluge of commercial e-mail.

That Hamidi's messages temporarily used some portion of the Intel computers' processors or storage is not enough; Intel must, but does not, demonstrate some measurable loss from the use of its computer system.

Nor may Intel appropriately assert a property interest in its employees' time. Nor can the fact Intel staff spent time attempting to block Hamidi's messages be bootstrapped into an injury to Intel's possessory interest in its computers.

Intel connected its e-mail system to the Internet and permitted its employees to make use of this connection both for business and, to a reasonable extent, for their own purposes. In doing so, the company contemplated the employees' receipt of unsolicited as well as solicited communications from other companies and individuals. That some communications would, because of their contents, be unwelcome to Intel management was virtually inevitable. Hamidi did nothing but use the e-mail system for its intended purpose--to communicate with employees. The system worked as designed, delivering the messages without any physical or functional harm or disruption. These occasional transmissions cannot reasonably be viewed as impairing the quality or value of Intel's computer system. We conclude that Intel has not presented undisputed facts demonstrating an injury to its personal property, or to its legal interest in that property, that support, under California tort law, an action for trespass to chattels.

DISSENT: Intel Corporation has invested millions of dollars to develop and maintain a computer system. It did this not to act as a public forum but to enhance the productivity of its employees. Hamidi sent as many as 200,000 e-mail messages to Intel employees. The time required to review and delete Hamidi's messages diverted employees from productive tasks and undermined the utility of the computer system.

It is well settled that the law protects a person's right to decide to whom he will speak, to whom he will listen, and to whom he will not listen. Of course, speakers have rights too, and thus the result is a balancing: speakers have the right to initiate speech but the listener has the right to refuse to listen or to terminate the conversation. This simple policy thus supports Hamidi's right to send e-mails initially, but not after Intel expressed its objection.

The principles of both personal liberty and social utility should counsel us to usher the common law of property into the digital age.

## DISCUSSION QUESTIONS

(1) How is Hamidi's unsolicited e-mail different from spam?

(2) What rights should Intel have in use of its e-mail system? What rights should Intel employees have? Former Intel employees?

(3) Is Hamidi's right of free speech appropriately restricted by the rights of others not to listen?

## RENO v. ACLU
### 521 U.S. 844 (U.S. Supreme Court, 1997)

At issue is the constitutionality of two statutory provisions enacted to protect minors from "indecent" and "patently offensive" communications on the Internet. Notwithstanding the legitimacy and importance of the congressional goal of protecting children from harmful materials, the statute abridges "the freedom of speech" protected by the First Amendment.

[T]he "Communications Decency Act of 1996" (CDA) contains provisions that are informally described as the "indecent transmission" provision and the "patently offensive display" provision.

On February 8, 1996, immediately after the President signed the statute, 20 plaintiffs filed suit against the Attorney General and the Department of Justice challenging the constitutionality of [the CDA]. District Judge Buckwalter entered a temporary restraining order against enforcement insofar as it applies to indecent communications. A second suit was then filed. After an evidentiary hearing, that Court entered a preliminary injunction against enforcement of both of the challenged provisions.

Neither before nor after the enactment of the CDA have the vast democratic fora of the Internet been subject to the type of government supervision and regulation that has attended the broadcast industry. Moreover, the Internet is not as "invasive" as radio or television. Users seldom encounter content "by accident." "Almost all sexually explicit images are preceded by warnings as to the content," and "odds are slim that a user would come across a sexually explicit sight by accident."

Finally, unlike the conditions that prevailed when Congress first authorized regulation of the broadcast spectrum, the Internet can hardly be considered a "scarce" expressive commodity. It provides relatively unlimited, low-cost capacity for communication of all kinds. The Government estimates that "[a]s many as 40 million people use the Internet today, and that figure is expected to grow to 200 million by 1999."

Regardless of whether the CDA is so vague that it violates the Fifth Amendment, the many ambiguities concerning the scope of its coverage render it problematic for purposes of the First Amendment. For instance, each of the two parts uses a different linguistic form. The first uses the word "indecent," while the second speaks of material that "in context, depicts or describes, in terms patently offensive as measured by contemporary community standards, sexual or excretory activities or organs."

Given the absence of a definition of either term, this difference in language will provoke uncertainty among speakers about how the two standards relate to each other and just what they mean.

The vagueness of the CDA is a matter of special concern for two reasons. First, the CDA is a content-based regulation of speech. The vagueness of such a regulation raises special First Amendment concerns because of its obvious chilling effect on free speech. Second, the CDA is a criminal statute [which] threatens violators with penalties including up to two years in prison for each act of violation. The severity of criminal sanctions may well cause speakers to remain silent rather than communicate even arguably unlawful words, ideas, and images. As a practical matter, this increased deterrent effect, coupled with the "risk of discriminatory enforcement" of vague regulations, poses [great] First Amendment concerns.

[T]he CDA thus presents a threat of censoring speech that, in fact, falls outside the statute's scope. Given the vague contours of the coverage of the statute, it unquestionably silences some speakers whose messages would be entitled to constitutional protection. That danger provides further reason for insisting that the statute not be overly broad. The CDA's burden on protected speech cannot be justified if it could be avoided by a more carefully drafted statute.

We are persuaded that the CDA lacks the precision that the First Amendment requires when a statute regulates the content of speech. In order to deny minors access to potentially harmful speech, the CDA effectively suppresses a large amount of speech that adults have a constitutional right to receive and to address to one another. That burden on adult speech is unacceptable if less restrictive alternatives would be at least as effective in achieving the legitimate purpose that the statute was enacted to serve.

In evaluating the free speech rights of adults, we have made it perfectly clear that "[s]exual expression which is indecent but not obscene is protected by the First Amendment." "[T]he fact that society may find speech offensive is not a sufficient reason for suppressing it."

It is true that we have repeatedly recognized the governmental interest in protecting children from harmful materials. But that interest does not justify an unnecessarily broad suppression of speech addressed to adults.

The breadth of the CDA's coverage is wholly unprecedented. [T]he scope of the CDA is not limited to commercial speech or commercial entities. Its open-ended prohibitions embrace all nonprofit entities and indi-

viduals posting indecent messages or displaying them on their own computers in the presence of minors. The general, undefined terms "indecent" and
"patently offensive" cover large amounts of nonpornographic material with
serious educational or other value. Moreover, the "community standards"
criterion as applied to the Internet means that any communication available
to a nation-wide audience will be judged by the standards of the community
most likely to be offended by the message. The regulated subject matter may
also extend to discussions about prison rape or safe sexual practices, artistic
images that include nude subjects, and arguably the card catalogue of the
Carnegie Library.

[T]he CDA places an unacceptably heavy burden on protected speech.
[T]he judgment of the district court is affirmed.

## DISCUSSION QUESTIONS

(1) What steps could be taken to protect children from "indecent"
content on the Internet, consistently with the Constitution?

(2) What ethical obligations do Internet users have in presenting
content to others through this new medium?

## A&M RECORDS v. NAPSTER
### 239 F.3d 1004 (9th Cir., 2001)

Plaintiffs are engaged in the commercial recording, distribution and sale of
copyrighted musical compositions and sound recordings. The complaint alleges that Napster, Inc. is a contributory and vicarious copyright infringer.
The district court enjoined Napster "from engaging in, or facilitating others
in copying, downloading, uploading, transmitting, or distributing plaintiffs'
copyrighted musical compositions and sound recordings, protected by either
federal or state law, without express permission of the rights owner." We
entered a temporary stay of the injunction pending resolution of this appeal.

In 1987, the Moving Picture Experts Group set a standard file format
for the storage of audio recordings in a digital format called MPEG-3,
abbreviated as "MP3." Digital MP3 files are created through a process
colloquially called "ripping." Ripping software allows a computer owner to
copy an audio compact disk directly onto a computer's hard drive by com-
pressing the audio information on the CD into the MP3 format. The MP3's
compressed format allows for rapid transmission of audio files from one
computer to another by electronic mail or any other file transfer protocol.

Napster facilitates the transmission of MP3 files between and among its
users. Through a process commonly called "peer-to-peer" file sharing, Napster allows its users to: (1) make MP3 music files stored on individual computer hard drives available for copying by other Napster users; (2) search
for MP3 music files stored on other users' computers; and (3) transfer exact
copies of the contents of other users' MP3 files from one computer to
another via the Internet. These functions are made possible by Napster's
MusicShare software, available free of charge from Napster's Internet site,
and Napster's network servers and server-side software.

Plaintiffs claim Napster users are engaged in the wholesale reproduction and distribution of copyrighted works, all constituting direct infringement. The district court agreed.

Plaintiffs must satisfy two requirements to present a *prima facie* case of direct infringement: (1) they must show ownership of the allegedly infringed material and (2) they must demonstrate that the alleged infringers violate at least one exclusive right granted to copyright holders. Plaintiffs have sufficiently demonstrated ownership. The record supports the district court's determination that "as much as eighty-seven percent of the files available on Napster may be copyrighted and more than seventy percent may be owned or administered by plaintiffs."

We agree that plaintiffs have shown that Napster users infringe at least two of the copyright holders' exclusive rights: the rights of reproduction; and distribution. Napster users who upload file names to the search index for others to copy violate plaintiffs' distribution rights. Napster users who download files containing copyrighted music violate plaintiffs' reproduction rights.

Napster contends that its users do not directly infringe plaintiffs' copyrights because the users are engaged in fair use of the material.

The district court considered factors which guide a court's fair use determination: (1) the purpose and character of the use; (2) the nature of the copyrighted work; (3) the "amount and substantiality of the portion used" in relation to the work as a whole; and (4) the effect of the use upon the potential market for the work or the value of the work. The district court concluded that Napster users are not fair users. We agree.

Courts have been reluctant to find fair use when an original work is merely retransmitted in a different medium. This "purpose and character" element also requires the district court to determine whether the allegedly infringing use is commercial or noncommercial. The district court determined that Napster users engage in commercial use of the copyrighted materials largely because (1) a host user sending a file cannot be said to engage in a personal use when distributing that file to an anonymous requester and (2) Napster users get for free something they would ordinarily have to buy.

Direct economic benefit is not required to demonstrate a commercial use. Rather, repeated and exploitative copying of copyrighted works, even if the copies are not offered for sale, may constitute a commercial use. In the record before us, commercial use is demonstrated by a showing that repeated and exploitative unauthorized copies of copyrighted works were made to save the expense of purchasing authorized copies.

"While wholesale copying does not preclude fair use per se, copying an entire work 'militates against a finding of fair use.'" The district court determined that Napster users engage in "wholesale copying" of copyrighted work because file transfer necessarily "involves copying the entirety of the copyrighted work." We agree.

A challenge to a noncommercial use of a copyrighted work requires proof either that the particular use is harmful, or that if it should become widespread, it would adversely affect the potential market for the copyrighted work. If the intended use is for commercial gain, that likelihood [of market harm] may be presumed. But if it is for a noncommercial purpose, the likelihood must be demonstrated.

Napster harms the market in "at least" two ways: it reduces audio CD sales among college students and it "raises barriers to plaintiffs' entry into the market for the digital downloading of music."

Napster contends that its users download MP3 files to "sample" the music in order to decide whether to purchase the recording.

The district court determined that sampling remains a commercial use even if some users eventually purchase the music. [T]he free downloads provided by the record companies consist of thirty-to-sixty second samples or are full songs programmed to "time out," that is, exist only for a short time on the downloader's computer. In comparison, Napster users download a full, free and permanent copy of the recording.

Napster also maintains that space-shifting is a fair use. Space-shifting occurs when a Napster user downloads MP3 music files in order to listen to music he already owns on audio CD. Napster asserts that we have already held that space-shifting of musical compositions and sound recordings is a fair use. [Those precedents] are inapposite because the methods of shifting in these cases did not also simultaneously involve distribution of the copyrighted material to the general public; the time or space-shifting of copyrighted material exposed the material only to the original user.

Napster, by its conduct, knowingly encourages and assists the infringement of plaintiffs' copyrights. Contributory liability requires that the secondary infringer "know or have reason to know" of direct infringement. Napster had both actual and constructive knowledge that its users exchanged copyrighted music.

In the context of copyright law, vicarious liability extends to cases in which a defendant "has the right and ability to supervise the infringing activity and also has a direct financial interest in such activities."

Napster's future revenue is directly dependent upon "increases in userbase." More users register with the Napster system as the "quality and quantity of available music increases." Napster financially benefits from the availability of protected works on its system.

The ability to block infringers' access to a particular environment for any reason whatsoever is evidence of the right and ability to supervise. Turning a blind eye to detectable acts of infringement for the sake of profit gives rise to liability.

Napster's failure to police the system's "premises," combined with a showing that Napster financially benefits from the continuing availability of infringing files on its system, leads to the imposition of vicarious liability.

[A]ppellees [A&M Records] have substantially and primarily prevailed on appeal. Appellees shall recover their statutory costs on appeal.

## DISCUSSION QUESTIONS

(1) If you ever used a Napster file-sharing system, do you believe you behaved unethically? Why, or why not?

(2) Educators and students often make "fair use" of copyrighted material in classrooms and libraries. Why is that acceptable, but Napster file-sharing is not?

# HOW TO READ A COURT DECISION

A court decision is the written report of a legal proceeding in one of the courts in our judicial system. To understand it, look for the following:

## Parties

Who are the adversaries in this legal dispute?
Who initiated the law suit (the plaintiff)?
Who is being sued (the defendant)?
Who initiated an appeal of the lower court decision (appellant)?
Who is responding to this appeal (the appellee)?

## Facts

What happened in the world before these parties entered the legal system?
What events or activities led to the legal dispute here?

## Legal history

What was the claim of the party initiating the law suit?
What happened in the lower courts before the parties got to this appeal?
What did the lower court(s) decide?

## Issue

What is the central issue in this dispute?

## Holding

How did this court finally decide the matter?
What is the answer to the issue question?
What is the "bottom line" in this dispute?

## Reasoning

What reasoning did the court use to reach this holding?
What possible objections does the court identify and how does it respond to
   them in its reasoning?

## Concurring opinions

Did any of the judges write a separate opinion agreeing with the holding of
   the majority, but offering different reasons?
What reasons do they offer that differ from the main opinion of the court?

## Dissent

Did any of the judges write a separate opinion disagreeing with the holding
   of the majority?
What reasons are given in the dissent for the disagreement?

*NOTE: Due to editing for this volume, not all of these elements are
included for each decision.*

# LEGAL CITATION

**Party Names**

The citation begins with the names of the parties on both sides of the issue. The case name is typically shortened to include only the first person if there are multiple parties.

EXAMPLE: Roe v. Wade

Roe is short for "Jane Roe," one of the plaintiffs in the case. Wade is the District Attorney of Dallas County, the defendant.

**Citation**

A standard citation form is used in the state and Federal courts in this country. Cases are collected in print books called "reporters."

Volume Number: The first number is the volume number of the book containing the case.

Court: The abbreviation in the middle of the citation indicates the particular court in which the case was heard.

Page Number: The last number in the citation is the first page of the reported decision.

Year: The year in which the case was decided by the court.

EXAMPLE: 410 U.S. 113 (1973)

410 means volume 410.
U.S. means United States Reports, the official reporter for all decisions of the United States Supreme Court.
113 means that the report of the decision starts on page 113.
1973 means that the decision was announced in 1973.

For more information on Legal Citation:

http://www.law.cornell.edu/citation/

## WHERE TO FIND THE COMPLETE TEXT OF COURT DECISIONS

The full texts of many decisions are now available free on the World Wide Web, at several sites. Some of the best places to start in looking for decisions:

http://www.findlaw.com/
http://www.law.cornell.edu/

# GLOSSARY

**amicus curiae**: friend of the court; interested person or group who is allowed to file a brief supporting a certain position in a case before the court, even though not a party to the lawsuit (plural: amici)

**appellant**: the party appealing a lower court decision to a higher court

**appellee**: the party responding to an appeal of a lower court decision

**arguendo**: in the course of arguing; for the sake of argument

**certiorari**: agreement by an appellate court to review the decision of a lower court

**Court of Appeals**: the first level of review in the Federal (national) court system; in state court systems, the Court of Appeals is sometimes the name for one of the courts in that system, although states vary in their naming practices for courts

**declaratory judgment**: a declaration by a court, e.g., that a statute is unconstitutional

**demurrer**: a claim that the facts stated by an opponent, even if true, would not be sufficient to prove the legal matter at issue

**enjoin**: to require someone to do or abstain from doing something

**finding**: a conclusion on a factual matter that a court needs in order to reach a further conclusion about the issues

**injunction, injunctive relief**: the remedy or solution sought by parties to a lawsuit that consists of a court order to do or not to do something

**habeas corpus**: literally, "you have the body;" a writ demanding that the government provide good reason for holding someone in custody

**jurisdiction**: the authority of a court to hear a legal matter, based on physical location, subject matter, and other factors

**law**: A rule that must be followed in a system of government; laws include statutes passed by legislatures (both State and Federal) as well as holdings of the courts

**monetary relief**: the remedy or solution sought by parties to a lawsuit that consists of the payment of money

**ordinance**: a law passed by a city's legislative body (such as the city council) regulating behavior in that city

**petitioner**: the party filing an appeal to a higher court

**remand**: send back. A high court typically rules on issues in dispute and then remands the case to the lower court to make final decisions.

**respondent**: the party responding to an appeal filed by the other party in an appeal to a higher court

**standing**: the authority or legitimacy of a party to be heard by a court concerning a case or controversy

**statute**: a law enacted by a legislature, following the procedures of that government

**U. S. District Court**: the "lowest" court in the Federal court system, which ordinarily first hears a case and hears the evidence presented by all parties, including testimony of witnesses and physical evidence

**vacate**: to set aside, render void, annul

**writ**: an agreement in writing, normally to commence a legal proceeding

# TABLE OF CASES